Playing for Keeps

We are accustomed to think of play and
seriousness as an absolute antithesis.
It would seem, however, that this does
not go to the heart of the matter.

—JOHAN HUIZINGA, *Homo Ludens*

Playing for Keeps

A History of Early Baseball

WARREN GOLDSTEIN

20TH ANNIVERSARY EDITION

Cornell University Press • Ithaca and London

First published 1989 by Cornell University Press
First printing, 20th Anniversary Edition, 2009

Printed in the United States of America

Library of Congress Cataloging-in-Publication Data

Goldstein, Warren Jay.
    Playing for keeps : a history of early baseball / Warren Goldstein.—20th
anniversary ed.
        p.   cm.
    Includes bibliographical references and index.
    ISBN 978-0-8014-7508-5 (pbk. : alk. paper)
        1. Baseball—United States—History—19th century.   I. Title.

  GV863.A1G66   2009
  796.357'0973—dc22

                                                                    2008049987

Cornell University Press strives to use environmentally responsible suppliers and
materials to the fullest extent possible in the publishing of its books. Such
materials include vegetable-based, low-VOC inks and acid-free papers that are
recycled, totally chlorine-free, or partly composed of nonwood fibers. For further
information, visit our website at www.cornellpress.cornell.edu.

Paperback printing   10   9   8   7   6   5   4   3   2   1

For Donna

Contents

Preface to the 20th Anniversary Edition   ix
Acknowledgments   xxiii

Prologue   I
Histories of the Game   I
A Note on Method   6
Origins   10

I   THE CULTURE OF ORGANIZED BASEBALL, 1857–1866

1   The Base Ball Fraternity   17
Rites of Play   17
"Hard Work and Victory"   20
Players and Workers   24
Cultural Antecedents   27

2   Excitement and Self-Control   32
Dangerous Excitement   32
Agents of Control: Rules, Umpires, and Women   34
The Problem of Competition   40

3   The "Manly Pastime"   43
Men and Boys   43
The Fly Rule   48
Ethics of the Game: Reform vs. Custom   53
Fruits of Reform: "Ambitious Rivalries and
   Selfish Victories"   58

II   AMATEURS INTO PROFESSIONALS, 1866–1876

4   Growth, Division, and "Disorder"   67

The Coming of the "Good Old Days"   67
Growth and Fragmentation   72
Cultural Conflict and Division   75

5   "Revolving" and Professionalism   84

The Decline of the National Association   84
Baseball Capital and Baseball Labor   94

6   The National Game   101

Home and Away   101
The Birth of the Cincinnati Red Stockings   103
Uniform Identities   108
Management, Triumph, and Defeat: The Red
   Stockings of 1869 and 1870   112

7   Amateurs in Rebellion   120

The Amateurist Critique of Professional Baseball   120
"Restoring" the Pastime   126

8   Professional Leagues and the Baseball Workplace   134

"Baseball Is Business Now"   134
The Origins of Baseball Statistics   142
The National League   147

Epilogue: Playing for Keeps   151

Notes   157
Selected Bibliography   179
Index   181

Preface

I remember the moment vividly. It was 1979, and I'd come to have lunch with my closest adviser in graduate school so we could discuss the momentous subject of my doctoral dissertation. I had found an intriguing combination of sources—a payroll ledger from a New Haven lock factory, as well as the diary of a young Irish worker in the same factory—and had already used them to write a pretty good paper. I broached the idea that these might be the ingredients for a successful study of labor, community, and working-class consciousness.

As we worked our way around the salad bar in the Silliman College dining hall at Yale, Richard Fox turned to me, plate in hand, and said, "There are dozens of studies like that already, and there'll be plenty more. You should do something different—something you love. Why not write about baseball?" I stood there, stunned at this outrageous notion. What was he thinking? Baseball, as we both knew, had only gotten in the way of my academic life. I once had to reschedule the lecture I was supposed to give as a teaching assistant in Richard's class because my (then) beloved Yankees had gotten into the playoffs and I was running back and forth to Yankee Stadium, not getting home until the early morning hours. Another time, I tried to write a review of some recent books about sports by academics but ended up completely blocked. The project died.

"Richard," I finally managed to croak out, "you want me to commit professional suicide!" "No, no," he protested. "It'll be great!" I don't remember any more about that lunch. I do remember the year I spent working on a prospectus and my ill-fated hunt for an adviser. A famous political historian who had advised my undergraduate senior essay so disliked my draft that he marched down the hall into the American studies office, slammed it down on the secretary's desk, and declared to anyone in earshot that he refused to be associated with such an absurd project. My department convened a special meeting and named a committee and a chair, and I was on my way. Sort of.

I didn't really know what shape the project would take, only that it would be a social and cultural history of nineteenth-century baseball and include attention to play as work and to the game as business, urban, and immigration history. The most perceptive criticism of my prospectus came from a fellow graduate student, Chris Wilson, now at Boston College, who likened it to a magician putting swords through a basket: here's the labor history sword, and now I shall insert the immigrant sword. The problem was that those intellectual swords made my subject disappear.

Friends and acquaintances thought that I either had the greatest topic on earth or had lost my marbles. My mother fell into the "You're writing about *what?*" category. "For this you needed to go to Yale?" she asked, pained that she could no longer kvell to her friends. How was *baseball* worthy of an Ivy League Ph.D., for goodness' sake?

Unintentionally, unconsciously, I was recapitulating, in intellectual terms, the earliest years of the organized game, when adult male ballplayers struggled to have their play recognized as "manly sport" instead of a "boy's game." People didn't exactly edge away from me at graduate student parties, afraid that my potentially self-destructive decision might be catching, but I did soon find myself perched (and occasionally hanging for dear life) on a rather lonely intellectual limb, which added a little extra angst to the commonplace that, whatever else they are, dissertations aren't much fun.

Unlike most of my fellow graduate students, I got to read mountains of baseball journalism from the 1850s and 1860s. Although I needed reading glasses by the time I was done (the type was *small*), I enjoyed getting inside the New York Mutuals and Brooklyn Atlantics. And when I found Harry Wright's letter books at the New York Public Library, I knew I had my hands on the kind of archival material historians kill for. (The dominant figure in early top-flight baseball in New York, Wright managed the pioneering 1869 Cincinnati Red Stockings, as well as the Boston Red Stockings in baseball's first professional league.) But it took me a long time to figure out how to write about this mass of material, which I photocopied and glued into makeshift chronological scrapbooks that I then filled with longhand notes. Twenty years later, I still cannot discard this research. My file box of typed, transcribed Harry Wright letters still strikes me as a historical treasure trove, and I've moved with it seven times.

I had planned, at first, to take my history from the 1850s up to the founding of the American League in 1901, but after two years of research I was only approaching opening day of the 1877 season. It was time, no matter what, to begin writing. Plus, the founding of the National League in 1876—just a quarter of a century earlier—offered a nice end point. The very first word I wrote was *competition*, which struck me as just right, since I was arguing that baseball's appeal came less from how fun it was than from how much it resembled work. It certainly had become so for me, just as it surely must have for its top-flight practitioners, known as *players* but who were really *workers*.

It didn't have to be professional suicide, I suppose. The late and much-lamented Roy Rosenzweig had, in 1983, opened up the field with his groundbreaking *Eight Hours for What We Will: Workers and Leisure in an Industrial City, 1870–1920*, a book that showed how leisure played an important, identifiable, even quantifiable role in the lives of Worcester's workers and their families. My fellow graduate student and friend Elliott Gorn was writing a terrific dissertation about nineteenth-century boxing. And David Brion Davis, who sat on my committee, proudly told me that he had advised the very first dissertation about the history of baseball, by none other than the dean of baseball historians, Harold Seymour. But if Seymour was the dean, the college over which he presided was mighty small when I started my research in 1979. John L. Paxson and Foster Rhea Dulles had written general sports histories, and most people writing in the field were mainly digging out the basic, doing very little in the way of interpretation—or connecting that history to American economic, political, cultural, labor, intellectual, diplomatic, technological, or women's history. Allen Guttman was the exception, of course. In *From Ritual to Record: The Nature of Modern Sports*, published in 1978, he offered sophisticated analyses of baseball history in particular. In 1974 Steven Riess had finished his dissertation (and I spent many hours reading it in microfilm), but his book *Touching Base: Professional Baseball and American Culture in the Progressive Era* did not come out until 1980.

The hunt for thoughtful books about sports led me to C. L. R. James, whose *Beyond a Boundary* combined memoir and anti-imperial analysis of Jamaican cricket. Unfortunately, though, it didn't offer much in the way of models for American baseball. I also looked to Lawrence Ritter's classic oral history, *The Glory of Their Times*, Roger Kahn's magnificent *The Boys of Summer*, Jim Bouton's hilarious *Ball Four,* and to the exquisite essays of the *New Yorker's* Roger Angell. These writers persuaded me that baseball had enough emotional substance to justify spending years of my life learning to write about it; they gave me not a clue how to go about my own writing. At the time Bill James was still self-publishing his annual *Baseball Abstract* and sending it to individual customers. (Ballantine didn't start publishing this indispensable book until 1981.) James was essentially unknown; the Society for American Baseball Research did not exist, and the word *sabermetrics* had not been invented. He was doing calculations not quite by hand, but by calculator, and the *Abstract* featured *typed* pages and tables. The *Historical Baseball Abstract* may have been a gleam in James's eye, but the first version came out only in 1985. And while James had academic readers, he offered no guidance to academics looking to work the same territory. Historian Benjamin Rader's groundbreaking textbook, *American Sports: From the Age of Folk Games to the Age of Televised Sports,* didn't appear until 1983, the same year I finished my dissertation. And Melvin Adelman's classic *A Sporting Time: New York City and the Rise of Modern Athletics* was a dissertation in progress when I started mine.

The wonderful, recently deceased historian Jules Tygiel tells how, even as he realized in 1973 that the Jackie Robinson saga was "a tale still worthy of re-examination and re-telling," he "dared not, however, mention [his] idea to too many people." After all, he reflected wisely in 1983, "baseball is not the stuff upon which successful careers in history are normally made." That's why he first wrote a study of the nineteenth-century San Francisco working class (sound familiar?). When I read those words, the hair on the back of my neck stood up. In the 1970s, as Tygiel, I, and others were considering sports history, we were making fateful professional decisions.

When I got my degree in 1983, the job market for historians may have been at its worst point in a generation. I'd taken a long time to finish my dissertation, and my work was quirky. Although I came from a first-rate graduate program, I applied for dozens of entry-level jobs and got only one interview. One. And I never even received the letter of rejection. I had to call and hear it from the secretary. As the other form-letter rejections piled up, I couldn't help but conclude that writing about baseball history hadn't done me much good.

I spent the next five years outside of academia working for a variety of nonprofits, on behalf of nuclear disarmament, expanded childcare, and human rights. I did sign a book contract with Cornell University Press in 1985, mainly because the then-history editor Peter Agree agreed to get my manuscript read by historians who appreciated what I was trying to do. To my great good fortune, he sent it to Roy Rosenzweig and Ron Story. The latter was famous among young sports-minded historians for his legendary collection of documents on the 1919 Black Sox scandal. Both understood that I was trying to bring the tools of social and cultural history to baseball's formative years, to situate the game in a new context, and to enter the lived experience of early ballplayers and their audiences. They saw that I wanted to understand how the world of play was connected to the world of work that structured ballplayers' lives before they came to the ballfield. Even more, they encouraged me to speculate about the meaning of my material, to take a few risks, and to prune the jargon out of the manuscript so that people without a Ph.D. could read it.

By 1989, when the book was published, the literary and historical mainstream had expanded its boundaries a bit, and *Playing for Keeps: A History of Early Baseball* garnered a batch of reviews in popular as well as scholarly venues. Robert Pinksy was critical of the prose—you can't win them all when the future poet laureate of the United States reads your writing—but otherwise gave it a brief rave in the *New York Times Book Review*, and historian David Nasaw gave it a lengthy and positive review in the *Nation*, one of the first times the venerable leftish weekly had ventured into sports with anything like appreciation. The standard view on the left was that professional sports (except for the briefly heroic Jackie Robinson–era Brooklyn Dodgers) filled the same role as religion: opiate of the people, false consciousness, distraction for the working class.

Friends and acquaintances gave it to their husbands and teenaged sons. Sales were good and Cornell soon issued a paperback featuring the best reviews on the back cover. It didn't hurt that the book won the North American Society for Sports History book prize that year. And after eighteen years, it's still a marvel to me that the book has stayed in print, some years selling a little more, some years a little less, but over the past decade, it has sold steadily, which has afforded me a small yet significant, ongoing pleasure. I occasionally hear from fellow historians using it in a class; I make it optional in my undergraduate sports history class and assign it in the graduate class in sports history I teach from time to time.

I can't prove it, but I like to think this book had something to do with making sports history academically "respectable." In personal terms, I'd begun making my way back into academia while working on *Playing for Keeps*, first getting hired as a half-time sabbatical replacement in the American studies program at SUNY College at Old Westbury, then getting a full-time visiting position, and finally a tenure-track job. Around the country history departments began offering sports history courses, mostly to boost enrollments but with the happy result that sports historians were finding jobs.

Publishers began to get in on the action. Elliott Gorn, who had landed a real job out of graduate school, had already planted a flag on the summit of historical respectability by publishing his much-reprinted, justly renowned article, " 'Gouge and Bite, Pull Hair and Scratch': The Social Significance of Fighting in the Southern Backcountry," in the *American Historical Review* in 1985. Cornell University Press published his now-classic *The Manly Art: Bare-Knuckle Prize Fighting in America* in 1986. He then signed a contract with Hill & Wang to write a general history of American sports, and I joined him as coauthor; *A Brief History of American Sports* came out in 1993. The trend accelerated in the 1990s, with the publication of new textbooks, biographies, monographs, and more popular work. As the encyclopedia craze hit academic publishing, I began getting requests to write about baseball figures, modern sports history, and even baseball itself.

By the early 1990s baseball history had come into its own. I think this phenomenon had to do with a number of converging factors. First, it's difficult to overestimate the importance of Bill James, whose lively prose and even livelier mind brought a new, more populist generation of fans into the serious study of baseball strategy and baseball history. James gave fans the tools to rethink the shibboleths found too often on daily sports pages. Without him I doubt that the Society for American Baseball Research would have come into being. Along with James we need to credit the indefatigable John Thorn, who for decades published *Total Baseball*, the true bible of baseball statistics as well as a crucial forum for good baseball history.

The emphasis in the new social history on the experience of ordinary Americans opened up the possibility for historians to write about many different aspects of people's lives. Not only were their work, unions, and political allegiances important, but also historians came to appreciate the significance of recreation, drinking, family, and sex. As I've already suggested, I couldn't have written this book without the example and perhaps the encouragement of Roy Rosenzweig. The career of the historian Rob Ruck catches this movement as well. His 1977 master's thesis, written under the guidance of David Montgomery, dealt with the origins of the seniority system in the steel industry. His 1983 doctoral dissertation became the book *Sandlot Seasons: Sport in Black Pittsburgh* four years later. Tygiel and Ruck both began as labor historians (just as I had wanted to) and ended up using that expertise to do sports history.

Even though he once fired my wife and battled the least powerful workers at his wealthy university, A. Bartlett Giamatti must be credited in the rise of baseball history. Renaissance scholar, Yale president from 1978 to 1986, president of the National League from 1986 to 1989, and commissioner of baseball for a brief, tumultuous 154 days until his untimely death at 51, Giamatti wrote lyrically about baseball and merged the worlds of academia and major league baseball. I know Giamatti's interest in the game made people look at me differently, even though, as I often pointed out to these now admiring scholars, Giamatti began writing about baseball only long after he'd earned tenure.

Inspired in part by Giamatti's example, more academics and academic presses began to acknowledge their inner baseball fan and suited up. The early 1990s saw publication of James Edward Miller's *The Baseball Business: Pursuing Pennants and Profits in Baltimore*, Charles Alexander's *Our Game: An American Baseball History*, and Benjamin Rader's terrific one-volume history *Baseball: A History of America's Game*. Bruce Kuklick wrote a lovely, biblically titled book about Philadelphia baseball, *To Every Thing a Season: Shibe Park and Urban Philadelphia, 1909–1976*, while Andrew Zimbalist wrote the best book for noneconomists on the economics of baseball, *Baseball and Billions: A Probing Look inside the Big Business of Our National Pastime*. The high literary culture *Gettysburg Review* devoted most of its 1992 summer issue to baseball fiction, poetry, and essays, including my own foray into baseball literary criticism.

I don't know the exact lineage, but there must be some reason women's baseball burst onto the scene that year and a little later. The film *League of Their Own* certainly helped, but so did Lois Browne's *Girls of Summer: In Their Own League*, Barbara Gregorich's *Women at Play: The Story of Women in Baseball*, and Gai Ingham Berlage's *Women in Baseball: The Forgotten History*.

University presses—most notably Illinois and Nebraska—began book series in sports history. In this same period I began getting frequent requests from presses to review manuscripts on baseball history, sports history, the history of baseball cards, baseball in various wars, minor league baseball, baseball biographies, and the like. The floodgates were open. And like all movements, this one made it possible for bad books to join good ones. I remember reading the same manuscript for three different presses. It wasn't any better the third time around, but by then presses were putting out mediocre books on the theory that any baseball book would sell.

Any assessment of the popularity and respectability of baseball history has to look to the phenomenon of Ken Burns. In 1990 I got a call from Burns's producer, Lynn Novick, who'd just finished reading *Playing for Keeps*. She told me Burns ("Do you know his work?") was starting work on a big television documentary on the history of baseball and invited me to be a scholarly consultant on the project. Well, the truth was I'd never heard of Ken Burns, but the project sounded like an enjoyable way to make a few bucks. Then, a few months later *The Civil War* became American television history, and I realized I'd be working with the most famous historical documentarian in the country. It turned out that I would also be collaborating with a remarkable group of people whose work I'd admired for years and with others whom I grew to admire: the historian Geoff Ward (Ken's coauthor and screenwriter); Bill James and John Thorn; the historian William Leuchtenberg, the *New Yorker's* Roger Angell (well, I was in a room with him once for an hour or so); and the essayist Gerald Early. As the only academic baseball historian who also taught mainstream American history I had a small but apparently valued role in the process, in which I critiqued the script, presented results of my own research, and offered a broader historical perspective on some of the baseball events.

One thrilling week Ken brought us to Walpole, New Hampshire, to watch and critique the entire twenty-three-hour rough cut of the film. Ken and his team had thoroughly reinterpreted and restructured the history of the game, all organized through the lens of racial segregation and reintegration via Jackie Robinson. The Robinson story lay at the absolute center of the film, and Ken told it beautifully. But he offered a social history of the game as well, telling the story of black baseball better than it had ever been told on screen before, giving the great Negro League players their due, and digging up extraordinary archival material to flesh out the story. This was true for the rough cut I saw that time in Walpole, and it was true of the finished film as well.

Finding Buck O'Neill and putting him on-screen to draw on his seemingly inexhaustible trove of stories did more to introduce nonspecialists to African American ballplayers and the Negro Leagues than any other work before or since. O'Neill, who died in 2006 at 94, told stories about Satchel Paige and Jackie Robinson that no one had ever published before. And while most of us knew the outlines, even many of the details, of the Jackie Robinson story—mainly due to Jules Tygiel's masterful *Baseball's Great Experiment: Jackie Robinson and His Legacy*—Ken's team also got Rachel Robinson to say more about Jackie than she'd ever told anyone. In fact, Ken said that even though he'd been making films for twenty years, he'd never been so moved by an interview. When they finished, he said, tears were streaming down his face and those of his crew.

Burns also told the story of baseball's labor relations better than anyone and merged the race and labor stories in an extraordinary section on the St. Louis Cardinals outfielder Curt Flood, who sued to overturn baseball's antitrust exemption and not only lost (in the last Supreme Court decision on the subject, *Flood v. Kuhn*) but watched his comrades abandon him in the courtroom—all but Jackie Robinson, that is. Burns understood the centrality of the reserve rule to the growth of the baseball business and charted the battles between players and owners until the players finally defeated the nineteenth-century relic. Ken sided with the players, and it changed the story.

He filled out the incredibly capacious story of the game with sections on ballparks, ballpark food, baseball music, bat and ball manufacturing, and dozens of other riffs. The result was a remarkable success. True, critics didn't like having to watch an eighteen-and-a-half-hour film to review it, and lots of fans in the heartland didn't like the emphasis on New York (and Boston) teams. Many baseball historians found it frustrating, to a greater or lesser extent, noting dozens of places (out of many thousands) where photographs or footage didn't match the narrative and highlighting a number of factual errors. Most of the historians wanted more social history, too. I wanted a riveting film that incorporated as much social history as possible and didn't cater to nostalgia. Fully acknowledging my own investment in the film, I think *Baseball* succeeded brilliantly on this score.

In retrospect, I think the most serious error in the film was its lack of attention to Latin ballplayers, whose rapidly increasing numbers in the major leagues jumped more than 25 percent while *Baseball* was in production and shot up another 60 percent by 2007. The percentage of Latinos in the majors surpassed that of African Americans in 1996 and has widened pretty steadily ever since. Burns missed the trend, but he was hardly alone; the rest of us working on the film did so as well. Some did not, however. Since the 1980s Rob Ruck had been exploring the connections between Latin and Negro League baseball, and, after writing about black sports in Pittsburgh, he traveled to the Dominican Republic to write a wonderful exploration of Dominican baseball, *The Tropic of Baseball: Baseball in the Dominican Republic*. Beautifully written and combining oral history and layered historical analysis of baseball, Ruck's work set a new standard for international baseball history and showed the reality of baseball's demographics in the last dozen years and likely many more.

Since Burns's film the University of Nebraska Press has been the most aggressive publisher in the field, republishing classic memoirs and other out-of-print gems, such as Roger Angell's *Five Seasons*. Nebraska has also published a three-volume documentary history of the game, books about minor league baseball, Native American ballplayers, African American ballplayers, the classic Mark Harris novel *Bang the Drum Slowly*, as well as the publications of the Society for American Baseball Research and the biannual journal *Nine: A Journal of Baseball History and Culture*. Trade presses also jumped into the fray, publishing such journalistic luminaries as David Halberstam (*Summer of '49* and *October 1964*) and James Reston Jr. (*Collision at Home Plate: The Lives of Pete Rose and Bart Giamatti*).

Now the book tables at the Organization of American Historians and American Historical Association annual meetings all feature the latest and forthcoming baseball titles as marketing teasers; no one bats an eye. Some of the milling historians may still look down their noses. It is also true that departments never advertise for someone who studies or teaches sports history. (I know of one department with more than one sports historian and another that told me one was plenty.) The AHA, which accommodates "areas of scholarly interest" such as numismatics and "society, social system, and values" (whatever that means), does not make room for sports. The OAH, however does list "sports/recreation" as an area of interest, and, while some prejudice against sports history remains, there is no doubt that the world has changed since *Playing for Keeps* first appeared.

Anyone republishing a book two decades later has to ask what needs changing or updating—or correcting. Because the publisher and I agreed not to change anything except the cover and instead add this introduction and a selected bibliography, I ought to address what has happened in the quarter-century since I began writing this book.

I think Robert Pinsky would be happier with the prose in the books I've published since *Playing for Keeps*, but there's not much to be done about what's already between these covers. I will say, however, that while I expected to cringe at some of my oldest published sentences, I must either be getting less critical in late middle age or the young man wrote better than I remembered—and feared. I'd write the book differently now, but then again I might not have the same patience I had in 1981 to sift through the arguments over the "fly rule." So, with a certain amout of hubris, I offer you not exactly the new and improved version but a proud survivor of the early days in a now enormous field.

"Why bother?" you may ask. "Hasn't this flood of new scholarship rendered early work more or less irrelevant?" At the risk of still more hubris, I'll explain why the book remains relevant. First, almost no one has gone back to reread and re-analyze—and therefore to reinterpret—the basic sources I used in *Playing for Keeps*. My presentation and analysis of the baseball coverage in the sporting press and the Harry Wright Papers remains the best available. A number of people have written about Henry Chadwick—most notably Tygiel, in his terrific book of essays *Past Time: Baseball as History*—and the early years, but not many have done the archival research that would enable them to reconstruct a different history. Tygiel disagrees with my account of the origin of baseball statistics; I remain unpersuaded by his account, but readers are welcome to read his argument against mine.

Second, most descriptions of the early game quickly gloss over some truly fascinating material. Most authors are in a hurry to get to the founding (at least) of the National League. No book I know spends as much time as *Playing for Keeps* on the inner workings of the early New York baseball clubs and the combination of psychology, business sense, and fraternal feeling that structured players' and fans' experiences of the early game.

Third, there's an unusual and, to me, important argument embedded in this book. It is a critical account of the nature of history, historical explanation in baseball, and how fans (and scholars) experience the game. I argue that there are at least two histories of the game—one linear, chronological, and material, the other cyclical, generational, and emotional. The common confusion between them explains our frequent inability to see the history of the game with any degree of clarity. That insight struck me as novel when I first wrote it, and I am more than ever convinced of its value today.

The only part of the book that strikes me as genuinely out of date is the section on baseball's origins. I tried to acknowledge the shifting nature of the origin story by writing, "We must, however, begin somewhere, and the most convenient—and most widely accepted—starting place in the history of organized baseball is the Knickerbocker Base Ball Club of New York." Ever since I wrote that sentence, scholars have been locating earlier baseball games, setting the sport further back in time. And David Block, in *Baseball before We Knew It: A Search for the Roots of the Game*, has done transatlantic research that debunks the common belief that baseball originated in the English children's game rounders and demonstrates (at least for now) that baseball actually descended from medieval ball games and then specifically from English base-ball, a children's game that appeared in the 1740s. Interestingly, the fact that rounders was a contemporary of baseball affected little of the subsequent history of the game itself; baseball promoters and reporters consistently strove to make baseball into a manly sport instead of a children's game. In a newer telling, I would note that baseball's "reformers," led by Henry Chadwick, were in reality pitting a newer, more difficult version of the game against the older "children's game." But the difference from rounders, it turns out, was not central to the development of the game.

In sum, I think *Playing for Keeps* remains relevant, unusual, a good read, and the most in-depth account of the game's formative years, mostly in the New York area, but also in its early professional years, as seen through the career and person of Harry Wright.

Finally, I'd like to say a bit about the significance of the last two decades in the study of baseball history. The single biggest change is that the field is now so large that anyone teaching a course in it would have difficulty choosing books to assign. We are still at the stage where more of the basic territory is being staked out, though perhaps not for much longer. And while I haven't written any sports history (other than reviews) for fifteen years, I love the new size and sophistication of our once tiny field.

The greatest gains in recent history have been in exploring and fleshing out the baseball history of ethnic and racial minorities largely excluded from, or only allowed limited participation in, the white major leagues. Black baseball has received extraordinary attention in the past twenty years, ranging from nonacademic oral histories to a flood of local research to some remarkable efforts to put Negro League baseball into a larger context, most recently and notably Neal Lanctot's *Negro League Baseball: The Rise and Ruin of a Black Institution.* But any issue of *Nine* shows how much more there is to know about individual events, the sports culture of particular towns and cities, and about poorly understood or relatively unknown baseball figures who have faded in memory. The Society for American Baseball Research publishes the annual *Baseball Research Journal*, as well as *The National Pastime* (both through the University of Nebraska Press). The Annual Cooperstown Symposium on Baseball and American Culture began publishing its proceedings about a decade ago. The *Elysian Fields Quarterly* publishes a heady mix of memoir, literature, history, and journalism. You will have no problem finding articles and books on Native American baseball—and on baseball in South Africa, Australia, Japan, Latin America, and just about anywhere else.

At long last Latin baseball has begun to receive due attention from North

American scholars. Roberto González Echevarría published *The Pride of Havana: A History of Cuban Baseball* a decade ago, well after, I should add, achieving fame as a literary scholar. But here, too, the tide appears to have turned, as the energetic young scholar Adrian Burgos Jr. has spent his entire academic career writing about Latin and African American baseball and whose *Playing America's Game: Baseball, Latinos, and the Color Line*, published in 2007, helped earn him tenure at the University of Illinois–Champaign-Urbana. Perhaps even more important, Burgos was part of a research team that received a $250,000 grant from the National Baseball Hall of Fame and Museum (underwritten by Major League Baseball itself) to produce a comprehensive history of the Negro Leagues and African American baseball. He researched Latinos in the Negro Leagues and African American ballplayers' involvement in Latin American baseball, both of which were substantial stories. Burgos became one of the coauthors (along with Tygiel and Neil Lanctot) of the 2006 book that resulted from this extraordinary project, *Shades of Glory: The Negro Leagues and the Story of African American Baseball*. I suspect there's more to come along these lines, but the flood of material raises one large, and final, question for me. What may we expect from the next conceptual jump in the history of the game? When will the history begin producing the kind of analysis aiming mainly to repopulate the game with those who have been absent from the history to date? And when will baseball history acquire the density of the best American cultural history? This isn't meant uncharitably; it's the pattern in all new fields. Even though *Playing for Keeps* takes on some pretty big issues— why baseball became so popular, the origins of the professional game, an explanation of baseball statistics, and the nature of baseball history—it was also an example of scholarship in a young field. An exquisite example of the kind of history I have in mind—history that will move the field into a more mature phase—is an essay by Tygiel, who had already done the field extraordinary service with *Baseball's Great Experiment* but who achieved new heights in the perfectly titled *Past Time: Baseball as History*. It is painful to lose anyone who dies before his time, as Tygiel did at 59 last year—all the more so as he was showing us how to take baseball to an entirely new level. In the essay "The Shot Heard 'Round the World," Tygiel confidently assumed that baseball has as much to teach us as any other cultural artifact and provided a social, cultural, racial, media, and foreign policy analysis of the most famous home run in modern baseball history, Bobby Thomson's pennant-winner against the Dodgers in 1951. Brilliantly intertwining these different threads into a compelling narrative of a truly emblematic game on the cusp between two baseball eras, Tygiel's essay serves as the historical equivalent to Don DeLillo's astonishing fictional recreation of the home run in the fifty-page prologue to *Underworld*. Since baseball history of this caliber wasn't even conceivable twenty years ago, I will conclude here and circle back to Richard Fox in that dining hall long ago. "No, no," he insisted. "It'll be great!" And it was.

Acknowledgments

In the last few years the social and cultural history of sport has become a more or less respectable field for scholarly inquiry. Ten years ago, when this book was conceived, the intellectual climate was quite otherwise. I am most thankful to the scholars and friends who were willing to risk taking seriously a serious history of baseball.

More than fifteen years ago Leo Ribuffo and Sarah Stage introduced me to the study of American history. I have been waiting a long time to offer them public thanks. About the same time my friends Marc Gunther and Jerry Kleiner inducted me into their baseball fraternity. Neither of them ever dreamed that I would repay them for what they taught me about baseball by writing a book about a period of baseball history in which the New York Yankees did not even exist. Both nevertheless spent countless hours giving me the benefit of their considerable critical skills and deep understanding of the game. The late Marshall Rachleff, whose passion for justice and American history were exceeded only by his love of baseball and the Detroit Tigers, pushed me in the only way he could—hard—to write this book. I am grateful for the all too brief time during which I experienced his astonishing courage, laughter, and wisdom as he battled leukemia to a standstill for more than a decade.

David Brion Davis contributed to my education as a historian in many ways, but especially through his enthusiasm for intellectual risk-taking and his astute and careful readings of my work. In a profession increasingly shaped by the demands of the marketplace, Kai T. Erikson stood out as a humane, committed scholar and teacher. It was my remarkable good fortune to work with him. All historians now laboring in unconventional areas of cultural history are deeply indebted to the late Warren Susman for his pioneering and underappreciated achievement in expanding the definition of what may be considered fit subjects for historical investigation. Happily, I and my work were the direct beneficiaries of his principles, generosity, and insight when he agreed to chair a panel on work and play at the 1982 meeting of the American Historical Association. He was taken from us too soon.

Peter Agree, history editor at Cornell University Press, has shown unflagging interest in getting this book into print, even in the face of authorial foot-dragging. I am grateful for his confidence in me. I also thank Barbara H. Salazar, senior manuscript editor at Cornell, who edited this book with impressive thoroughness, patience, and skill.

My brother Ralph Goldstein managed to put up with my stubborn computer illiteracy long enough to teach me word processing and thereby to earn my lasting thanks. Jean-Christophe Agnew read and offered valuable comments on early chapters. Ronald Story gave the entire manuscript an extraordinarily generous reading.

Three scholars made especially noteworthy contributions to this book. Melvin Adelman's kindness to those working in sports history must be a minor legend by now. He sent me his own research on early baseball in New York, copies of hard-to-find articles, and chapters out of his book, and he is one of the very few people capable or willing to talk with me about the 1860 Atlantics or the Mutuals of 1867.

Roy Rosenzweig's thorough, detailed, appreciatively critical reading of my manuscript remains the finest piece of criticism I have ever received on any written work. I still don't quite know how he does it. I hope that the final product meets the expectations of his comments.

For permission to quote from letters and other materials in the Harry Wright Papers and the Henry Chadwick Scrapbooks, both in the Albert G. Spalding Collection, I thank the Rare Books and Manuscripts Division, The New York Public Library, Astor, Lenox, and Tilden Foundations.

Finally, I thank Elliott Gorn, who raised the standards of American sport history with his fine history of boxing, *The Manly Art*, and who took time out from his own writing to go over this book with me chapter by chapter. To find a good friend, first-rate scholar, and patient editor all in the same person has been a rare pleasure.

One other person has lived with this book as long, if not as willingly, as I—my wife, Donna. For her faith in me, for her love of baseball and Cooperstown, and for what she has taught me about "playing for keeps," I am more grateful than I can say.

WARREN GOLDSTEIN

Riverhead, New York

Playing for Keeps

Prologue

Histories of the Game

The historian who studies the development of organized baseball is frequently struck by a sense of déjà vu. So many of the controversies of modern baseball are repetitions of earlier disputes that one wonders, finally, if baseball really has a history, or at least a history understood as change and development. "These modern ballplayers," begins a familiar lament, "care about nothing but money. They don't care about their team, or their city, or their fans. In my day [in my father's day, in the good old days] they were different." But were they? This fan certainly would have no trouble finding others to agree with him. And he would feel support for his complaint if, reading the sports pages one morning, he ran across a column by a veteran player claiming that "somehow or other they don't play ball nowadays as they used to some eight or ten years ago. . . . I mean that they don't play with the same kinds of feelings or for the same objects they used to."[1] Somewhat less encouraging to the modern fan would be the date of the veteran's letter—January 9, 1868.

The problem for the historian is to make sense of nearly identical claims separated by a century during which baseball underwent enormous changes in scale and organization. We may begin by noting that such statements are less thoughtful analyses of contemporary baseball than they are emotional commentaries on the game, particularly on satisfactions that it evidently no longer provides to its followers. One strategy, therefore, is simply to ignore them, or to treat them as obstacles in the path toward discovery of the "real" history of

I

the game. Most baseball histories adopt this method, and some are fine accounts of the growth of the modern professional game. Others, far less interested in what "really" happened, rely on their own (or other people's) memories and feelings about the game, and write memoirs. Some of these personal, idiosyncratic accounts of the game, usually set during the authors' youths, are among the loveliest and most insightful books inspired by baseball.[2]

But if we are interested—as I am—in the history both of the structure and of the experience of the game, neither choice is adequate. We need a method that, capable of grasping structural change and development, can also account for and assess the significance of the intense and often remarkably similar emotions regularly evoked by the game. One such approach is to recognize that baseball has (at least) two very different kinds of histories: one linear, chronological, and cumulative, the other cyclical, generational, and repetitive. This latter historical form can help us to understand the fan's lament. Much of the game's history has been concerned with very basic tensions that resist resolution. When those conflicts are relived by each new generation of players and fans, they may be expressed in different ways, but the tensions remain. That is why baseball history has an eerily repetitive quality; as Yogi Berra is rumored to have remarked, "it's déjà vu all over again." It is also one of the reasons that the game is experienced and remembered so intensely. Feeling many of the same excitements, fears, and ambivalences that fans and players have been feeling since baseball began, each participant in the game is also in a relationship with every other participant in the game throughout its history. Despite the hundred-year gulf between them, our modern fan and the veteran of 1868 would immediately recognize what the other was feeling about baseball.[3]

The combination of unresolvable tensions and generational turnover has exercised a stabilizing influence on the experience of the game. Players' and fans' first encounters with baseball typically occur in childhood, and childhood memories form a deep reservoir of feelings about play treated with the utmost seriousness. Children cannot understand the expression "It's only a game." To what, in their world, could the "only" be referring? Playing baseball as a child, though serious, is never work, never paid, and that is one reason adult fans complain constantly (and have always complained) about professional players' salaries. Although the argument is usually couched as an objection to the magnitude of those salaries, its emotional force clearly derives from the very fact that men, usually very young men—"unforgivably young men," in Roger Angell's words—earn any money at all by playing baseball. "In my day," maintains our modern fan, "the players played for the fun of the game—not for what they could make at it." That the fan is almost certainly wrong (that is, if he grew up later than the 1860s) is an important but not the only point. It is equally important to understand in what sense the fan is right. When he was a boy the only players he knew did play for fun, and he did not have the mental categories to understand that major-league ballplayers were different. In this light, the famous plea of the little boy for Shoeless Joe Jackson to "say it ain't so" ought to be understood as a wish for the ballplayer to deny his involvement not only in the Black Sox scandal but also in what, to the distraught boy, must have appeared by far the greater scandal—playing ball for money rather than for fun.[4]

For most fans baseball history is a combination of remembered feeling and "the facts," and despite their well-known obsession with statistics of the game, fans' memories of specific statistics (such as a favorite player's batting average during a particular year) are usually less accurate than forcefully held. What is telling about baseball memories is where they come from. The most passionate comparisons, recalled events, remembered stories usually fall into the category of the personally distant or very recent past. The distant personal past usually means childhood; these memories rarely come from the fan's adolescence or young adulthood—the time when young fans learn (among other things) that play is for children, that adults work, and that their heroes have jobs, contract disputes, and little attachment to the "home" town and team. That the standards fans use to judge baseball—the game and the players—are so clearly drawn either from the world of the child (player) or from that of the adult (nonplayer) indicates just how difficult it is for fans to engage memories and experiences drawn from the time when they lost their innocence. That only the most self-reflective baseball literature deals with this process of discovery and disillusion suggests its deeply unsettling nature. And yet it is precisely the adolescence of organized baseball that is the subject of this book, two decades remembered by no one, which nonetheless contained the seeds of the game's next hundred years.

In the late 1850s, organized baseball was a club-based fraternal pastime grounded in the respectable local culture of urban artisans, clerks, and small proprietors. By the mid-1870s, it had become a substantial commercial undertaking depending on business management, gate receipts, and the paid labor of baseball players. This book is an intensive examination of the culture and structure of organized baseball during these years. It is not an attempt to substantiate Jacques Barzun's claim that "whoever wants to know the heart and mind of America had better learn baseball." It neither celebrates "America learning to play" baseball nor chronicles the decline of "true sport" into "just another business." It presents no elaborate definitions or typologies of "leisure," "recreation," "play," "games," or "sport" in an effort to be "scientific." Baseball has always included elements of work as well as play; one of the principal burdens of this book is to explain the work and play of the game, to show how they merged, how they conflicted, and how they changed.

By the early 1860s sharp differences had already emerged among players, clubs, spectators, and the press over how much emphasis ought to be placed on the game itself—on practice, skillful play, and playing to win—as opposed to the "social" side of the game—post-game dinners, club balls, and playing for "fun and exercise." Parallel conflicts had also arisen. Players and commentators became obsessed by the felt need to retain and demonstrate their "manliness" on the ballfield (and in their clubs) as they played, with increasing seriousness, what had been until quite recently a boys' game. Within the baseball fraternity, "boyish" behavior became synonymous with the more expressive, less self-controlled, at times rowdy behavior of the urban, "unrespectable" working classes.

The tensions that structured the experience of early baseball—manliness vs. boyishness, self-control vs. excitement, playing for fun vs. playing for keeps—were held together mainly by the powerful ties of fraternalism within the baseball world. By the late 1860s, however, what I call the "modernizers" within the game—those most committed to top-flight competitive play—had come to dominate organized baseball and were taking it decisively toward open professionalism.

Baseball spread dramatically throughout the Northeast and Midwest in the half-dozen years following the Civil War, so that by the end of the decade it had probably begun to deserve to be called the national game. At the same time, the life of the baseball club had undergone a profound change. Professional "clubs" were really small businesses now. Club "members" had become spectators of the club's "players," employees under contract who had frequently been "imported" (in the language of the time) from another city.

The baseball world had never been very far removed from the world of work. As early as 1860 the language reporters used to describe a successful team was the language of self-disciplined, productive craft labor. The late 1860s saw the introduction of the ideology and practice of management in professional baseball, and the relationships between players and "managers" began to resemble those between workers and employers in other nineteenth-century businesses. Club captains exercised wide authority over the conduct of their players on and off the field, while club rules—which had been collectively determined and enforced guidelines for club behavior— became instruments of labor discipline. The legendary Cincinnati Red Stockings of 1869, known mostly for their all-professional nine and undefeated season, embodied these deeper changes in the game: the "nationalization" of baseball, the changed relationships between clubs and players, and the success of a new kind of baseball management.

As the National Association of Professional Base Ball Players was organizing in early 1871, a number of men from some of baseball's oldest clubs—clubs that had been out of the competitive mainstream for years—mounted an amateur challenge to the professional game. Emotionally grounded in a mythically harmonious and Edenic past, this effort, though it appealed to many fans and practitioners of the sport, underestimated the extent to which baseball's modernizers had already transformed the game. The amateur arena quickly became all but indistinguishable from professional play, and the amateur association soon collapsed. Nor was the professional association much of an organization; it lasted only five years before it was supplanted by the National League of Professional Base Ball Clubs in 1876. During these years, however, professional clubs completed the conceptual transformation of baseball play into work performed by employees under contract to boards of directors, directed and disciplined by "management." Their skills in demand, players earned relatively high salaries at this time. For baseball businessmen, who were having a difficult time making the game into a stable and profitable enterprise, players' salaries were obvious targets. National League owners' introduction of the infamous "reserve clause" in 1879 was designed to eliminate players' freedom in the marketplace and thereby permanently to limit the size of their salaries. For the next century and more, the principal struggle in professional baseball has remained that between players and owners over control of the game's labor market.

It is only by looking at the development of baseball as an arena of work as well as play that we can understand the linear and material history of the game. By listening closely to what the baseball fraternity thought and said—and did not say—about these developments, we can follow the game's cyclical and emotional history. Both histories will enable us to see how organized baseball came to be played for keeps.

A Note on Method

Contrary to what might be expected, there is no dearth of accessible source material on nineteenth-century baseball. True, more exists for the latter part of the century than for the 1850s and 1860s, and there are better archival collections for an institutional history of the game than for a cultural or social history of baseball. But since names of ballplayers generally appeared in the press by the late 1850s, much work can still be done with city directories and census schedules to determine more precisely just who these ballplayers were, what they did for a living, and where they came from.[5]

As social historians have known for some time, it is difficult to find sources that show what ordinary people in the past thought and felt about their lives. Nevertheless, that is precisely what I am most interested in here—the way early baseball was felt, perceived, thought about, and experienced. For this reason I have focused on the written word and not on statistical analysis. A wealth of writing about baseball appeared during the early years of its organization, most of it in newspapers. It was concentrated in the sporting press, and I have, accordingly, put most of my attention there.

It is not enough, however, simply to point out that I have "relied" on contemporary newspapers, in the manner that, say, a political historian consults newspapers for news of political events and conflicts. While I do use reporters' accounts of games and club activities as guides to events in the baseball world, they are much more useful as *documents* of baseball culture in the 1850s and 1860s. Any writing reveals more than its author intends, and I have usually been more concerned with the way game stories were structured, the language reporters used, and the tensions their language reveals or suppresses than in the outcomes of the games they describe.

Since this work is concerned with the experience and consciousness of baseball, contemporary reporting and commentary make excellent sources. Journalism was much more involved with its subjects in the mid–nineteenth century than it is now. Journalistic "objectivity" was far from the standard universally accepted; reporters did not feel constrained to write only about "the facts." It was not at all unusual for reporters to praise the people they wrote about or to condemn them in vigorous terms. In this respect sports reporting resembled the political and crime journalism of the period.[6] It was, in fact, connected to both of these genres, most clearly in the person of George Wilkes.

Wilkes's crowded career is difficult to summarize briefly. Born in 1817, perhaps the son of a cabinetmaker, Wilkes became deeply involved in New York journalism and workingmen's politics by the 1840s. He worked with Mike Walsh as an editor of the *Subterranean*, served a four-week term in the Tombs on a libel conviction, and cofounded the *National Police Gazette* in 1845. In his enthusiastic efforts to expose crime, vice, and corruption, he was, according to one historian, "a spirit more nearly akin to the rogues whose careers he so carefully traced in his *Police Gazette* than he would perhaps have been prepared to admit." After an interlude in California in the early 1850s, when he worked for a time as a speechwriter and political strategist for his friend and fellow New York expatriate David Broderick (a state senator in the early 1850s and United States Senator from 1857 to 1859), Wilkes returned to New York journalism. Through a complicated series of deals, maneuvers, and arguments, Wilkes became associated first with the eminent racing paper *Spirit of the Times*, then with a competitor, *Porter's Spirit of the Times*, and finally founded his own *Wilkes' Spirit of the Times* in 1859. The other papers soon folded, and Wilkes's sheet became the premier sporting periodical of its time.[7]

Wilkes' Spirit of the Times put aside the salacious crime stories of its editor's youth and claimed it would publish nothing that could not be read aloud in the respectable Victorian family parlor. "In the discharge of this duty," wrote Wilkes, "the most scrupulous care will be taken, as heretofore, to exclude any expression incompatible with the presence of the paper in the refined family circle." Although its extensive commentaries on prizefights put this goal out of reach, Wilkes was moving in that direction. His later renunciation of prize-fighting and the paper's move "uptown to a middle class setting where . . . [boxing] was viewed as morally and aesthetically distaste-ful" was foreshadowed by his appeal to the respectable family circle. Wilkes was leaving behind most of the bawdy, raucous forms of urban street culture, and the baseball coverage in his paper reflected his own cultural and class choices.[8]

But in the late 1850s and early 1860s Wilkes was clearly ambiva-lent about such choices. Like the rest of the sporting press, *Wilkes' Spirit of the Times* provided extensive coverage of the theater. The sporting press, in fact, was the theatrical press at this time. *Porter's Spirit of the Times* billed itself as "A Chronicle of the Turf, Field Sports, Literature, and the Stage," as did its parent *Spirit of the Times*. Wilkes's paper featured the same subtitle when it began publication. His principal competitor among sporting sheets, Frank Queen's *New York Clipper*, was subtitled "American Sporting and Theatrical Journal." Both papers published theater schedules along with their calendar of sporting events, and it is likely that reviews of dramatic performances provided the critical climate that helped give rise to the involved, often vehement style of 1860s baseball journal-ism. Both papers also spent more time on horse racing and boxing than on the fledgling organized game of baseball.

The *New York Clipper* made no attempt to distance itself from the more roguish aspects of urban culture. Serialized tales of crime and seduction ran regularly on its front page.[9] Curiously, however, this paper's baseball coverage was indistinguishable from that of its main competitor. In fact, one of the striking characteristics of the baseball journalism of those years was its uniformity from paper to paper. Reporters frequently wrote for more than one publication, and one could pick up almost any paper and find virtually identical language, tones, and attitudes. Baseball coverage ranged from short accounts of games to long stories on important matches, from descriptions of club social activities to discussions of changes in club personnel. Papers published letters from clubs, players, and fans, and held mail for baseball clubs and players.

Yet some commentators' voices carried a disproportionate amount of weight in the baseball world. Chief among them was Henry Chadwick, longtime baseball correspondent for the *New York Clipper*, the *Brooklyn Eagle*, and the *New York Sunday Mercury* and an influential figure in the early history of the game. Born in 1824, the half-brother of the English sanitary reformer Sir Edwin Chadwick, Henry Chadwick came to the United States at the age of thirteen. He wrote about cricket for a while in the 1850s but made his real contribution as a sportswriter in baseball reporting and commentary. A prolific writer, Chadwick edited scores of annual guides to the game and authored numerous books on baseball and other sports. Throughout his career Chadwick remained a vigorous proponent of particular ways of playing, analyzing, and recording the game, of changes in baseball rules and structures, even—and perhaps most important—of a version of baseball morality. His writings constitute an indispensable source for the study of the early game.[10]

One of my principal assumptions is that this body of writing can be used to enter the lived experience of organized baseball in the 1850s and 1860s. Baseball writers were intimately involved in the baseball world of their day. They played the game and sometimes, as in Chadwick's case, belonged to a club. They participated in baseball politics, attended club social affairs, and accompanied clubs on visits to other cities. The most vocal promoters of the newly organized game, they expected—and received—privileged treatment from players and clubs. On the field itself, they sat in a special position between players and spectators, at a table known by the early 1860s by the term still used today: the "press box." They were instrumental in developing systems of scoring, and played a key role in developing, publishing, and disseminating baseball's statistics. Most were unabashed fans of the game and had little sense of a distancing, "professional" journalistic ethos.

Given this involvement in all details of the game, it is unlikely that, over a period of years, their accounts of baseball games and other events in the baseball world could have been consistently inaccurate or radically distinct from the experience of the players and spectators. Reporters depended on both, after all, for stories and readers. They may not, in other words, have been particularly *reliable* informants about specific games, but they did nearly always offer *relevant* observations. If we approach their reports and commentaries as documents to be read rather than definitive accounts of events, this otherwise pedestrian source begins to reveal a good deal about the way people experienced the game.

Some years ago, in a remarkable lecture about "wife-selling" in eighteenth-century England, E. P. Thompson talked about the need to "break" the dull and matter-of-fact language of newspaper stories in order to get at the emotional realities of the event being described. Nineteenth-century newspaper stories usually did not employ very complex language or imagery, but if read carefully, with an eye to pattern, structure, theme, and use of language, they yield much more than their narrative simplicity suggests at first glance. I cannot claim to have broken the code of nineteenth-century baseball reporting with Thompson's ingenuity. I have nevertheless acquired some confidence in this way of approaching otherwise recalcitrant texts.

Origins

A popular but little-heralded children's game in antebellum America, baseball existed in a wide variety of forms and was known by as many names: "base," "one-old-cat," "stool ball," "rounders," "feeder," "bat and ball," and many others. All of these games involved a tossed ball, a batter who tried to hit the ball with a stick of some kind, and one or more "bases" to which the batter ran in a circuit after striking the ball. Most of the games had been played in England at least as early as the eighteenth century, and games known as "baseball" date from those years. "Base" and "base ball" were also known in the United States in the late eighteenth and early nineteenth centuries.[11]

The best known of the ball games, and the genuine forerunner of American baseball, was the English game of rounders. This children's game provided for four bases laid out in a diamond-shaped configuration, a "feeder" who tossed the ball to the "striker," and "outs" when a striker missed the ball three times, batted a ball that was caught, or was hit by a thrown ball when running the bases. Rounders' status as baseball's immediate predecessor was both obvious and uncontroversial until the late nineteenth century, when Abraham G. Mills, then president of the National League, proclaimed at a New York baseball banquet that the national pastime had grown from American origins. His audience at Delmonico's responded with shouts of "No rounders!" and a small tempest began to brew. Something of a debate developed between two grand old men of the game—Henry Chadwick, the preeminent baseball writer of the latter nineteenth century, and Albert G. Spalding, the sporting goods millionaire, owner of the Chicago White Stockings, and former baseball official.[12]

While the English-born Chadwick maintained that baseball's paternity lay in rounders, Spalding argued vociferously for the American origins of the game. Abraham Mills chaired the commission assembled in response to Spalding's call to decide what he later called "that vexed controversy." Based solely on the recollections of an elderly former resident of Cooperstown, New York, Mills's report concluded that the late General Abner Doubleday had drawn "the first known diagram of the diamond, indicating positions for the players . . . in Cooperstown, N.Y., in 1839."[13] As no evidence has yet been produced to substantiate this account and a huge amount of evidence, both direct and indirect, contradicts it, it merits no further attention.

Still, we cannot ignore it, for this controversy continues to play a part in histories of the game. Modern historians insist on debunking the "Doubleday myth" as they begin their hardheaded examinations of the game. Yet disproof of such myths or their definitive banishment turns out to be beyond the powers of baseball historians, who find themselves ever more frustrated by the intransigent persistence of untruths.[14] No historian is entirely immune to the temptation to correct clear falsehood in the name of truth, but we do need to recognize that competing versions of baseball history have been part of the way the game has been played, watched, and thought about ever since its earliest years. This book is not an effort to establish the "real" or "definitive" history of early organized baseball, and does not aim to supplant all others. It is explicitly *a* history of early baseball, one that explores—among other things—the tendency of the game to invoke and incorporate its own history. I am less interested in destroying illusions than in seeing why people have created or attacked baseball mythology. Mythmakers and debunkers have been engaged in essentially the same endeavor: they appeal to history to validate and institutionalize their own experience of the game.

We must, however, begin somewhere, and the most convenient—and most widely accepted—starting place in the history of organized baseball is the Knickerbocker Base Ball Club of New York. Visions of beginning recorded baseball history probably had little to do with bringing together a group of men to play baseball on a vacant Manhattan lot sometime in 1842. Content to remain nameless, the group, though forced out of their old playing field by urban development, continued to play informally until 1845. In that year a young bank clerk named Alexander Joy Cartwright proposed that the players form a club. His fellows liked the idea, and, constituting themselves as the Knickerbocker Base Ball Club, they drew up a constitution, wrote down their playing rules, and rented a field and dressing rooms in the Elysian Fields of Hoboken, New Jersey. These fields were readily accessible by ferry from Manhattan; New Yorkers had been using them for social and recreational purposes for years.[15]

After an 1846 contest with the New York Club (about which very little is known) in which they were trounced by a score of 23 to 1, the Knickerbockers did not compete again on the ballfield until 1851. Doubtless they were chagrined by the lopsided defeat, but in any case competitors were scarce. The New York Club appears to have disappeared after its victory, and the Knickerbockers remained baseball's only club until 1850, when they were joined by the Washington Club. These clubs played two "matches," as formal games between clubs were called, in each of the next three years, and by 1854 two more clubs, the Eagles and the Empires, had entered the lists in New York.[16]

The mid-1850s saw baseball clubs spring up all over New York and Brooklyn: in 1855 there were eleven clubs in the two cities, and others in Newark and on Long Island. By 1856 there was talk of calling a convention of baseball clubs, and the idea came to fruition the following year under the leadership of the Knickerbockers. In 1858 players founded the rather hopefully named National Association of Base Ball Players. Because it is just about here that this history begins in earnest, a few general observations about the newly organized game are in order.

First, the version of the game codified by the Knickerbockers was but one of many played throughout the United States at the time. The Olympic Town Ball Club of Philadelphia, for example, had been organized in 1833 to play a kind of rounders known as town ball. Only in 1860 did the club members decide to adopt the game played by the Knickerbockers and other New York clubs. This decision, in the words of a contemporary journalist, prompted "mutterings both loud and deep," and the "honorable retirement of most of their old members." More common was a kind of baseball played principally in the New England states known as the "Massachusetts game" (to distinguish it from the "New York game"). Differing from the New York game in several important particulars—the bases were laid out in a square rather than a diamond, an inning was over when just one batter was put out, and the winner was the first side to score 100 runs—the Massachusetts game dominated New England baseball until the early 1860s, when a number of older clubs switched their allegiances and new clubs were formed to play what had become known by then as the "National Association game."[17]

Second, the very earliest baseball clubs competed neither as frequently, as regularly, nor as fiercely as modern ball clubs. Club members met regularly to play among themselves, but formal matches with other clubs were relatively rare events until the late 1850s. The game was embedded in a set of fraternal rituals and club activities in the 1850s and 1860s. Only later did the baseball contest emerge as the focal point for players, spectators, and the press.

Finally, despite important differences from modern-day baseball, the New York game would be recognizable to the present-day spectator. There were the same nine players on a side, the same configuration of bases, and then as now the batter—called the "striker"—endeavored to hit the ball thrown by the pitcher in a place where it could not be caught. Players were put "out" in familiar ways: they were out if they were forced at a base, if they were touched with the ball, if they swung at and missed the ball three times, or if a batted ball were caught on the fly. "Called strikes," however, were issued at the discretion of the umpire, there were no called "balls," and the batter was out if a fielder caught the batted ball on the first bounce. Fielders wore no gloves, masks, or shinguards. The pitcher stood only forty-five feet away from home plate (as opposed to sixty and one-half feet now) and delivered the ball underhand. Umpires were responsible for deciding disputed points of play: whether a runner was safe or out, whether it was too dark to continue playing, and when to call a strike on a batter. The Knickerbocker rules made the winner the first team to score twenty-one "aces," or runs, but in 1857 the new association adopted the modern rule providing for a nine-inning game.[18]

Because there were few called strikes and no balls, the rules favored the offense, and scores were extremely high by modern standards: twenty or thirty runs per side were the norm. Even so, reporters and knowledgeable fans preferred a low-scoring game in which defense and offense were more evenly balanced. Games usually began around three o'clock in the afternoon and lasted anywhere from two to four hours, with the majority probably taking between two and three hours. Crowds ranged from a few friends to upwards of five to ten thousand spectators for big games, such as the 1858 all-star matches between Brooklyn and New York at the Fashion Course race track.

Scholars sometimes refer to the early game as "quaint" or "amusing," and the version played in the 1840s and early 1850s may well have been so. But by the late 1850s defensive and offensive strategy alike had become quite sophisticated. Though pitchers threw underhanded, they could throw the ball very fast, and reporters commonly argued the advantages of pitching with control and cunning instead of depending on pure speed. Good fielders turned double plays frequently; runners stole bases and good catchers threw them out. Now that we have a sense of the game on the field, let us turn to the rather less familiar fraternal culture in which early baseball was embedded.

PART I

The Culture of Organized Baseball, 1857–1866

I

The Base Ball Fraternity

Rites of Play

The men who played early baseball considered themselves members of "the base ball fraternity," a fraternity organized around the baseball club. Although the language of the baseball club is still used today, even with respect to professional teams, it has been obsolete for a century. The earliest baseball organizations were genuine social clubs, in which baseball playing was an important but far from the only activity. As one club constitution put it, "the objects of the Club shall be to 'improve, foster and perpetuate the American game of Base Ball,' and advance morally, socially, and physically, the interests of its members."[1]

Baseball clubs had much in common with other male fraternal organizations in antebellum America. They were governed by constitutions, by-laws, and officers. Members paid dues and met regularly, either in their "club rooms" (usually located in a hotel or tavern) or on the playing field. Membership ranged from a dozen to more than two hundred. Depending on the number of members, clubs designated a "first nine" (the nine best players), a "second nine," and sometimes a "third nine." Most also had what was known as a "muffin nine," comprising the club's worst players.[2]

Competition between clubs during these years was quite formal. Although most clubs had regular "practice days," from one to (in one case) four days a week, and played "practice games," not all clubs played matches, and some played many more than others. Players and the press distinguished between "practice games," "friendly games," and "social games," on the one hand, and more competitive "matches" or "match-games," on the other. In order to arrange a match, a club first issued a written challenge to the club it wished to play; the challenged club then decided whether to accept the challenge. Matches could consist of a single game, but a club usually challenged another to a "home-and-home" series, best two out of three games.[3]

The captains of the opposing nines would agree on a mutually acceptable umpire, the press would be notified of the upcoming match, and occasionally the games would be advertised. Some matches were played for special prizes, but prizes were usually awarded only in large tournaments. The prize for victory in most matches was the game ball. At the end of the game, a spokesman for the losing club would present the ball to the winners with a short speech, to which a representative of the winning club would respond in kind. The ball was then retired, inscribed with the date and the score, and put in the winners' trophy case, usually located in their clubroom.[4]

Presentation of the ball did not end the affair. Throughout the 1850s and much of the 1860s, a match game was followed by a meal hosted by the "home" club, commonly at a local tavern, restaurant, or hotel. The festivities, which included toasts, speeches, and songs, sometimes lasted well into the night. These postgame social activities were mentioned in game stories, and from time to time they received detailed coverage. The fraternity kept track of the best hosts. A game with the Atlantic Club, for example, appears to have guaranteed its opponents (who were usually its victims) the "well-known hospitality" of this Brooklyn club. Such hospitality frequently included alcohol. At a match between the Atlantics and Eckfords in 1862, a third club provided a "fine collation including champagne." And an informal game a month later "was concluded in true base ball fashion, cheers and 'tigers' being exchanged in a hearty and earnest manner, and the 'lager and segars' were also hospitably dispensed." The *Clipper* observed good-naturedly of a game in 1860 that a "keg of lager" may have contributed to the apparent inability of the players to remember the score.[5]

When clubs traveled to a neighboring city or town, as many did once or twice a season, they were always entertained by the host club. The further they traveled, the more extravagant their treatment. Arriving in Baltimore at 4:00 A.M. for a match later that day, the Brooklyn Excelsiors were met by a committee of their hosts, the Baltimore Excelsiors, by whom they were escorted to Guy's Monument House, where all sat down to a splendid breakfast. . . . During the morning they were escorted in carriages to the various places of interest throughout the city, every attention it was possible to bestow upon them being given them by the gentlemanly members of the Baltimore Excelsiors. Indeed from the time of their arrival to their departure not a cent's expense were they allowed to incur, and whenever they desired to visit any place, carriages were at once placed at their disposal; in fact, nothing that the most generous hospitality could suggest, or yield, was wanting to make their time pass agreeably, and in this respect the Baltimoreans were most successful and victorious, taking the palm from every previous occasion the Excelsiors have hitherto enjoyed. About an hour before the time appointed for the commencement of the game, the Brooklyn party were escorted to Holliday street, where a city car, gaily decked with flags, and drawn by four horses, was in readiness to take them to the ground.

The game itself was lopsided, as the "masters of the game" from Brooklyn crushed their hosts, 51 to 6, but no one seemed to care. What mattered was the evening's entertainment:

> . . . the company, to the number of fifty and more, sat down to a most sumptuous entertainment. . . . After full justice had been done the good things there spread before them, and the appetites created by the exercise in the field had made things rapidly disappear, Dr. Hawks, President of the Baltimore club, in a few appropriate remarks welcomed the Excelsiors, and closed by toasting them as the Champion club of the United States. . . . Dr. Jones, of the Brooklyn Excelsiors, ably responded to the toast in his usual eloquent style, but begged to be excused from receiving the compliment of the "champion club," and closed by offering as a sentiment, "the Excelsior club of Baltimore," which was responded to most heartily by three times three from the Brooklyn boys. Other toasts followed. . . . And so the time passed, until . . . evidence of the dawn's appearance.

After spending the rest of the day sightseeing, the Excelsiors departed for Philadelphia, where they easily defeated a "picked nine," or allstar team, and enjoyed similar festivities.[6]

Combining their baseball with other forms of socializing during the season, clubs stayed active through the winter months as well, even when they played no baseball at all. In fact, the early 1860s equivalent of the hot-stove league consisted of the numerous social events of the prominent New York and Brooklyn clubs: balls, suppers, hops, promenades, skating parties, "soirees," and the like. Each club seems to have had an annual ball, an occasion for a different kind of performance, but still a performance, and one that engaged no small amount of competitive spirit.

At the second annual ball of the Eckford Club of Brooklyn, for example, the ballroom was "elegantly and profusely decorated with an abundance of bunting," along with the colors of a dozen area clubs. Frank Pidgeon, the "veteran captain" of the club's first nine, displayed his prowess on the dance floor, "officiat[ing] at the head of the floor managers in regular Parisian style." Press coverage was as enthusiastic as if the Eckfords had just hosted a major tournament. "It affords us sincere pleasure to chronicle the entire and perfect success of the Eckford's second annual reunion," the story went on, "and we hope that the club and their 'troop of friends' will long live to arrange and indulge in the joys of many similar festive occasions."[7]

Members of baseball clubs were proud of their ability to attract women both to observe their baseball skill and to participate in their social events. Fearful that their sport would be dismissed as "boys' play," they were especially happy to draw women to undeniably adult social occasions. The press, in turn, was eager for evidence of this sort. The *Clipper* observed that the Eckfords had "long been noted for the number of ladies who assemble upon their grounds, as spectators of their playing." If "the full attendance at last winter's re-union" was any indication, at their balls, too, "their fair friends always assemble in unusual numbers." Similarly, the winter social calendar of the Bowdoin Base Ball Club of Boston was a tribute to the club's members, who "gave evidence," according to the *Clipper*, "that they were as much at the 'home base' in the ball room, with the ladies, as on the ball grounds with their friendly opponents."[8] The rites of play extended from the ballfield to the ballroom, structuring the life of the baseball club.

"Hard Work and Victory"

That baseball club members participated in a wide range of social activities off the field did not mean that they failed to take their baseball seriously. On the contrary, players and commentators alike understood that first-rate baseball play depended on frequent practice, mastery of one or two positions by each player, and a disciplined co-operation on the ballfield. Baseball reporters stressed the advantages of regular practice, and commonly attributed victory or defeat to practice or indolence.

After being thrashed by the Knickerbockers, for example, the Empire Club earned little sympathy: the losers "gave evidence of a want of practice altogether, and like all who go into matches without due practice, merit the defeat they sustained." A *Clipper* reporter scolded the Atlantics for their "relaxed state of discipline" and advised them of "the necessity of their at once introducing a prompt reform in this respect, by giving more attention to the practice requisite to insure success." Noting that a Philadelphia club's members were "working like beavers" to prepare for matches in New York, another reporter asked rhetorically, "What are our Clubs . . . doing? Simply nothing." On the other hand, when the Star Club overwhemed the New York Gothams 41 to 16, *Wilkes' Spirit of the Times* noted this "practical and striking illustration of the advantages of continuous and regular practice." Because the Stars had begun practice on April 1, by mid-May they were "a unit, each backing each other up, in every and all positions, like clock-work." A victory for the Gothams, who had not practiced all season, "would be strange, indeed."[9]

Skill was only rarely connected to "natural talent" or "innate ability." The play of the Athletics in 1865 was "a practical and pertinent illustration of the efficacy of constant and steady *practice*: for to it almost solely are the Athletics indebted for a large proportion of their success and fame." In the Excelsiors' case, two defeats in 1863 "roused them up" the next season, not to acquire better players but "to the knowledge of the facts that a better organization of their first nine and more practice are necessary to insure that success the reputation of the Club and the well-known individual skill of its members deserve." Similarly, "superior muscle" may have helped the Harvard freshmen defeat the Brown sophomores in 1863, but the *Providence Journal* emphasized the "longer and more thorough training of the Harvard boys." Even a very bad ditty dedicated to the Columbia Base Ball Club of Bordentown, New Jersey, advised matter-of-factly in its closing stanza: "Practice, then, and when you play, / You'll be sure to win the day."[10]

But practice alone was not enough. Baseball commentators had a more sophisticated approach to training very early in the history of top-level competitive baseball. Clubs, they urged, should practice so as to concentrate on the skill of the first nine by playing the "first nine against the field"—that is, the starting lineup against everybody else. That way the best players would get used to each other and to their set positions. Most of the contenders for the informal championship of these years appear to have taken this advice to heart. In early May 1865, for example, the Atlantics drew a thousand spectators (on a Monday afternoon) to watch the first of a series of "instructional games between the first nine and the field."[11]

These methods had important consequences. First, a focus on the most skillful players made practices one-sided; other players had less chance to develop their skill or simply to play the game with their fellow club members. In this light, club social activities and post-game entertainments take on additional significance: they helped maintain the allegiance and participation of members who played little or not at all.

Second, this kind of practice contributed to the growing specialization of ballplayers as adepts at one or two positions. Failure to promote such specialization exposed a contending club to serious criticism. In one 1860s game the players' "positions were, as usual, different to those the majority of the same players had before occupied." It was "entirely out of the question," the reporter continued, "to suppose that special excellence in playing any one point of the game can be obtained unless the players, appointed to the position, permanently occupy it. A first base player, for instance, should be known as a first base player only, and the same as regards the other bases, the pitcher, catcher, and short field [shortstop]." An account of a match for the championship of Massachusetts in 1859 made a similar point: "It was evident to everyone present, that the distinguishing features of these Clubs were their admirable discipline and training, each player having his place, and being perfectly at home in it. Our city clubs would do well to imitate their country friends in this particular."[12]

Finally, good baseball playing demanded a high degree of cooperation among the players as well as individual skill. Consistent success depended on players' familiarity with each other's style of play. The play of the Eckfords in a "grand match" in 1860, for example, made it "unnecessary to offer any comment; they are in a most perfect state of practice, and . . . enter the field and play as a unit. An exhibition of their Nine's playing is worth going some distance to look at, and we regard it as about the perfection of base ball playing."[13]

What is striking about these commentaries from baseball's early years is that they employed almost exclusively the language of work: discipline, training, skill, specialization. By and large, such language was appropriate. The better New York and Brooklyn clubs practiced three times weekly, while the 1865 Philadelphia Athletics practiced four days a week. Increasingly during these years, particularly on competitive clubs, players did specialize at one or two positions. And without a doubt, the most successful nines owed their victories to practice, acquired skill, and highly coordinated play.

Neither reporters nor players tried to insulate their game from the language or ideology of work. A club just organizing in 1860 announced that it had begun practice, and would soon "be most happy to meet in the field any challenging club, when they will strive to render themselves worthy of their motto, 'Hard Work and Victory.'" The club motto is particularly arresting. No hint of frivolity or casualness, no suggestion of fun, and no appeal to health disturbed the terrain it claimed. And although that terrain was physically outside the workplace—it was, as a matter of fact, in the Elysian Fields of Hoboken, New Jersey—it was in other ways quite close to it. Nor was this club alone. Members of the Fulton Club could be found every Monday "hard at work" on their grounds in Hoboken. Members of that Philadelphia club, it will be recalled, were "working like beavers" to prepare for a match in 1863.[14]

The language of work was used to describe the play of individual games as well. The Putnams, for example, "were slow in getting down to their work" in a game against the Eckfords, and found themselves eight runs behind after three innings. Teams that had fallen behind in a game and were trying to catch up were often described as going "into their work." Exhorting his team to make up a four-run deficit, the captain of the Atlantics urged his players: "Stop fooling, boys, and go into your work."[15]

Reporters, in other words, showed little interest in the experience of "true sport" or "pure play." When they praised or criticized particular players and clubs, they appealed not to a concept or realm of leisure and play but rather to the standards of the workplace—a workplace in which craftsmen still exercised considerable collective autonomy over the pace and organization of their labor. By evaluating baseball play in the language of work, reporters were not breaking new ground. Their readers were not surprised to see the language of productive labor used to describe baseball playing. (In fact, some of the same language was used to describe prizefighting.) The language never heard or read was the language of "pure" play or "pure" recreation. The concept of pure recreation was only beginning to be created at this time. The development of play and leisure as a separate sphere of activity was largely a product of the latter half of the century, as we shall see.

Players and Workers

The experience of baseball play in the mid–nineteenth century was not very far removed from the experience of work, especially from the world and culture of the urban workplace. Some clubs were based in specific shops or workplaces, such as the prominent Eckford Club of Brooklyn, which drew its members and players from the shipwrights and mechanics of the Henry Eckford shipyards. Other clubs appear to have been grounded in certain trades or occupations. The Baltic, Jefferson, and Atlantic clubs of the late 1850s were based in the food trades, which seem to have contributed disproportionately large numbers of baseball players. Clerks were also well represented in the ballplaying fraternity, perhaps especially in Washington, D.C., where government clerks filled the membership rolls of the local clubs.[16]

In any attempt, then, to generalize about the composition of the fraternity as a whole, we must keep in mind that certain clubs were centered in particular trades, workplaces, or neighborhoods. Nevertheless, there is still value in looking at the general membership. In New York and Brooklyn, where we have the most extensive data on ballplayers' occupations, patterns were relatively stable between 1855 and 1870. Roughly one in five club members during this time belonged to a highly ranked occupation (a profession or a "high white collar" position); about a third were skilled craftsmen; while a little less than half (between 44 and 48 percent) were "low white collar or proprietors." There were so few unskilled workers that their significance lay mainly in their scarcity. In any given year, between 75 and 80 percent of the baseball fraternity could be found in occupations running from journeymen and clerks to master craftsmen and small shopkeepers. When we focus on the most active ballplayers during this period, as opposed to overall membership and occasional ballplayers, we find fully 90 percent of these men in the middle groupings. The absolute numbers of ballplayers begin to get rather small, so statistical breakdowns have less meaning, but it does seem that, especially in Brooklyn, it was skilled craftsmen who dominated the game on the playing field.[17]

In Chicago, where the baseball fad reached its height in the latter half of the 1860s, bookkeepers and clerks appear to have substantially outnumbered skilled and unskilled workers on club nines. Nevertheless, as in New York and Brooklyn, the middle occupational groupings continued to account for roughly three quarters of active club players. In New Jersey during the late 1850s, skilled workers outnumbered clerks and small proprietors on the ballfield; combined, these two groups made up a little more than 60 percent of the total.[18]

Baseball clubs represented in the National Association of Base Ball Players were at the center of the baseball fraternity and received most of the press coverage. These were the clubs that played the most, sponsored the most postseason social events, and furnished the most skillfully played exhibitions of the sport. But the sporting weeklies would also publish brief notices of other games when correspondents provided them, for many men played the newly popular game without belonging to a club. Baseball nines (or teams)—as distinct from baseball clubs—seem to have formed wherever men came together in organized groups: workplaces, voluntary associations, military organizations, colleges. The most fertile sources of baseball nines were volunteer fire companies and workplaces. Workers in the printing trades in particular—pressmen, compositors, engravers, and typographers—appear to have been the most active nonclub players.[19]

Among those whose matches were reported in the press were the compositors and pressmen of the *New York Daily Times*, the Oceana Hose 36 and the Lafayette Engine Co. No. 19, Hose Company No. 55 and Engine Company No. 34. Engravers of the American Bank-Note Company frequently played their counterparts at the National Bank-Note Company. Very few of these nines ever joined the National Association. Evidently the relatively new ballplaying fraternity had less appeal than the preexisting fraternity of the firehouse or workplace.[20]

Typographers received extensive press coverage from their journalistic brethren, and were understood as a distinct category of ballplayer. "Base Ball in Rochester among the Typos," read a typical headline to an 1860 report of a match game between "nine valiant men from *The Express* office" and their opposite numbers from the *Union.* By 1866 printers were playing each other at the "Typographical Grounds" in Brooklyn. Not coincidentally, printing was one of the better organized trades in the 1850s and 1860s, and the National Typographical Union's Local 6 of New York was the strongest local in the union. These skilled workers had craft traditions, rituals, and fraternal activities that went back a good many years. Apparently preferring occupational homogeneity on the ballfield, "typographical base-ballers" rarely played matches with nines outside their trade. More typical was the 1866 match in which two clubs of "typos" played for the championship of the trade in Philadelphia.[21]

The baseball fraternity, then, was something of a mixture of classes, neither exclusively a middle-class nor a working-class sport. That is not to say that the fraternity was a democratic melting pot, in which men from all walks of life could rub off their class distinctions in competition on the diamond. This view—a staple of baseball ideology in the early twentieth century—was no more true of baseball's early years than of any other. The game was born into a particular social context, and distinct class and cultural elements of that context nurtured the game in its infancy. Artisans and clerks, for instance, accounted for most of the players on workplace nines. Of the skilled craftsmen represented in the baseball world, a disproportionate number came from trades that had so far escaped the complete industrialization and restructuring into "sweated" workplaces characteristic of furniture, clothing, and shoe manufacturing in antebellum New York.

Printers—compositors, pressmen, typographers—were relatively well paid among skilled workers in New York, and maintained a sense of pride in their craft. The Eckford shipbuilders included relatively prosperous master craftsmen as well as journeymen in a trade that, at least in New York, was still governed substantially by artisans themselves. And among the food trades, butchers in particular managed to retain an unusual amount of control over Manhattan's principal markets and, as a result, over the pace and conditions of their work.[22] We know less about the clerks and shopkeepers who joined baseball clubs, though there is evidence that the food trades supplied a number of baseball's small proprietors and some indication that clerks in dry goods firms, as well as in New York City government, played quite a bit of baseball.

That so many of baseball's best players were skilled craftsmen, men who, depending on their trade, still retained significant control over their work rhythms, helps to explain how players could have given so much time to baseball practice. (So does the early closing time of the food markets.) Many historians of the game have suggested casually that baseball must have been a middle-class sport because players had to take time off from work, but this description fits relatively few of the fraternity's best and most active players.

Cultural Antecedents

Baseball's demographic profile provides the background for understanding the culture into which the game was born. The new pastime's cultural antecedents lay in the swirling street life and frequently boisterous amusements of the urban (particularly New York) lower classes in the four decades before the Civil War. Fueled by extraordinary urban growth and massive immigration from abroad, shaped by technological innovation and the transformation of artisanal production, riven by sexual segregation, political factionalism, and nativism, the urban working-class popular culture of these years had a richness and density that historians have been mining for more than a decade without exhausting. Tracing the origins of this world lies beyond the scope of this book; nor is it possible to do justice to its multifariousness in a few paragraphs. A quick look at some of its distinctive institutions will serve.

In New York's Bowery were concentrated theaters and sideshows, brothels and oyster houses, saloons and gambling houses, markets and dance halls. Patronizing these institutions, working in them, or making their headquarters at them were members of volunteer fire companies, street gangs, political organizations and factions, and volunteer military companies. The degree of overlapping membership among these characteristic plebeian groups will never be known precisely, but undoubtedly it was substantial.[23]

They shared a number of important qualities: they placed great importance on the integrity of their particular group, which possessed very clear boundaries of occupation, political faction, neighborhood, ethnic group, or some other measure of membership; they were frequently engaged in a physical rivalry with similar groups, whether through ritualistic competitions, spontaneous defense of honor, or drunken brawling; they shared a history of original "respectability," a quality they had lost by the late 1830s or early 1840s; each group served as an arena in which working-class men experienced and demonstrated "cultural autonomy and manly independence."[24]

Commentators have remarked on the resemblances between fire-company competitions and team sports, but the sport with the closest ties to antebellum working-class culture was prizefighting. Saloon-keepers promoted boxing matches, and fighters made their headquarters in chosen bars. Boxers were recruited by fire companies and by political machines, and frequently belonged to New York's street gangs. During the heyday of this culture, baseball was literally unheard of.

By the late 1850s, however, the urban landscape had changed. The volunteer fire companies had fallen into such disrepute that many cities across the country were replacing them with professional forces. But before they disappeared from New York, volunteer firemen took up baseball, providing a kind of cultural bridge between this new sport and the earlier, more rough-and-tumble world of working-class leisure. Their baseball activities received less press attention than typographers', but the firemen clearly contributed a great deal more to the emerging culture of organized baseball. The New York Mutuals, for example, one of baseball's leading clubs into the 1870s, were founded in 1857 by Mutual Hook and Ladder Company No. 1.

Most striking are the cultural similarities between the two institutions. First, the names of early baseball clubs and fire companies were virtually indistinguishable. Names of fire companies tended to cluster around place names and nicknames (Buckeye, Missouri, Knickerbocker, Atlantic [Avenue]); Indian names (in New England); patriotic names (Washington, Franklin, Liberty, Union, Lafayette); names referring to water (Neptune, Oceana, Cascade); and names suggesting admirable qualities (Invincible, Perseverance, Alert, Friendship, Good Intent). A few New York companies conjured up more flamboyant images: the Black Joke, Red Rovers, Honey Bees, and Shad Bellies. Baseball clubs followed almost identical patterns in choosing their names, and to a remarkable extent seem simply to have copied the firemen. Water references naturally held less attraction for baseball clubs, which compensated by reaching into the heavens (Star, Constellation, Satellite, Meteor) and into the classical past (Olympic, Minerva, Neptune, Sparta). Ballplayers chose Indian names more frequently (Powhattan, Pocahantas, Mohawk), and occasionally named their clubs after trades or workplaces (Typographical, Eckford, Henry Eckford, Fulton Market, Chestnut Street Theatre). If not all baseball club names had antecedents in fire companies, nearly all fire-company names were picked up by baseball clubs.[25]

Patterns of baseball sociability closely parallelled those of the volunteer fire companies. The following description will sound familiar:

> Firemen turned out in full regalia for the ceremony known as "visiting," . . . in which one fire department would play host to other fire companies for a few days. . . . A typical visit began with a triumphal departure from the engine house, bands playing and banners (presented "on behalf of the female friends of the company") waving, and a march through the city to the rail yards or docks. . . . On arriving, the visitors would be met by a delegation of firemen from the host city, and paraded to their quarters. . . . The next few days would be spent in a round of receptions, processions, trials of equipment, and endless collations ("wine and toasts passing freely around").[26]

The postgame socializing enjoyed by baseball clubs was clearly modeled on that of the fire companies, even to the kind of food preferred at the dinners. "Chowder suppers" were characteristic of both institutions. Similarly, the annual fireman's ball preceded the annual balls of the early baseball clubs by several decades. The proceeds of the 1858 Brooklyn–New York all-star matches—the first time spectators paid to see a baseball game—were donated to the firemen's fund for widows and orphans. The Elysian Fields, where the Knickerbockers rented their grounds, were hosts to a full range of working class leisure activities at this time, from firemen's parades and chowder suppers to union meetings.

Politicians' interest in baseball equaled their efforts to organize the fire companies and prizefighters only toward the end of the century. William Marcy Tweed, however, was more foresighted than most. A member of the Mutual Hook and Ladder Company, he later served as a longtime director of the New York Mutuals baseball club as well. The Mutuals' close links to Tammany Hall eventually brought the club into serious disrepute.

When baseball clubs gathered on the ballfield for a match, their players wore uniforms based on those of the firemen. Their belts were all but identical; the most visible resemblances between the two were their distinctive shirt fronts. Both wore rectangular or shield-shaped double-breasted panels, on which were carried the insignia of the club or company. Peck & Snyder, the premier sporting goods retailer in New York City, advertised firemen's belts and shirt fronts along with its line of baseball clothing. Whole firemen's uniforms were displayed next to the uniforms of baseball players.[27]

Volunteer military companies, which survived until the Civil War, also provided important cultural antecedents for the baseball fraternity. One historian has even gone so far as to call the volunteer militia "the first national pastime in the Middle West." Like firemen and ballplayers, militia members wore distinctive uniforms (in fact, their uniforms were far gaudier than those of their ballplaying or fire-fighting counterparts), undertook elaborate "visits" between cities, held annual balls, engaged in public display and competition, and came in for public disapproval when such competitions degenerated into drunken melees.[28]

However much baseball drew on previous traditions of working-class leisure, its exhibitions were considerably less violent, less drunken, and on the whole less raucous than its cultural predecessors. Baseball clubs included more middle-class members than fire companies, men who frequently held leadership positions within their clubs. Perhaps the combination of skilled workers and a complex team sport put a premium on a kind of self-disciplined cooperation ill-suited to the more expressive style of prizefights or fire-company competitions. Baseball seems to have appealed to the more "respectable" members of the working classes. Early baseball reporting emphasized the game's respectability as much as its character as skilled work.

Men of the middle classes responded to the appeal of respectable sport. For if middle-class members of the baseball fraternity offered their clubs little in the way of first-rate baseball skill, they contributed much to baseball culture. Most obviously, perhaps, the extended—and expensive—socializing between clubs could not have been paid for out of club dues, which ranged from $2 to $5 a year. Wealthier members clearly subsidized such activities.

It was not only their interest in flowery toasts and "splendid chowders" that drew middle-class men into the baseball fraternity. The Victorian middle-class attitude toward sport and physical recreation had begun to shift in the 1840s and 1850s, a development with important consequences for the history of all American sports. Although historians debate the precise causes of this change, it appears to have been linked to concerns about the growth of cities and sedentary occupations, a Protestant moral code emphasizing individual self-control, and a growing faith in social progress. Increasingly during these years, according to Elliott Gorn, these Victorian ideals were seen as realizable through physical education and respectable sport.[29]

So the new concern for physical health led many men to embrace fresh air, exercise, and "manly sports" in the 1850s. The sporting press was full of articles about the benefits of exercise and all kinds of outdoor sports. Particularly during the late 1850s and early 1860s, baseball was defended, praised, and advertised as a "healthful recreation"—in Henry Chadwick's words, an "invigorating exercise and manly pastime."[30]

Finally, middle-class club members brought to their baseball playing and socializing the characteristic Victorian fear of unregulated passion and concern for self-control. This central component of American middle-class and respectable working-class culture has been insufficiently appreciated by students of American baseball. Early baseball players are usually pictured as priggish "gentlemen" whose "quaint" notions of "genteel sportsmanship" and "fair play" were quickly (and rightly) outgrown by the more "realistic" and competitive masses.

Although this view is exaggerated, it is not unfounded. Baseball was straddling a cultural boundary during those years, a position it has never managed entirely to escape. The game appealed simultaneously to the culture of the urban streets—a culture that was losing some of its principal institutions by the late 1850s—and to the respectable and newly vigorous culture of middle-class Victorian men. Participants in the baseball fraternity would find these two cultures difficult to reconcile.

2

Excitement and Self-Control

Dangerous Excitement

"Excitement is the great desideratum in our Metropolitan community," declared the *New York Clipper* in 1860, and baseball games were an important source of that sought-for excitement. According to the *Clipper*'s major competitor, the excitement "attendant upon the prominent contests" of the Knickerbocker and Gotham baseball clubs in the previous decade had boosted the popularity of the fledgling game of baseball in New York. "It is well known," the article continued, "that where a lively, well-contested and exciting game is in progress, there will ever be found crowds of interested spectators."[1] Recognizing the importance of attendance figures, sportswriters, who usually saw themselves as promoters of the game, rarely missed an opportunity to mention the "numerous assemblage," the "immense concourse," or the many hundreds and thousands of spectators at a match.

But the excitement—or expectation of excitement—that brought people to the ballfield was not always benign. For when players and spectators got excited, they began to tread on dangerous ground. An appreciative crowd could turn ugly, and in that case, complained the secretary of one of the most prominent clubs of the era,

what . . . can any club do? Can we restrain a burst of applause or indignation emanating from an assemblage of more than 15,000 excited spectators, whose feelings are enlisted as the game proceeds, by the efforts of this or that player or players?

He who has witnessed the natural excitement which is ever the attendant of a vast miscellaneous assemblage . . . knows full well that it is an utter impossibility to prevent the crowd from expressing their sentiments in a manner and as audibly as they please.[2]

Players, too, could get excited in a close game and play poorly or unfairly, lose their tempers and dispute the umpire's decisions, argue with or "blackguard" opposing players or even their own teammates. Any number of things could bring on this desired but dangerous excitement.

In a game between the Brooklyn Atlantics and the New York Mutuals in 1863, nearly everything seems to have contributed to the uproar. Several accounts described the unusually intense emotions engaged by the game. One began with the heat of the day and the patience of the crowd, especially the "hundreds" of gamblers "who would stand the heat even of the infernal regions rather than forgo the excitement attendant upon their peculiar occupation." Until the ninth inning the game was remarkable only for the generally poor fielding on both sides. But when the Mutuals, down by eight when they batted in the bottom of the ninth, began to score runs, "considerable 'chaffing'" broke out "among the members of the two clubs." Such talk was "not safe or advisable among quick-tempered men," the reporter observed, for "it was nothing before personalities began to be introduced, and anything but friendly remarks made by both parties, one to the other."[3]

By the time the Mutuals had come within one run of the Atlantics, the emotional equilibrium of the players and spectators was long gone. "Our descriptive powers fail in attempting to portray the scenes that now began to occur," wrote the *Mercury* reporter. Both clubs and "their friends" became "excited to an unusual degree." With a man on first, the Atlantic pitcher pitched more than fifty balls to William McKeever, hoping to induce him to swing at a bad pitch or to lure the runner off base. Not surprisingly under the circumstances, McKeever's patience wore thin; he "allowed his temper to get the better of him, and . . . lost the advantages his usual control gives him." The reporter took the occasion to opine that players who could not control their tempers should "give up play" in all important contests, although he did acknowledge the part played by "the high betting, that these championship contests lead to." He then chided the Mutuals, who ought to have remembered that it was a trying position for the Atlantics to be placed in, and had their members kept cool and silent, attending only to their game, and gone on with their play, leaving to the umpire, whose sole duty it was, to decide any disputed questions, all would have been well, and the Atlantics would not have been led into the committal of the actions they were; but in as much as the Mutuals did not act in this manner, but, on the contrary allowed themselves to become as excited as the Atlantics were, and without the same excuse, they became, in a measure, responsible for a great deal of the trouble that occurred.[4]

Some of the "most excited" Atlantic players then tried to have the game called, citing the "poor excuse" of darkness; the "terribly-excited crowd," which presented a "threatening aspect" to the umpire; the "excited" Mutuals, who helped provoke the Atlantics; and the gamblers' search for "excitement," which helped precipitate the commotion.[5] Had the Mutuals "kept cool and silent," had McKeever controlled his temper, and, one suspects, had the temperature been lower as well, the trouble would probably have been avoided.

The principal villain of the afternoon was the excitement produced by the day, the crowd, the game, and the players. The victim of the day was "the best interests of the game," which had received a "serious blow." But there were other victims as well, and their losses were the ones that counted most in the world of mid-century baseball: almost everyone involved in the game—both sets of players and most of the spectators—had lost self-control.

Agents of Control: Rules, Umpires, and Women

Baseball club members dealt with the problem of self-control in a variety of ways. Club rules were quite explicit. In his model club constitution published in the first edition of the subsequently annual *Beadle's Dime Base-Ball Player*, Henry Chadwick suggested fines for the following offenses: "profane language," either in club meetings or during "field exercise"; "disputing the decision of the umpire during field exercise"; "refusing obedience to the Captain during field exercise, and while he has lawful authority"; absence from a business meeting without sufficient excuse; and failure to come to order in a meeting or in field exercise. Suspension and expulsion were the penalties for repeated absences or failure to pay fines and club dues.[6]

A look at a half-dozen club constitutions and by-laws suggests that clubs usually fined members for four field transgressions: swearing, disputing the umpire's decision, offering one's opinion on a play before the umpire made his decision, and disobeying the captain. These offenses had one thing in common: the player who committed any of them got "carried away," or temporarily lost control of himself. (The idea that a player might calmly and deliberately swear or disobey his captain is nowhere indicated in the contemporary literature.) The fines were small enough—from 10 to 50 cents—to suggest that they were meant as fund-raising rather than truly punitive provisions. Clubs fined members for being late to or absent from meetings, but Chadwick's recommendation that no fines be levied for nonattendance on practice days, "experience having shown that such are almost useless . . . principally from the valid excuses offered by the participants," appears to have been widely adopted, if in fact he was not merely codifying prevailing practices.[7]

Rulesmakers and promoters of the game alike recognized that the excitement they sought on the ballfield was likely to lead to a loss of self-control. They upheld an ideal of "gentlemanly behavior," but they recognized it as an ideal unlikely to be realized. They anticipated lapses, and surrounded them with a ready-made set of correctives: little rituals to bring the errant member back to the fraternal fold. Since fines were often collected before players left the field, they were probably used to purchase postgame refreshments. On practice days minor infractions were treated good-naturedly, and major ones appear to have been quite rare. The earnestness that pervaded so much of the culture and literature of the period, even the literature of sport, was seldom in evidence among members of baseball clubs.[8]

Club rules, however, could not be relied upon to govern players' conduct during a match; in that situation proper behavior was considered at once important and elusive. The fraternity's solution to this problem was the umpire. From the earliest years of organized baseball playing, the umpire's position has been recognized as at best arduous and at worst impossible. Chadwick observed that the "position of an Umpire is an honorable one, but its duties are anything but agreeable, as it is next to impossible to give entire satisfaction to all parties concerned in a match." Nevertheless, "upon his manly, fearless, and impartial conduct in a match mainly depends the pleasure that all, more or less, will derive from it."[9] It was up to the umpire to enforce fair play and honorable conduct, and perhaps most of all to maintain an impartiality demanded (and expected) of no one else at the match.

The umpire's duties were to establish and interpret the boundaries of the game within the process of play itself, to translate the rules from the static pages of a manual into the far more difficult, fluid situation of a match with real spectators, players, and foul lines that existed on grass and dirt. And his rulings were final. As reporters repeated tirelessly, the rightness or wrongness of an umpire's decisions was not a subject of dispute; because those decisions were made by the umpire, they were *always* right.[10]

As the judge of fair balls and fair play, he wielded language that had not yet lost its suggestion of proper and improper conduct, as is intimated in this instruction: "Whenever a disposition is evinced on the part of either side of the contestants in a match to prolong the game until darkness puts a stop to it, in order to secure an advantage obtained, but which, by fair play, would in all probability be lost, the Umpire should decide the game either by the last innings that had been fairly played, or draw the game." If a team could gain an advantage over its opponents by manipulating a loosely drawn rule, the umpire was expected to enforce the rule strictly so that no such advantage could be obtained. Section 37 of the March 1860 rules, for example, provided for strikes to be called on the batter if he refused "to strike at good balls repeatedly pitched to him, for the apparent purpose of delaying the game or of giving advantage to a player." The umpire was first to warn the batter, then to start to call strikes on him. Often, with runners on base, batters would wait for either the pitcher or the catcher to miss the ball so that the runners could advance. This practice was roundly condemned as "contemptible" in the *Clipper* and as "trickery" in *Beadle's*. Batters were exhorted instead to "play the game manfully," and the guarantor of "manful" play was the umpire.[11]

The anomalous position of the umpire helps explain why it was generally considered "unpleasant," his duties "onerous." He was to remain a solitary figure above the game, immune to the powerful attractions of fraternity and partisanship. "The moment he assumes his position on the ground," wrote Chadwick, he was "to close his eyes to the fact of there being any one player, among the contestants, that is not an entire stranger to him; by this means he will free his mind from any friendly bias." He was to "avoid conversation with any party during a match game, and also turn a deaf ear to all comment on his decisions." Such a position was highly artificial, and the distance it required must have been difficult to establish. The umpire had to be a "member of a Base Ball Club governed by these rules," and most often he was a well-known player who knew the contending players, had played with or against them many times, and could expect to do so again.[12]

In the course of a match, this disinterested arbiter must have appeared an oddity to players and spectators alike: his reasons for being there bore little resemblance to theirs. Although chosen by the captains of the opposing teams, he immediately assumed a position above all other participants, and claimed for himself, indeed became the repository of, precisely those qualities most likely to be lacking in everyone else on the field. In a game built around clubs, whose members thought of themselves as a highly social "fraternity," the umpire stood alone. In the midst of a competition that pitted players against each other and made partisans out of onlookers, the umpire stood cool, aloof, impartial. In a game requiring constant judgment and interpretation, only he had the authority to judge. Outside of the game in some ways, he intervened in every contact between the contestants. And as competitive struggle continually threatened players' and spectators' self-control, as it drew them into "unmanly" and "boyish" behavior, the umpire came to embody manliness and self-control.[13]

Because umpires were constant reminders of what players and spectators were not, it is understandable that they were sometimes treated with less than absolute respect. As early as 1859 a reporter noted with surprise the "general satisfaction" that greeted an umpire's decisions "in these days of finding fault with umpires." Even so, failure to accept an umpire's decisions in honorable silence received harsh treatment in the press. A Rochester club that had withdrawn from the field to protest an umpire's "prejudice" against them wrote to the *Clipper* to explain their case, asking—in vain—for support. "Even if the decisions were as partial and unjust as you state they were," went the reply, "still, that does not justify your retiring from the field. . . . *Be the decisions of an Umpire what they may, they should be silently received and abided by to the end of time.*" Finally, the paper warned, "another such withdrawal from a game for such a cause would prevent any Club in this vicinity from playing with your party." Finding it necessary to make a similar point even to a member of the well-known Empire Club of New York, the *Clipper* made the connection between player behavior and "gentlemanly" behavior: "Every good ball player, and for that matter every gentleman, should receive the decisions of the umpire without a word of comment."[14]

To all appearances, however, the combined effect of club rules, umpires, and "love of fair play" was not strong enough to ensure that the ballfield would remain orderly and decorous during a game. Ballplayers and their supporters sought the patronage and influence of women to assist in this task. Just as women's presence at club social events was taken to be a guarantor of ballplayers' maturity, or manliness, their attendance at games was considered evidence of baseball's worthiness, popularity, and respectability. Some clubs provided special accommodations on their ball grounds for women spectators, ranging from seats (men generally sat on the ground or stood) to tents and parasols to special sections in a grandstand. Clubs took pride both in the care with which they treated their "fair friends" and in the fact that their sport attracted female patrons. The members of the Eckford Club, for example, "have always enjoyed a standard reputation for the attraction which their playing offers to the ladies, and for the liberal number who grace their ground on all occasions of match games." Frederick Boughton of the Atlantics claimed that "on the field it has always been our pride and pleasure to preserve good order, and to render every accommodation and courtesy in our power to our friends of the press, the ladies, and to all evincing any interest in . . . base ball."[15]

Baseball clubs and promoters wanted women at games as evidence of the game's popularity. Many spectators would be drawn by the legitimacy that only women could confer on the game. Most important, however, women were supposed to help men control themselves on the ballfield. Like the umpires (and like their supporters among the press), women personified standards of behavior that could, theoretically, keep men's behavior within certain boundaries.

"Let our American ladies visit" the ballfield, sermonized the *Clipper*, and the most rough or rude among the spectators would acknowledge their magic sway, thus conferring a double favor upon the sports they countenance, because the members of our sporting organizations are usually gentlemen and always lovers of order, but they can no more control the bystanders than they can any other passengers along a public highway. When ladies are present, we are proud to be able to say that no class of our population can be found so debased as not to change their external behavior immediately, and that change is always for the better.

Women had not yet understood that if a young man joined a sports club or went hunting and fishing, "his morals and his manhood" would be much safer "than they might be during an evening saunter along Broadway"; he would learn to "despise all dissipation." Men needed the "confidence and approval" of women "as a kind of social regulator in the joyousness of our fun, to prevent it from becoming too boisterous." Men who played baseball expected to get carried away, anticipated that their fun could get "too boisterous," and feared that the "*self-control* of contending clubs and parties" would not hold up under the strains of competitive sport, but most of them were not willing to give it up. Vesting broad powers in the umpire was one response to this problem. Another was to bring women into the ball grounds and to count on them to be the restraining influence on what would otherwise be potentially unregulated passion. Women, in this familiar Victorian scheme, were to domesticate the ballfield.[16]

As the artisan, frequently household-based economy of the eighteenth and early nineteenth centuries was transformed by masters and markets into a system of production based on separate workplaces, shops, and factories, Victorian women and men created the separate "spheres" for which their culture is so well remembered. Middle-class women particularly, barred from the public realm, claimed the physical, emotional, and moral terrain of domesticity. Middle-class and "respectable" working-class men, on the other hand, inhabited a public world, the productive part of which offered dramatically shrinking rewards, whether measured in money, independence, or pride in craft. At the same time, the new cultural standards of the bourgeois world emphasized the "manly" virtues of self-control, sobriety, and familial responsibility. The irony, of course, is that these values (which we think of as quintessentially Victorian) became enshrined just as the industrializing economy was closing off the very possibilities they promised. We should not be surprised, then, that large numbers of workingmen, as Elliott Gorn points out, "slid back into less morally rigid ways. The sporting underworld could stir the envy of those who felt themselves deprived of the freedom and openness they perceived in working-class culture."[17] Although the baseball world overlapped the "sporting underworld" at times, for the most part it lay relatively close to the border of respectability, on both sides of the line. Whether impelled by envy or backsliding or memory, ballplayers continued to play the game, and newspapers continued to cover it.

The Problem of Competition

That all of these agents of ballfield self-control—club rules, umpires, women—proved unequal to the task leads us to the problematic status of competition itself. After all, none of the problems of overexcitement or uncontrollable behavior would have arisen without a competitive struggle. This was very well understood by the men who wrote about the game. In fact, one of the striking characteristics of the baseball community in this period was the profound unease with which many players and commentators faced the desire for victory on the ballfield. Competitive team spectator sports were just beginning at this time. Of necessity, people faced this new phenomenon with preexisting intellectual and emotional categories, categories formed in part by New York's recent history of public conflict: street-gang battles, fire-company fights, militia brawls, and theater and draft riots. Competition in politics had likewise become deadly serious with the shots at Fort Sumter.

Ballplayers did what they could to anticipate, dissipate, or circumscribe the "ill-feeling" prompted by intense competition. Some clubs even chose not to pursue match victories. Others did, however, and in the most vigorous ways. Like the clubs and players themselves, the press was often caught in the dilemma, and reporters' commentaries on these aspects of the game are the best place to find the confusions and tensions that structured the experience of mid–nineteenth-century baseball.

At times reporters carefully emphasized just how hospitable the clubs were, or how much good fellowship was expressed at their dinners, or how much mutual admiration was expressed in the toasts. If we resist the temptation to attribute these efforts simply to Victorian etiquette, we can glimpse the unease players felt about the conflict that had just taken place on the ballfield, and about the fact that many of those at the table had just been defeated on the playing field. Game stories often pointed out the "ill-feeling" engendered by a particularly tense match. Seen in this light, the postgame "entertainment" was more than a chance to "do justice to a good chowder," include the nonplaying members, or toast the glories of the game of baseball. It was also an attempt to repair the rents in the social fabric, to rejoin the members of the fraternity who had just been aligned against each other. Postgame "ceremonies" were in fact rituals by which the recently divided and occasionally disordered ballfield was reclaimed in the name of the baseball fraternity and its standards of good fellowship. Wounds inflicted during the conflict were salved, especially the "sting of defeat." After the Newark Eurekas had been beaten by the visiting Philadelphia Athletics, the host club "entertained their guests most hospitably, drowning in a warm-hearted exchange of mirth and good fellowship, all recollections of defeat." Efforts of two Philadelphia clubs to erase the "ill-feeling . . . too strongly expressed in the eighth innings" by cheering each other at the end of the game were "sincere," remarked the reporter, "if the remarks of Mark Antony upon the assassination of Julius Caesar were an eulogy upon the conspirators." But determined to show that "the ire displayed was absolutely temporary," the players "left the field, many of them arm in arm with each other." [18]

The social interests of the players and other club members acted as checks on the importance of the game itself. Reporters, for their part, were frequently much less interested in the actual contest than in the emotions surrounding and permeating the game. It was not unusual for *Wilkes' Spirit of the Times* to observe, as it did of an Atlantic–Mutual game in 1864, that the "most creditable features of the match were the friendly feelings that prevailed throughout, the Mutuals receiving their defeat as ball players should do." [19] The sentence unintentionally raises all kinds of questions. Were "friendly feelings" unusual at a match? Why were reporters concerned about the "creditable features" of the game? "Creditable" to whom, and in whose terms? And if one of these "creditable features" was the Mutuals' acceptance of defeat in an approved manner, and if this acceptance deserved special notice, how often did ballplayers not receive defeat as they "should do"?

It is impossible to give precise answers to these questions. What is clear, however, is that when players failed to measure up to this standard of behavior, their violations could attract much more attention than the game itself. In 1866, for example, the Harvard College baseball club visited New York and played four matches with clubs in the area. The Excelsior game drew a large crowd, but the story in one paper was concerned almost entirely with the "discourteous and gross" comments made by some spectators, partisans of the Atlantics, about their rival, the Excelsiors. Taking upon himself the responsibility of delivering an "underlying moral" to the Atlantics, the reporter argued that although the club members "were certainly not accessories to this manifestation of envy and ill-feeling," they had a "severe task before them." Winning games was not enough, he warned. "They have more than the simple duty of maintaining themselves as champions, for it devolves upon them also to discountenance and make amends for the indiscretions of their too warm supporters." Though the game escaped interruption, its details were submerged by the reporter's outrage at those "whose actions and expressions place courtesy under such a cloud, abash good sense, and even put to the blush the commonest decency." Of the contest itself, "but little can be said in the brief space at command." As far as the reporter was concerned, the "contest" was not the real story of the afternoon.[20]

3

The "Manly Pastime"

Men and Boys

The baseball fraternity's concern for self-control was linked to a notion of manliness—of "manly" behavior on and off the ballfield. If there was a sphere from which baseball players, club members, and promoters tried to insulate their game, it was that of "boys' play," a category sometimes opposed to "men's sport." One way of distinguishing baseball as a legitimate and serious activity for grown workingmen was to insist on its manliness and to bar "boyish" conduct from the game. As a behavioral ideal, as a boundary, and at times as a weapon, the concept played a critical role in the early history of baseball.[1]

A brief but extremely revealing history of the game began the first edition of *Beadle's Dime Base-Ball Player* in 1860. Opening with a description of rounders, Henry Chadwick quickly proceeded to point out its defects. "It is a very simple game," first of all, "one designed only for relaxation during the intervals between study in school," and was thus "entirely devoid of the manly features that characterize base ball as played in this country." So simple was it that "boys and even girls can play Rounders without difficulty." Alexander Cartwright's 1845 rules for baseball had eliminated a number of rounders' features, principally the practice of putting a runner out by hitting him or her with a thrown ball—the "first innovation on the primitive rules of the game familiar to every schoolboy in the Eastern and Middle States." This simple description of the game was clearly overloaded with language—"very simple," "schoolboy," "primitive," "entirely devoid of manly features"—meant to bludgeon the reader into agreeing with Chadwick's dismissal of rounders. Baseball, on the other hand, "requires the possession of muscular strength, great agility, quickness of eye, readiness of hand, and many other faculties of mind and body that mark a man of nerve. . . . Suffice it to say that it is a recreation that anyone may be proud to excel in, as in order to do so, he must possess the characteristics of true manhood to a considerable degree."[2]

Chadwick's overpowering concern was that baseball, "this invigorating exercise and manly pastime," be distinguished from the "primitive," "simple game" designed "only for relaxation of schoolboys" which was much more widely known and played in the United States in 1860 than baseball. If the simple statement of baseball's uniqueness had been persuasive, there would have been no need to give such a charged synopsis of its evolution. But since the game was better known as town ball, one-o-cat, two-o-cat, or any of a large number of other names attached to games that fell under the loose rubric of "base ball," the history became necessary—and, consequently, so did the large differences between rounders and baseball. That the games differed less than Chadwick claimed helps to account for his rhetorical overkill. But what is most interesting about his distinctions is the feelings and concepts on which he relied as he drew them. In consigning rounders to childhood, Chadwick appealed to manhood, and to a particular version of manhood. While rounders invited "relaxation," baseball was an "invigorating exercise" that demanded all the "faculties of mind and body that mark the man of nerve." Skill in rounders was of little interest to Chadwick, but "anyone may be proud to excel in base ball," for "to do so he must possess the characteristics of true manhood to a considerable degree."

Despite organized baseball's best efforts to separate the "national game" from its origins in children's games, it has been beset by tensions between boys and men which date from the earliest baseball organizations. At the second convention of ballplayers in New York, the March 1858 meeting at which the organization took the name of the National Association of Base Ball Players (NABBP), the assembled players voted that "no Club shall be represented in this Association by any delegate under twenty-one years of age." Although the resolution applied only to delegates, it effectively kept the junior clubs from taking part in the proceedings, and they made their displeasure known. But the legislated boundary remained permeable. Inasmuch as the NABBP did not recognize them as clubs, some junior clubs re-cruited members of senior clubs to play with them in match games in 1860, to the consternation of their opponents. Eventually the thirty-five junior clubs met in convention and adopted their own constitu-tion, the main objective of which was a provision "excluding, in match games, all persons belonging to any other Club than the one he represents, whether such club be or not be a member of the [Junior] Association."[3]

Most of the attention focused on this practice was concerned with the unfair advantage gained by the junior club whose nine included one or more senior players. Far more interesting, however, was the fact that some senior players continued to play in junior games. Whatever official bodies decided, the lure of playing with younger players, either because older players could dominate them or because such games offered less pressure and more fun, proved too strong for older players to resist. In this light, the NABBP's exclusion of junior clubs looks very much like an attempt on the part of senior players—many of whom were only in their early twenties—to legitimize their own play as "manly sport" by distinguishing it officially from the play of boys.[4]

"Manly" and "boyish" were charged words in mid–nineteenth-century America, perhaps even more so in that of the baseball frater-nity. No single word carried more virtue or praise in sporting lan-guage than "manly," and few words carried so much disdain as "boyish." "Manliness" in particular was such a fundamental category in the evaluation and characterization of a whole range of activities, ideas, and behavior that it rarely received explicit attention. Although writers and reporters usually assumed that what it meant to be manly could be taken for granted, they so overused "manliness" that the term may have been a less adequate guide to behavior than they liked to think. The realm of "manliness" was defined by what lay outside it: anything that was not "manly" was roundly condemned. Here too, however, their language betrayed them. So much vehemence infused this effort as to suggest that the ideal of manliness was as fragile as it was vague.[5]

Reporters frequently attacked what they considered "boyish" be-havior at games, on the part of both players and spectators. Some-times the offenders were in fact boys, who apparently lacked the self-control of the ideal spectator. Two thousand spectators, "mostly juveniles," attended an all-star match between junior players of New York and Brooklyn in 1861, and, as the *Clipper* put it, "the behavior of the majority of them does not speak favorably for their love of order." Similarly, at a game between the Eckford and Union clubs in 1862, the "boys outside of the grounds upon the embankment caused a great deal of disturbance and noise, their bad conduct annoying the players of both clubs. . . . We are aware," the report continued, "that it is [a] difficult job . . . to subdue these 'Young Eckfords' and embryo ball players, . . . but we would suggest that a few officers might quiet them somewhat, and perhaps develop less pugnacity in their dispositions." And Henry Chadwick could scarcely contain his surprise at the "order and decorum" prevailing at the Junior Convention.[6]

But often, perhaps most often, the boundary was more conceptual than chronological, more concerned with the "manly" or "boyish" behavior of adults than with the activities of real boys. From the late 1850s to the mid-1860s, the legislated distinctions between men and boys became ever stronger, while the boundary continued to be full of holes. The Junior Association met every year, elected its own officers, and organized its own championship. Periodically, however, junior clubs petitioned successfully to join the National Association and left the junior circuit, while senior clubs commonly recruited new players from the junior clubs. The Excelsior Club, for instance, used the junior Stars much as a modern major-league team uses its farm system. So "juveniles" were constantly being imported into the "man's game." Finally, although junior clubs could not belong to the senior association, young players could and did join senior clubs.[7]

The boundary that really mattered, then—and the one most difficult to maintain—was that between "manliness" and "boyishness." Players clearly found the standards of "manly" play impossible to meet. Few, for example, managed never to dispute an umpire's call. All through the early 1860s newspaper accounts of games concluded with a formulaic mention of the "soundness and impartiality" of the umpire's decisions, and frequently with the equally formulaic observation that his decisions were completely respected. But as we have seen, umpires' decisions were not always received in respectful silence. Endlessly repeated comments about "impartiality" and "order" resemble invocations and wishes more than disinterested accounts, signaling the threat to manliness bubbling just beneath the surface.

This impression is not dispelled by the emphasis in the following 1860 report: "We must not forget to mention that the decisions of the Umpire were sound and impartial, and *silently* abided by in every instance." Anything else, the *Clipper* lectured a correspondent, "was simply boy's play, and entirely unworthy" of the players who had tried to explain "this and that in reference to the disputed point." Whether or not the offenders were in fact juveniles was beside the point; juveniles were invoked to censure the action.[8]

Yet players, spectators, and commentators sensed that one of the attractions of their game was its involvement in questions of youth and age, boyishness and manliness. At every level of the game, the boundary between them was redrawn. Even within senior clubs, players recreated the divisions between children and adults, "juveniles" and "old boys." When clubs divided for practice games, they frequently split into single and married teams, or Bachelors and Benedicts. Players were known and written about as veterans (the "Old War Horse" Peter O'Brien, "Old Reliable" Joe Start) and rookies, who were called "youngsters" or even, in one case, "our infant." Nearly every season saw a match between the "old nine" and the "new nine" of a prominent club. The strains that this continual division put on the language of youth and age were rarely clearer than in the following description of such a match among the Atlantics (whose home field was in Bedford, Long Island): "The 'Bedford Boys' had a good game among themselves on the 19th . . . when the new First Nine played a game with the 'veterans,' or old First Nine. The 'juveniles' won by a close shave, notwithstanding the old boys were ahead for eight innings."[9]

Two of the "old boys," Dickey Pearce and Charley Smith, were twenty-five and twenty-two years old, respectively. They, along with three other "veterans," played regularly in the first nine as well. But all of the players, juveniles and old boys alike, were the "Bedford Boys." At the same time that the baseball fraternity leaped to dispute any slight to its members or pastime, strove to banish boys and boyish behavior from the game, and promoted its sport as an acceptable, even respectable adult activity for spectators and players alike, every club member in these years thought of himself and his comrades collectively as "the boys."

Captains and umpires, especially umpires, were the only undisputed men in the game. Even they assumed the roles for only two or three hours before returning to the fraternal fold. Another source of the emotion that swirled around the umpire's position, then, was the feeling of players that the umpire—usually just one of "the boys"—had, in the interest of fairness, turned his back on his brethren to assume a position as a man among "the boys," a role as unnatural as it was temporary. But however contradictory ballplayers' attempts to be men and boys simultaneously may seem to us, to them the conflict was, quite plainly, *between* manly and boyish behavior.

The evident confusion and ambivalence within the baseball fraternity over the boundary between men and boys resembled the tensions between the culture of respectability and the culture of the street. Baseball straddled both boundaries, a position awkward enough to lead many members of the fraternity to choose one side over the other.

The Fly Rule

In the late 1850s and early 1860s the struggle over baseball's manly or boyish character took clearest form in a debate over a particular rule of the game—what was known at the time as the fly rule. Until the season of 1865, a batter was out if a fielder caught the batted ball, fair or foul, either before it touched the ground or after the first bound. Opponents of this style of playing, which they called the "bound game," favored a rule change specifying that the batter was out only if the batted ball was caught before it touched the ground, that is, "on the fly." This issue attracted a huge amount of attention in the sporting press. To contemporary ballplayers and those who spoke for them, the debate over the fly rule conveyed some of their strongest feelings about being men and ballplayers. It was the most heated controversy in the baseball world before the emergence of professionalism.[10]

Simply put, the reformers considered the bound catch a "boy's rule." By eliminating the bound catch in favor of the fly catch, they hoped to make baseball a more manly sport. Proponents of the fly game argued their case by example on the playing field, in the newspapers, and in conventions of the National Association of Base Ball Players. Six times, beginning in 1857, reformers urged the assembled representatives of the baseball clubs to change the rules. Rebuffed five times, they finally succeeded in the convention of 1864. In the meantime the press campaigned for the change in editorials, guide-books, and conventions. Headlines of the *Clipper*'s convention sto-ries highlighted the fly-game–bound-game controversy, most elabo-rately in March 1860:

MEETING OF THE CONVENTION
RE-ADOPTION
OF THE BOY'S RULE OF THE CATCH ON THE BOUND!
DEFEAT OF THE FLY GAME

"In regard to the failure to adopt the Fly game," the reporter con-cluded, "all we have to say is, that we exceedingly regret it; for, al-though we have no idea that it will retard the progress of the game in the least, it still leaves place in the rules open to considerable im-provement." That particular improvement would make the game more manly, reformers argued, but what exactly did they mean? Many argued that the fly rule would place baseball on a par with cricket, which had its own fly rule and was undeniably a manly sport. Baseball players' defensiveness toward the older, more established, more complex, "scientific," indisputably adult game of cricket lasted for quite some time. Baseball promoters talked out of both sides of their mouths, alternately celebrating baseball's manly character and assailing its principal boyish feature. The key to the manliness of the fly catch was that it made the game more difficult—it demanded more skill of the fielders.[11]

So vigorous were the reformers in their advocacy of the fly catch that even before the rule was changed, they exhorted players to es-chew the bound catch unless it was absolutely necessary. According to Chadwick, catching on the fly was unquestionably the "prettiest mode of catching"; besides, a "fielder has two chances in attempting a catch on the fly, for should he fail in the first instance, he has the resource of a catch on the bound afterward." These arguments were surrounded by and clearly subordinate to Chadwick's real concern— that the bound catch was frequently "a feat a boy ten years of age would scarcely be proud of." Skillful bound catches were "few and far between." Chadwick urged fielders to "try their utmost to take [the ball] on the fly, and not wait until it is almost touching the ground, and then, boy-like, try to take it on the bound. Nothing dis-appoints the spectator, or dissatisfies the batsman so much, as to see a fine hit to the long field caught on the bound in this simple, childish manner."[12]

The fly catch not only demanded more skill (especially in the days of barehanded fielders); occasionally it called forth from its advocates fears of virility wasted on the ballfield, as is suggested by the following rhetoric: "What is more annoying to an admirer of good fielding than to see a splendid hit to the center field, such as would merit a home run, entirely nullified by the puny effort of waiting until the force of the ball is spent on the ground, and then taking it on the bound."[13] In this sexual economy of the game, in which adult male (sublimated) sexuality was contrasted with boys' masturbatory practices, manliness at the plate—fine hitting—deserved a manly response from the field—catching on the fly.

"First class players," observed *Wilkes' Spirit of the Times*, always "scorned to adopt the boys' play of the easy bound catch. A missed fly-catch from a good attempt is far more creditable than an easy bound catch waited for." According to the *Clipper*, "no manly or skillful player will ever be guilty" of the "custom of sacrificing the catch on the fly to the more simple effort on the bound." Manliness was connected with skill, but they were not precisely the same thing. A manly player also understood the "propriety" of attempting a fly catch even if he could not be sure of making it. Manly play could mean taking "creditable" risks, even at the expense of the outcome of a game. If the game itself could eliminate the choice, and thus demand more skill, then it would be more manly. Manly ballplayers, presumably, would follow.[14]

Game reporting in the late 1850s and early 1860s distinguished between fly and bound catches, as did the detailed box score developed by Chadwick and used by the *Clipper*. The following fragments of a nearly play-by-play account of a match between the Excelsior and Empire clubs in 1859 illustrate the way reporters viewed the difference: "Benson . . . was well caught out by Leggett on the fly. . . . Leggett had previously been put out by an easy catch on the bound by Russell . . . Smith being caught out on the fly in splendid style by Reynolds, who judged the ball beautifully."[15] Only rarely did a bound catch earn praise; fly catches automatically merited compliments.

A series of games between the Excelsior and Knickerbocker clubs in 1859 provided an ideal opportunity for the press to sing the praises of the fly game. The Knickerbocker Club had initially proposed the fly rule at the first convention of ballplayers in 1857. Pioneers "in any matter pertaining to the welfare and progress of the manly pastime," according to the *Clipper*, the Knickerbockers played their own practice games by the fly rule. Now they wanted to demonstrate its merit to the fraternity at large. Predictably, the press thought the experiment a success:

> We venture to say that at the close of the match—the shortest on record—not a dozen players among the great numbers present, would have been found who would not have voted then and there for the immediate repeal of the boyish rule of the catch on the bound. The superiority of the others was so manifest, the play so much more brilliant, even under the disadvantage of some wild throwing, and otherwise muffin-like play, that few could gainsay the fact that the senior club had so long being [*sic*] trying to prove to their brethren, viz.: that the catch on the fly when adopted would make the game complete, and place it on a par, in fielding at least, with the best display of cricketing ever seen here.
>
> We warrant that at the next convention the delegation in favor of the new rule will be so large and strong that their opponents will not have a sight, . . . for we think the vote will be unanimously in favor of the catch on the fly.

Fly-rule play was "more brilliant" despite otherwise poor play; it made for a shorter game; its adoption could "complete" baseball by placing it on a par with cricket. The return game of the match lasted only an hour and fifty minutes ("the shortest on record"), and "was decidedly the most brilliant contest of the season, reflect[ing] the highest credit on the skill and ability of the Excelsior club, not only on account of the signal victory they achieved, but also for the highly creditable manner in which they achieved it."[16]

It is a measure of the fly rule's importance to its proponents that they were willing to publish such shameless propaganda with a straight face. One of the finest teams of the period, the Excelsiors were all but incapable of losing to the Knickerbockers. Their relatively low score (twenty runs as opposed to the Knickerbockers' five) suggests that they were going easy on the game's oldest club. Still, these games furnished the *Clipper* with a standard by which to judge the play of clubs that chose not to stress the fly catch.

Even though fly-game contests were not "regular matches," some clubs, especially the Knickerbockers and Excelsiors, continued voluntarily to play games under the fly rule. The Knickerbocker Club's correspondence from 1859 to 1862 was filled with requests from area clubs to play a "fly game of base ball." The *Clipper* claimed as early as July 1859 that "all the best clubs now practice the catch on the fly on their practice days," but if this were truly the case, Henry Chadwick would probably not have arranged a series of "prize games" to "test the merits" of the fly game five years later.[17]

Part of the explanation lay in the nature of the opposition to the fly game. Since it almost never received sympathetic treatment in the press, this opposition must be reconstructed from hints and fragments. Nevertheless, a relatively clear picture does emerge from this effort, a picture whose general outline appears repeatedly throughout the history of the game.

According to *Porter's Spirit of the Times*, some people objected to the fly catch "as being too much like cricket, some that it would hurt the hand more than by taking the ball on the bound." This complaint was not treated seriously by the *Clipper*, which argued (unfairly, given that fielders wore no gloves until later in the century) that only "want of skill" kept "the swiftest ball" from being "easily caught and held without injury to the hand, except a smart sting." While the press and other fly-game advocates constantly pressed to make baseball a more skillfully played game, a more difficult game, many members of the fraternity and a majority at the conventions before 1864 clearly wanted no such thing. Interestingly, however, their objection was not to the fly game per se but only to its being made mandatory. The same convention that rejected the recommendation of its rules committee in favor of the fly game in December 1860 easily approved a measure stating "that the Convention extends to such clubs as may prefer to play match or practice games on the fly, the privilege of doing so."[18]

Perhaps the exhibition fly games in 1859 and 1860 had convinced the delegates that they had little to fear from granting official status to such games. If so, they underestimated the resolve of their opponents, who were determined that the fly rule would "ultimately be the rule of the game." After all, the reformers argued, "the poor players cannot always be in the majority in the Convention." Chadwick held this position consistently, reporting the defeat of the fly rule in 1863 with the comment that "all, or nearly all, of those opposed to it belong to the muffin fraternity, whose fun the fly game would put a stop to altogether."[19] Was this an accurate characterization of the fly game's opponents?

With some important exceptions, it does seem that the best players, or at least the delegates of the clubs with the most successful nines, tended to favor the fly rule more than those from less successful clubs. But the opponents of the measure could hardly be classified uniformly as "muffins," a term usually reserved for the poorest players of all. And some clubs whose nines clearly did not belong to the first rank, most notably the Knickerbockers, were firm supporters of the reform. By and large, convention support for the fly rule came from the older and better Brooklyn clubs; as a group the New York clubs ranged from strongly opposed to mildly in favor. Between 1860 and 1864 the sentiments of the "country clubs"—those based in cities other than New York or Brooklyn, whatever their size—shifted dramatically, from overwhelming opposition to strong support.[20]

By 1860, a mere fifteen years after the first club was organized and the first set of rules written, the baseball fraternity had produced two rival groups. On the eve of the 1863 convention, the *Clipper* looked forward to "an exciting trial of strength between the two parties who advocate and oppose this style of game,"[21] but the struggle was also between two different visions of how the game ought to be organized, experienced, and played. Those who advocated the fly game also placed increased emphasis on skill, on a connection between manliness and the exercise of acquired baseball-playing skill, on practice, discipline, and match-game victories; in short, on the game itself. These reformers, or "modernizers," found opponents in those players and club members who did not separate the game from its matrix of social and club activities, who liked the game for its "exercise" and "fraternity" as much as for its technical skill and match victories. These "traditionalists" predominated in the fraternity until the mid-1860s, when they were decisively defeated on the fly rule, which was in any event more a symptom than the substance of the change they were resisting.

Ethics of the Game: Reform vs. Custom

In suggesting that there were, in effect, two different, opposing ethics of the game at this time, I am not maintaining that the boundary between the two was hard and fast, that players and spectators did not manage to combine elements of both. I am arguing that two identifiable clusters of values were competing in the baseball world, and that they tended to be held by different groups.

The press, led by Henry Chadwick, usually flew the reformers' banner. Reporters' scrutiny of the game and of the skill with which it was played became more intense between the late 1850s and mid-1860s. More and more matches received inning-by-inning, sometimes batter-by-batter attention. Chadwick promoted detailed statistical analyses of individual games and of the season's play of the best "first nines." In the second edition of *Beadle's* (1861) he published a schematic scoring system that, with modifications, is still used today, as well as a form for the detailed reporting of games. Baseball statistics absorbed a large part of that year's guide, as the proliferation of the game's statistics was already outstripping those of every other sport, including cricket. Chadwick made the connection between the organization and analysis of the game: "Every club ought to belong to, and be bound by the rules and regulations of the 'National Association of Base Ball Players,' and we do not wish to take the trouble, necessary to make this analysis, for those clubs who are not members of the National Association."[22]

That the National Association itself represented the modernizing tendencies in the game is suggested by its resolution in March 1859 to abolish the "custom of furnishing refreshments on the occasion of matches." As Chadwick explained, "this custom, which originated in a desire to promote friendly intercourse between the members of the several clubs, had degenerated into one, seriously detrimental to the interests of the game, owing to the spirit of emulation that arose among the clubs, each aspiring to excel each other in the expense and splendor of these entertainments." And in his sample club by-laws, Chadwick provided that "no expenses for refreshments on match-days shall be paid out of the funds of this club." The "interests of the game," according to its most influential reformer, needed protection from its "customary" social aspects.[23]

If we recall that the *Clipper* criticized the bound catch as a "custom" of which no "manly or skillful fielder will ever be guilty," we can see more clearly the significance of the modernizing forces in the game itself. Such "customary" practices were inappropriate at a time when many participants were more interested "in the progress and final perfection of the game we cherish." Still, postgame refreshments remained an important part of the game into the mid-1860s. As the decade progressed, however, and more and more games were reported in the baseball columns, less and less space was devoted to the "excellent collations" enjoyed by both teams after a contest. It is likely that the custom was gradually dying out (club balls, too, were rarely noticed after mid-decade), though visits to other cities continued to provide occasions for elaborate dinners and socializing.[24]

The tensions expressed over these social rituals were the same ones, slightly displaced, that crystallized around the fly rule. In fact, they were felt everywhere in the game. We can even see them in Henry Chadwick, the most stouthearted of reformers and modernizers, an unstinting baseball propagandist, who nonetheless insisted on the importance of decorum and "respectability" in the game. His attitude combined solicitude for the manliness and honor of the game with vigorous support for measures that undermined the context essential to that version of baseball respectability. Chadwick had his feet planted firmly in both ethics, but he put most of his weight on the reforming foot.

Like most of those interested in baseball rules—and Chadwick was fascinated by them, providing extensive, exegetical commmentaries on disputed points in the yearly editions of *Beadle's* and serving for years on the NABBP's Committee on Rules and Regulations—Chadwick wanted to change them to make the game "more perfect." Ballplayers do not seem to have joined the rules committee of their association to keep the game the same; the officers and committee members voted consistently and disproportionately in favor of making the game more difficult. These advocates, however, were not always the best players, and perhaps the issue of rules explains the otherwise surprising position of the Knickerbockers in the forefront of the modernizing ranks.

For the significance of the Knickerbockers in baseball history lies in the fact that they were not only the first club but the first to play by a set of written rules. It was their club and game rules that justified their claim of being "the pioneer of the present game of Base Ball." Twelve years later it was the Knickerbocker Club officers who issued the call for the first convention of baseball players. According to Chadwick, "the knowledge of the benefit that would accrue to the game, if a proper revision of the rules were to be had, and a new code established," led to this call "for the purposes of establishing a permanent code of rules by which all could, in future, be governed." And at that convention it was the Knickerbockers who, "with a view of making the game more manly and scientific, . . . proposed, that no player should be out on a fair struck ball, if it was only taken by the fielder according to the old rule, . . . but that the ball must be caught in the air before it had touched the ground, or the player was not out." The Knickerbockers' original interest in establishing and encouraging the rules of their manly sport, the manliness of which they themselves regarded as somewhat suspect, led them to support a rule change that in other ways ran against the way they thought about and played their game.[25]

Although occasional press notices referred to the great skill of the Knickerbocker nine, these accolades reflected the regard in which the baseball fraternity held the club rather than respect for its competitive ability. Though the Knickerbockers were appreciated for their past leadership and were still valued as upholders of the traditional ethic of the game, their field play did not even merit statistical analysis in Chadwick's baseball annuals. The fly-game matches they played with the Excelsiors were interesting only because the point being tested was the fly rule, not the comparative strength of the two teams. In fact, a reporter used entirely different, even contradictory sets of standards in judging such a game in 1860. In accounting for the defeat of the "veterans," 32 to 9, he opined that the Knickerbockers' "muffins" could probably have put up a better struggle than their first nine had done; but his concern over their poor play had evaporated by the end of the story: "Suffice it to say, that the game was one of the most amusing and enjoyable of the season; and as, after all, that is the great object of the game, recreation being the desideratum in base ball, we think it would be well to play more of such matches."[26]

But recreation was far from the only desideratum in baseball at the time. Not all clubs escaped censure for playing "for the fun of the thing," as Wilkes' Spirit of the Times put it in 1864. The "ancient and honorable Knickerbockers," as they were called in 1866, were different.[27] They served both the modernizers and the traditionalists as a repository of older, residual values, as a club to which journalists could ascribe, positively, the values that they were in reality doing their best to eliminate from the game. Even the modernizers remained ambivalent about the gradual purging of the noncompetitive elements of the game. Similar feelings probably motivated players as well.

Why else would the Excelsiors and Knickerbockers have continued to play an "annual series of friendly practice games" long after the clubs' skill levels had diverged radically? According to the *Clipper*, the final game of the 1863 season "was one of the most friendly and enjoyable affairs of the season," and was followed, appropriately enough, by "the whole of the contestants [sitting] down to an excellent supper at Perry's hotel, where a right merry and social time was had for an hour or two." "The Knickerbockers," observed *Wilkes' Spirit of the Times*, "play ball because they love it. They turn out for sport simply, and have plenty of it."[28] A game against the Knickerbockers enabled players who had otherwise abandoned the quest "for sport simply" to play the kind of game they had played when they— and the game—were younger and less manly.

A few other clubs occupied the territory presided over by the Knickerbockers. When the Baltic Club returned to the playing field after a brief disbandment at the beginning of the Civil War, a welcome was extended to its members, who "played ball for the sport and enjoyment of the pastime, and not for the purpose of victory." Similarly, the New York Base Ball Club was, according to one report, "a body of gentleman who are banded together for the purpose of indulging in the game purely as a means of recreation and exercise, and only play their nines against each other—not sending or receiving challenges."[29]

But the mantle of the Knickerbockers stretched only so far. Press commitment to competitive skill was growing during these years, as was that of players and spectators. In his discussion of the Active Club's 1863 season, a reporter noted that "in some of their contests we regretted to see their first nine display an amount of careless and indifferent playing, which was far from creditable to them. This playing and often losing a game just 'for the fun of the thing,' is a rather poor method of adding to a Club's fame or trophy case."[30] While the writer recognized that the club seemed to care more about fun than about fame and trophies, he was determined to persuade the Actives (and his readers) that such "indifferent" play caused them to lose respect as well as games. Clubs that stood no chance of winning the championship and did not compete for it escaped the disapproval aimed at the better clubs when they played poorly.

Although they rarely reflected on this phenomenon, baseball writers understood the difference between the kind of sport they were encouraging and a game that was structured on different values. They recognized that the players, even the very good players, had tendencies in both directions; that although they wanted to win games, they also occasionally enjoyed "fun and exercise" that contributed little to the "excellence of the nine." The reformers had chosen, however, to push the game whenever possible toward a more serious application to practice, toward finer, more skillful play, and toward victories on the playing field.

But the ambivalence that the reformers had to confront was formidable indeed, and it has never entirely disappeared from the game. What I have called the two ethics of the game, visible in the struggle over the fly rule, have been so deeply embedded in the history and experience of baseball that it is difficult to imagine a level or manifestation of the sport that has not been (and is not) structured by these two ethics and the tension between them. Despite the best efforts of spectators, commentators, and players (and later of owners and administrators) to control that tension by collapsing one side of it, by absorbing one ethic into the other, the game has proved remarkably recalcitrant.

Fruits of Reform: "Ambitious Rivalries and Selfish Victories"

If these tensions had been easy to resolve, then something like the "contest for the championship" would have been a relatively simple and straightforward feature of each season's play. It was in reality a good deal more complicated. Not only was there no systematic method of determining the "champion club." Even among the strongest clubs, whether to compete for the championship at all was, at least occasionally, a problematic issue. In 1861, for example, the Excelsiors played no championship matches at all, and three seasons later the Eckfords "resigned their claim to the championship" by not accepting the Atlantics' challenge. The Excelsiors and the Eckfords, two of the three strongest clubs of the late 1850s, had never played each other, "owing to some club difficulty that occurred between them" at the all-star matches in 1858.[31]

Unfortunately, some club difficulty cropped up frequently at championship matches—or often enough to disturb the most vocal boosters of such games. A match between two leading junior clubs in

1860, "a sort of contest for the championship of the junior clubs," was, "as far as the playing was concerned, . . . very creditable to both clubs." The problem was "the feeling that was manifested by some of the members of both clubs"—feeling that was "boyish in the extreme, to say the least." The *Clipper* reporter was ready to abandon the whole enterprise. "From what we have seen of the result of these matches for the championship," he wrote, "we are inclined to the belief that they are anything but beneficial to the interests and welfare of the game, for though they lead to the acquirement of a great deal of skill in the practice of the game, the ill feeling that is engendered is an offset that is more important as a matter to be considered."[32] Chadwick, it will be recalled, wanted to protect the "interests and welfare of the game" from overemphasis on expensive socializing. Here the emphasis on skill and competition threatened the game by giving rise to the "more important" ill feeling. In other words, the very effort to make the game more manly was giving rise to boyish emotions.

A few weeks later the *Clipper* editorialized on the subject. While some of the championship matches that year had been characterized "by the right kind of spirit, . . . generally speaking the excitement and spirit of rivalry attendant upon them has led to conduct that was anything but of a friendly character." Quoting from the statement of purpose of the NABBP, the writer claimed that the big matches hardly promoted "the cultivating of kindly feelings among the different members of Base Ball Clubs."[33]

That, in a nutshell, was the problem. Reformers pushed players to take the game more seriously, to perfect their "excellence as a nine," to "go on to ambitious heights of excellence crowned by victory," and yet simultaneously demanded that players "enter not upon the coming season for mere purposes of ambitious rivalries and selfish victories." These sentiments, appearing in consecutive paragraphs, confronted the contradictions between the two ethics, but appeared in an article structured on the assumption that the tension could be resolved in favor of what it called "the legitimate results of true sport—relaxation, pleasure, exercise, and health."[34] That assumption was incorrect; as long as both sides received such strong support, no such resolution was possible.

Thus, even while press accounts of "grand matches for the championship" grew longer, more frequent, and more detailed, commentators regularly pointed out the one-sidedness of the desire for victory and called for the abolition of these contests. Although the *Clipper* "now regard[ed] these matches as anything but conducive to the best interests of the game," its editor, Frank Queen, arranged a "Grand Base Ball Match" for a silver ball trophy between New York and Brooklyn all-stars later that year, and devoted prodigious quantities of print to advertising, covering, and analyzing it.[35]

Reporting on the status of the Olympic Ball Club of Philadelphia, a ballplayer of that city proudly pointed out that the Olympics were "the champion club of the city," but in "saying this," he continued, he did not intend to convey the impression "that the championship is the first ambition of its members." On the contrary, he argued, "whilst skillful play is worked hard for by all, and a successful contest highly gratifying, yet respectability has always been the ruling desire of the club."[36] This correspondent truly wished to subsume the "skillful play" of his heroes under the banner of "respectability," but whether respectability was its ruling desire is questionable. Consider this report in the *Clipper* of August 15, 1863:

> The discreditable scenes that took place towards the close of the game lead us sincerely to hope that this will be the last season that any of these championship games are played. It is unquestionably for the best interests of the game that matches for the championship, together with the title of champion, should be entirely done away with, and the sooner the leading men in the fraternity frown this class of matches down the better.
>
> They lead to the alienation of clubs from each other, that hitherto have been fast friends; they create a feeling of rivalry that results in endless disputes, and a great deal of ill feeling among members of the different clubs principally concerned in the contests; and above all they are the means of affording hearty encouragement to that spirit of gambling that knows neither honor, truth or justice in its efforts to obtain success. Surely these are evils, resulting from this class of games, sufficient to ensure the utmost efforts of all true friends of our national game in putting down the source of so great an obstacle to its future progress and welfare. . . . So much for the objectionable championship contests; now for a brief description of the game itself.

There can be no doubt that the reporter's distress was genuine. But rather than ignore the details of the game itself in favor of a denunciation, the *Clipper* introduced the "madness" and "discreditable scenes" by a three-line headline that referred only to the game—"AN EXCITING CONTEST AT BROOKLYN. / The Atlantic vs. Mutual. / THE MUTUALS VICTORIOUS BY ONE RUN"—and concluded with the usual box score. Press attitudes toward the championship increasingly showed all of the ambivalence of a piece on the upcoming season of 1863, headed:

> THE CONTEST FOR THE CHAMPIONSHIP FOR 1863
> The Documents Signed, and the Men Gone Into Training.
> *ATLANTIC VS. ECKFORD FOR THE CHAMPIONSHIP*

which observed that "in ball playing circles throughout the country, the contest for the championship has been the regular topic of conversation, and when the matches come off there will be certain delegations from every city in the North present, and no doubt the largest concourse of spectators ever seen at a match."[37]

Despite the worries about ill feeling, madness, and the spirit of rivalry, by the mid-1860s mainstream baseball was competitive, championship baseball—not baseball played for the fun of the thing. It absorbed most of the interest of the sporting press and drew the largest crowds of spectators. True to the game's contradictory history, however, this development, too, was attended by paradoxes. The increasing emphasis on the play of the game, instead of creating a separate, unserious sphere of recreation or leisure, a world of play set off from the world of work, served to intensify the resemblance of baseball playing to productive labor. The enormous emphasis on "manly skillful play" and the language of craft excellence must have appealed powerfully to the skilled workers who played such a large role in "first-class" baseball in New York and Brooklyn, who had no ideology to support a notion or sphere of pure recreation. Nor, as participants in a culture where manliness was a preeminent virtue, could they have felt comfortable playing according to a "boys' rule" or "boyish" standards of conduct.

So the effort to improve and "perfect" the "pastime" made it more serious rather than less, made it more difficult to play rather than easier, marked it off increasingly from casual recreation and made it increasingly indistinguishable from work. But although organized baseball attempted to distance itself from fun and exercise, these qualities clearly did not disappear from the game. In fact, by pushing organized baseball in this direction, reformers unintentionally created a larger arena of less worklike play. For though championship baseball attracted most of the press interest, it actually accounted for a diminishing proportion of games played. Participation in baseball clubs soared as the Civil War ended, and by the late 1860s the National Association conventions consisted of delegates from state baseball players' associations, not representatives of individual clubs. The levels below that of the contenders for the championship were expanding even as press attention was narrowing to the championship. Moreover, it is doubtful that any kind of baseball was played purely for victory or purely for fun and exercise. Such tensions have never fully disappeared from any level of the game, at any point in its history. They have been repressed or ignored but never eliminated. That is not to say that the game has never changed. On the contrary, the advocates of the fly game won a decisive and important victory over the baseball traditionalists of the early 1860s. They enshrined the values of skillful, competitive struggle for victory as the dominant ethos of organized baseball. Baseball's "progress" had little to do with the "inevitability" of the game's "evolution"—but it did leave the losers in that struggle very much behind. From the winners are descended the modern professional major leagues. The losers recreate themselves every season on sandlots, in pickup softball games, on the lowest rungs of municipal leagues.

But the winners were not always happy with what they had won. Press attitudes toward baseball's oldest surviving club suggest that the "ancient and honorable Knickerbockers," as they were referred to on the eve of baseball professionalization, served as the touchstone for an ethic that the modernizers were struggling to limit, even as they worried about the effects of their own reforms. "When the rivalry between clubs is carried to an extent that leads to mutual jealousy and ill-feeling," editorialized the *Clipper*, "it is about time that matches should cease to be played, and under such circumstances we advise all clubs to follow the example of the Knickerbockers, and ignoring all match games between club and club, confine themselves to pleasant and gentlemanly games among themselves, when they can enjoy the contests as a recreation and a healthful exercise. But we hope for better things."[38]

The hope was genuine. Whether it could be realized was another matter. For the victory over the fly rule and the growing importance of championship matches represented crucial advances in the game's linear history, paving the way for open professionalism. At the same time, the hope for better things was starting to circle back toward a remembered past, and we can just barely glimpse the beginnings of baseball's cyclical history.

PART II

Amateurs into Professionals, 1866–1876

4

Growth, Division, and "Disorder"

The Coming of the "Good Old Days"

With the emergence of professional baseball in the late 1860s, the game grew at a dizzying pace and underwent far-reaching internal changes. One of the most widespread responses to these changes was an invocation of a past allegedly purer than the complicated and difficult present. By 1867, Henry Chadwick's new weekly, *The Ball Players' Chronicle,* was complaining loudly about the modern evils of the game and wondering what had happened to the good old days. "Where are the veterans," Chadwick editorialized under the headline "The Abuses of Base Ball," "who used to make base ball matches and fair, manly play, synonymous terms?" The *Chronicle* reprinted a long letter to the Brooklyn *Times* from a correspondent who worried that the game

> seems to be no longer participated in for the mere pleasure of the thing, or to dispel the enervating effects of a sedentary occupation; and though we cannot but feel gratified at the fact that Brooklyn has, from the inception of the game, as played at the present day, held the laurels of the championship, it is a question if it would not have been as well for the interest of the game, as a National sport, had this honor been more equally divided.[1]

One need only recall, however briefly, the near-total lack of "chivalric sentiment" in the Atlantic–Mutual match of 1863 to suggest that these efforts to use an untroubled golden age as a standard by which to judge the present were concerned less with historical accuracy than with establishing (out of whole cloth, if necessary) an Edenic prehistory of the game.[2]

But Chadwick had other needs for baseball history at the same time. A second, equally strong theme in the 1867–1868 *Chronicle* was the degree to which baseball had improved in the previous decade. "Some ten years ago," he wrote, "and even later, it was a rare sight to witness a ball match, played anywhere, or by any parties, which was not marked by changes in the positions of the players in nearly every innings, and what was most objectionable, open disputes about the decision of the Umpire. Now the reverse is the rule." Crowds, too, "in times gone by," abused umpires by "derisive cheers," whereas now "we find such conduct emanating only from the lowest and most ignorant" spectators.[3]

As history, these arguments leave much to be desired. By 1859 and 1860 players on the best nines had assigned positions, and the accepted wisdom on the subject was well known. And as for disputing decisions of umpires, neither players nor spectators had stopped (or would ever stop) doing so, and Chadwick's attempt to blame contentious crowds on the "lowest and most ignorant," "boyish," and "partisan" onlookers was consistent with his efforts in the early part of the decade to blame all unseemly conduct on "boys" and "roughs." His purpose here was to show that the game was simultaneously more skillfully and honorably played and more respectably watched than it had been in the late 1850s and early 1860s. According to this Whiggish interpretation of baseball's history, each season was more brilliant than the last, play was better than ever, and the "success and permanency" of the game were assured. These two forms of "history" dominated Chadwick's baseball writing in the latter part of the decade. That they were contradictory seems not to have occurred to him.

A third way the baseball past found its way into the present started as winter filler for sporting papers. Accounts of old games, box scores and all, began to appear frequently in the *Chronicle* in December 1867, and Chadwick's statistical summaries of the season, stretched out over many issues, often went far back into a club's history. For some time matches between prominent clubs had prompted sportswriters to reflect on the history of the competition between the clubs, and sometimes to give detailed scores of the previous matches. Such coverage may have reflected the declining interest in (or frequency of) club social activities in the winter, and the consequent focusing of the baseball public's interest on the game itself—even old games. Or it may have been an attempt to measure the competing claims of the past and the present. The interest in statistics and the increasingly common "Review of the Season" also represented efforts to gain control over the season just past. More and more, seasons included dozens of games that even the most devoted fan or sportswriter could not possibly hope to witness.

Whenever he advanced an argument about the present or future of the game, Chadwick automatically appealed to the past. Baseball did not exist for him by itself in the present: it was always in relationship with old games, previous ways of playing, earlier players and clubs, even his old stories. And the more distant the past, the more likely that it would be appealed to in the present. The reprinted stories, for instance, were all from the 1850s. He rarely drew on the recent past, the years that would have provided a sense of continuity. In other words, Chadwick had difficulty describing continuous historical development or gradual growth; he needed breaks, radical differences, a Fall.[4]

Chadwick's "histories," then, must be read as records of a particular consciousness of the game—and, given his enormous influence on reporting, record keeping, and rules of play, that consciousness is of more than passing interest. It was not, however, the only way of looking at the game or its history. *Wilkes' Spirit of the Times*, for example, thought fulminations about baseball's "evils" priggishly moralistic, "overzealous," and "deharmonizing." But if this paper did not share Chadwick's sense of the game's moral declension, it did share his reliance on a version of the past with which to evaluate the present. Certain clubs were said to have had their golden age years ago, while one reporter pointed out the difference between the highly skilled play of the modern professionals and the "bad play" so common "under the old regime."[5]

Whether or not commentators saw baseball in these years as morally degenerate depended a good deal on their attitude toward the presence of money in the game. Modern fans may be consoled to learn that from the time of its entrance into baseball, money has provided the occasion for the most confusion, most bitter controversies, and most disparate views and experiences of the game. Most broadly conceived, baseball's relationship with money is the substance of the linear history of the game; the cyclical history chronicles the game's emotional relationships. It is neither possible nor desirable to separate these two histories entirely, even for analytical purposes, but it is possible and important to try to understand what was happening in each during these years to produce the tangle of fact and emotion that has complicated most attempts to look clearly at baseball's past.

Baseball myth has it that money entered the game along with the Cincinnati Red Stockings, the first all-professional team, in 1869. Baseball historians have effectively debunked this view, to the extent that even the keeper of the myth, the Baseball Hall of Fame, has changed this part of the story. Not only did professional baseball—that is, play for pay—predate the Red Stockings; money had entered the game over a decade earlier in the form of occasional admission fees, and such fees were firmly established by 1862. Clubs had played prize matches for large purses as early as 1859, held "benefits" for star players, paid salaries to a few, and raised money for charities.[6]

The appearance of money in baseball was closely linked to the beginnings of high-level competition. Admission was first charged in 1858 at a series of all-star matches between New York and Brooklyn at the Fashion Course in 1858. Borrowed from cricket clubs, which usually held benefits for their professional players, "benefits" for such players as James Creighton, Dickey Pearce, and Joe Start were thinly disguised means of offering payment to some of the clubs' best players. Creighton, the young pitching phenomenon of the early 1860s, was probably being paid by the Excelsiors as early as 1860, and the Philadelphia Athletics were paying a salary to Al Reach in the early 1860s.[7]

Although many writers argued later in the decade that money had both created and corrupted first-class competition, such accounts reversed the developments they sought to explain. It was the better clubs' commitment to top-level competition that brought this kind of money into the game. If clubs had not first agreed on the value of competition, they would have had no reason to break the National Association's rule against compensating players. Similarly, big prize matches took place only because of the excitement stirred up by competition. And if the competition between prominent clubs had not been such a strong attraction, spectators would not have paid to see their matches.

Interestingly, however, none of these manifestations of money in baseball aroused the indignation of the press, and there is no indication that players felt any distress over the first steps toward the commercialization of their sport. Organized baseball—as opposed to informal children's play—had always been involved with money: clubs rented grounds and assessed dues and fines; members bought uniforms and equipment, and financed dinners, balls, and excursions. Even gambling had been a part of the game almost from the start. Reporters often called attention to gamblers at games and to the betting odds in very matter-of-fact tones, suggesting that betting was an unremarkable element of the game. They also commonly used betting language and other financial metaphors to help structure their stories.[8]

In August 1865, *Wilkes' Spirit of the Times* assessed the relative strengths of the Mutuals and Atlantics in terms of the betting odds: "In this game, although the champions' [Atlantics'] friends were confident of their winning easily, many of them backing their opinions at the rate of 2 to 1, and even $100 to $40, their efforts did not warrant any such odds or any odds at all, as the Mutuals' fielding, batting, and entire playing was fully equal to their opponents'." The Atlantics barely won the game, 13–12, and the reporter punctuated his praise of the Mutuals by asking, "How are you, two to one?"—a comment doubtless echoed by many of the 18,000 spectators. Pretending to a position of impartiality above the favoritism of partisans and gamblers, the reporter betrayed his own involvement in the game. Gambling and its peculiar partisanship were far more seductive than he realized.[9]

Nor was he alone. Henry Chadwick, the great journalistic enemy of gambling in 1867, routinely reported five years earlier that a match between the Mutuals and Gothams had attracted much interest, "the odds, among the betting fraternity, being largely in favor of the Mutuals," and that, in the course of a match between the Newark Eurekas and the Mutuals, "the odds in the betting market were in favor of the Jersey boys." Throughout the decade, when a club was doing well in the course of a game, its "paper" was said to be offered at a "premium" or "above par"; if it did poorly, its "paper" was offered at a "discount" or "below par." If a club established an early lead, its "stock" went up.[10]

So just as baseball was never very far from the language, experience, and world of work, it never occupied a terrain fully apart from the world of the marketplace. This is not to argue that the game has always had the same relation to the commercial world that it does now, but to place the very real debates and controversies over professionalism in their proper context.

Growth and Fragmentation

So the preoccupation with money and professionalism in baseball was not simply about those two issues. One key to what it was about lay in the timing of Chadwick's reportorial and editorial outbursts on the subject. What, we may ask, was happening in the seasons of 1866 and 1867 that had not happened before? What specific developments helped to trigger the sudden concern for the welfare of the game?

First, after the Civil War, baseball activity increased enormously. New clubs formed at an extremely rapid rate; table 1 tells part of the story. At the first convention after the end of the war, the number of clubs represented was triple that of the previous year, thirty more

TABLE 1

Number of clubs and states represented at NABBP conventions, 1860–1866

Year	Clubs	States
1860[a]	62	6[b]
1860[c]	54	5
1861	34	2
1862	32	3
1863	28	3[b]
1864	30	3[b]
1865	91	10[b]
1866	202	17[b]

[a]March.
[b]Plus Washington, D.C.
[c]December.
Source: Henry Chadwick, ed., *Beadle's Dime Base-Ball Player* (New York, 1861), pp. 40, 46–47; (1862), pp. 31–33; (1864), pp. 33–36; (1865), pp. 35–37; *Wilkes' Spirit of the Times*, May 12, 1860, p. 157; December 20, 1862, p. 253; December 24, 1864, p. 260; December 23, 1865, p. 259; December 22, 1866, pp. 266–267; *New York Clipper*, March 24, 1860, p. 387; December 22, 1860, p. 284; December 27, 1862, p. 293; December 19, 1863, p. 287.

than at the largest prewar convention. The following year the number more than doubled, and in 1867 there were so many clubs that most were represented at the national convention by delegates from their state associations. The "Base Ball Directory" published each week by the *Chronicle* listed more than 200 senior clubs and another 175 junior clubs by November 1867.[11]

Even more important than the number of clubs were their geographical distribution and the relative positions of New York and Brooklyn. Of the more than two hundred clubs listed in the *Chronicle*'s directory, New York and Brooklyn clubs accounted for less than 15 percent. Two years earlier, however, at the 1865 convention, a third of the ninety-one clubs had been from these neighboring cities, as had the majority of clubs represented at conventions during the war years. From 1865 to 1867, as the proportion of New York and Brooklyn clubs was halved, the number of area clubs remained roughly the same—about thirty. So while the growth of organized baseball in the metropolitan area seems to have leveled off just after the war, other parts of the country—particularly the Midwest—were experiencing a huge upsurge. The center of gravity of the baseball world was shifting westward. It had already begun to move up and down the East Coast, but if the origins of National Association officers can be used as a rough measure, there was very little movement until 1865. With few exceptions, clubs of the New York metropolitan area dominated the three top offices of the association (president and first and second vice-presidents), and all of the conventions were held in New York City. In 1865, however, representatives of two "country clubs" (in Newburgh and Utica) held the vice-presidencies, and the following year these positions were occupied by delegates from Boston and St. Louis (by far the most distant city yet represented in the leadership of the association).

A New Yorker continued to hold the presidency until 1867, when Arthur Pue Gorman of the Olympic Club of Washington, D.C., was elected head of the organization, and his first vice-president came from Altoona, Pennsylvania. The next year the revolution was complete: for the first time the association's annual meeting was held outside New York City, in Philadelphia, and, as the *Chronicle* headline put it, "Ohio Takes the Presidency." Nor was that all. Wisconsin "took" the first vice-presidency, and the recording secretary's job went (for the first time) to someone west of the Eastern Seaboard, an editor from Rockford, Illinois, who represented the Forest City Club and the Illinois Association of Base-Ball Players. The new president, George F. Sands of Cincinnati, made it clear in his acceptance remarks that he regarded his election as symbolic of changes in the game: "I beg to assure you that I do not interpret your action as a personal compliment," he told the delegates, "but one accorded to the States West of the Allegheny Mountains, where our national game now flourishes to an extent unequalled in the rapidity of growth in popularity in the annals of base ball." [12]

On the one hand, this huge expansion of the game gave baseball commentators and promoters reasons for pride. Their sport was finally becoming what they had been calling it for years, the national game. On the other hand, there were hints that not everyone shared this unqualified enthusiasm. For, as the game's popularity spread geographically as well as through the social order of metropolitan New York, it came into more and more contact with people unfamiliar with the behavior Chadwick tried so hard to enforce on the New York and Brooklyn ballfields. Apropos of the National Club's tour, he observed that "in gatherings at other cities of the country, and especially in country towns and villages, we still find crowds of spectators so prejudiced and misguided by ignorance as to be guilty of the boyish conduct of hissing and hooting at an umpire, where his decisions do not suit their partisan views," and he called upon "every true lover of the game" to "come to its rescue" and "train up assemblages to good behavior on ballfields." Claiming that metropolitan audiences, after many years of effort on his part, had been "trained up" to the point where they practiced "a silent acquiescence in every decision of any umpire, right or wrong," Chadwick asserted that the only exceptions to this decorum "in or around the metropolis" were found in "the very lowest and most ignorant portion of an assemblage." [13]

Its questionable accuracy aside, it was a neat argument. Respectable players and spectators had been "trained" to act properly; those who had not internalized the "controls" of the game were "boyish," "low," "partisan," "uneducated," or untutored in metropolitan manners. Baseball's encounter with the "untrained" made Chadwick's class assumptions more explicit, even to the extent of translating regional differences into class language. Proud of what he considered to be the effect of his "training," he exulted in the triumph of silence, self-control, and respect for the umpire: successful internalized repression. But this achievement was unraveling. The game was absorbing new players and fans who fell on the other side of the boundaries of age, class, and region on which Chadwick drew as he sought an urban, adult, bourgeois self-control.

Some scholars have argued that for a variety of reasons—expense of transportation and admission, remoteness of the grounds, and length of working hours—baseball was a middle-class sport watched by middle-class fans, but this view requires us to ignore too much of what contemporary observers recorded about the game. Measured by its spectators, baseball was a far more democratic sport than its advocates liked to see. One of the ironies of the game's history is that, on the one hand, its ideologues and promoters have always maintained that one of its most important virtues has been the democratic mix of classes and ethnic groups (more recently, colors) in the stands, a microcosm, so they argue, of America itself; while, on the other hand, they have usually worked hard to enforce a standard of conduct at games based more exclusively on respectability and the genteel middle-class culture of white, native-born Americans.[14]

Cultural Conflict and Division

The plain fact was that as baseball became more popular, crowds grew larger and more boisterous. Reporters worried about the effects these new spectators would have on the experience of the game. Fear of uncontrolled conflict dominated accounts of big games, especially those in which disturbances did take place. Overt displays of partisanship evoked fear and contempt in reporters, who simultaneously worried that partisan feeling could not be controlled and judged such behavior with the language of class (and "adult") scorn. "Club followers" who attended matches not only to root for their favorite club but also to harass the opposition came in for special derision. In 1860 the Eckford Club seems to have attracted some of the most vocal supporters, fans whom the *Clipper* criticized for "disorderly conduct," while the Eckfords were censured for failing to "suppress" their fans.[15]

Nothing else in the coverage of the Eckfords ever indicated that the club was less respectable than any other. The club's social events received lavish attention in the press, and its president, the dockbuilder

Frank Pidgeon, was one of the fraternity's leading lights in the 1850s and 1860s. Although historians have tended to claim that the Eckfords were the premier "workingman's club" of the time, no contemporary accounts explicitly suggest as much. And between a fifth and a quarter of the members did no work with their hands at all. Still, a club based in the artisanal culture of the shipyards may well have had a class and neighborhood appeal more attractive to the city's less "respectable" working classes than that of, say, the Knickerbockers. In any event, the *Clipper* was convinced of this appeal and worried by its dangers, and its reporter compared club followers with the "runners in the Fire Department, [who] are under no control except their own evil passions." [16]

The other club that seemed to care little about attracting a rough crowd was the Atlantics, who took part in a famous interrupted match with the Excelsiors in 1860. Tarring the Atlantics with the same brush it used on the unruly crowd, the *Clipper* suggested that their loss of temper (occasioned by a succession of errors) was connected to the outcries of "their very questionable friends," and regretted that Captain Joseph P. Leggett of the Excelsiors, in withdrawing his men from the field, was not followed by the Atlantic nine, "as that was the only method of putting a stop to the outrageous conduct." Later the *Clipper* directly criticized the club for not doing anything to quiet the crowd, and accused it of "undertak[ing] to defend the action of the rowdy crowd that broke up the late match." The Atlantic defense combined a laissez-faire attitude toward the "applause or indignation" of the crowd with a hard-boiled approach to the pressure of a big game. There was also, as the *Clipper* noted, "a tone of braggadocia [sic] . . . not characteristic of that modesty we are led to expect from true merit." [17]

In espousing the virtues of modesty and self-control, the reporter was drawing on the moral resources of an ascendant evangelical bourgeois culture; the Atlantics' spokesman was relying on the less modest, more frankly partisan, and somewhat defensive "manliness" of an urban artisanal culture itself on the defensive during these years. The *Clipper* editorial on the match introduced an explicit class and ethnic element to the controversy. Seeking to account for the "riotous proceedings," the paper pointed to "the *spirit of faction* that characterizes a large portion of the community, and in which the foreign element of our immense metropolitan population, and their native offspring especially, delights to indulge." This spirit was poisoning the nation's politics, "giving rise to almost all the bitterness of party spirit and sectional strife." It seemed particularly powerful in the cities, where it was "the great curse of our noble fire department" and had "led to the almost total abandonment of the self-sacrificing and manly volunteer force of the department." Although "the factional spirit is the bane of every community wherein it is once allowed to obtain a foothold," the editorialist's ire focused on "the lower strata of our heterogeneous population," where "its poisonous breath" gave rise to the "human fungi" of urban gangs: the Dead Rabbits of New York, Killers of Philadelphia, and Plug Uglies of Baltimore.[18]

The *Clipper* called this bane the spirit of faction, and tried to blame it on immigrants and the lower classes, but the fact was that competition itself was dangerous. It was competition that threatened the "*self-control* of contending clubs" and replaced "kindly feelings with bitter hatred." Manly practitioners of the game were supposed to be able to control their passions on as well as off the ballfield, and players who did not or could not do so were uncomfortable reminders of the "boyish" behavior these men thought (or hoped) they had left behind. Such behavior frequently tempted even "mature" players, who had hardly "grown out of it." Participation in "the fraternity" demanded a high level of repression—a denial of the very urges that fueled high-level competition and motivated players to struggle hard enough to win. Not surprisingly, the balance was difficult to maintain. That is one reason the rhetoric directed at lapses from this ideal behavior was so harsh. It was aimed, literally, at "boys" and at "the lower strata," "low and ignorant" spectators, and "roughs." But as we have seen, many members of the fraternity, especially the players themselves, were not far removed from boyhood. Few active players were over thirty through the 1860s, and most were under twenty-five. As young men attempting to adhere to a difficult discipline, players and their supporters tried to strengthen their claim on adulthood by deriding "childish" or "boyish" behavior.

But the fact that the same rancor was directed at the lower classes suggests that the question of "maturity" or "manly" behavior had a class content as well. It further suggests that the language of age and class could be used (at least from the top down) interchangeably, perhaps especially when the scorn originated with a combination of middle-class professionals and "respectable" skilled craftsmen, and was aimed downward at the unskilled workers, laborers, and street arabs who did not belong to their clubs and did not aspire to the self-controlled respectability of their betters.

There were other reasons why the language of age and class overlapped during these years. First, as trades were being reorganized and industrialized by masters and entrepreneurs in antebellum New York, employers in the more fragmented and sweated trades relied heavily on the poorly paid and unskilled labor of boys and women to replace the skilled male workers who had been the mainstays of the crafts. Boys, then, represented a threat to the livelihood and republican independence of many mid-century artisans. That the employers—and not the boys themselves—were at fault was not lost on such workers; it was nonetheless difficult for such men not to resent or condescend to the boys who participated in a man's world. That so many of the new unskilled workers were Irish immigrants contributed to the intensity of this conflict.

Second, ballplayers may have been trying to distinguish their play from the less respectable sport of that stock figure of New York's working classes in the 1840s, the Bowery B'hoy, also known as the Bowery Boy. Closely identified with the boisterous culture of the fire companies, the theater, and the street, the B'hoy was a "sentinel of the new army of the unemployed, . . . a kind of popular hero, proud of his sporting ways, willing to defend them against all comers with a punkish gaze." The B'hoy represented the very culture on which baseball drew in its earliest years, just as it tried to distinguish itself from the rougher, more expressive, less self-controlled elements of that culture. The language of men and boys, in short, was also the language of men and b'hoys.[19]

In the third quarter of the nineteenth century, writes Eric Hobsbawm, there appeared a "fissure" in "what was increasingly becoming 'the working class' . . . [which] separated 'the workers' from 'the poor,' or alternatively 'the respectable' from the 'unrespectable.'" As important outside the shop as in, this fissure divided the sporting world as well. Hobsbawm argues that the boundaries of the most politically powerful and socially cohesive elements of the "respectable" working classes "pretty well coincided with . . . the world of clubs," among which he lists "Mutual Aid Societies, fraternal benevolent orders (generally with strong rituals), choirs, gymnastic or sports clubs, even voluntary religious organizations at one extreme, labor unions and political associations at the other."[20] It is not my intention here to argue the political potential of baseball club members. I do suggest, however tentatively, that the artisan members of baseball clubs may have been at once some of the most self-conscious and "self-improving" of skilled workers, men whose emphasis on self-control and self-discipline and skill on the ballfield was linked not only to the way they viewed their work but also to their sense of social position in the world outside the shop.

Participation in a baseball club or on a baseball nine may have been an expression of the most distinctive qualities of skilled and self-conscious workers: pride in achieved skill and its exhibition, self-directed efforts at discipline and "improvement," participation in the masculine ("manly") world of "respectable" fraternal activities, and a strongly protective feeling about the arena in which these accomplishments could be enjoyed. Yet despite Chadwick's dream of well-trained audiences, the game remained intimately involved with the other side of working-class culture. Club followers cared less for the niceties of respectable decorum than for "their" club's victories. As an expression of the brawling, relatively unrepressed, more sensually demanding side of artisan culture, such spectators—and players —played an important part in the spread of baseball's popularity in the 1860s. Their frank and vocal partisanship cemented ties between clubs and neighborhoods or towns and contributed to the excitement of close-fought, high-level competition. That partisanship, and not a higher feeling for the "best interests of the game," drew people into enclosed grounds and subsidized the grounds entrepreneurs in the early 1860s and the professional clubs later in the decade.

To the chagrin of baseball's promoters and moral guardians, those partisans, the "rough element," the unsavory fans who enjoyed large quantities of alcohol, noise, general commotion, and unregulated emotion, have never been banished from the ballpark. Too much of baseball's appeal was (and still is) to feelings repressed only with much difficulty. The game could even engage different parts of the same person as well as distinct segments of a large population. Well-known and highly regarded veterans occasionally departed from the standards of respectable behavior. The lure of letting go was too strong always to be resisted. But the game's diverse attractions were (and continue to be) discussed and debated as though they appealed to disparate audiences. The potential for disorder and violence was said to attract "roughs," while the promise of manly displays of nerve and skill spoke to the "respectable" patrons. This analysis was correct but it was incomplete. These differential appeals also spoke to conflicting tendencies within every member of the baseball fraternity, no matter how "respectable," no matter how "low."

The continuing role of alcohol is instructive. Throughout this period the saloon remained a common and generally unremarkable part of baseball's fraternal life. The Mutuals, for example, held their regular meetings in The Study, a Hudson Street saloon that also served as headquarters for the Active Club. Postgame dinners were frequently held in saloons, and the press showed little unease with the subject of social drinking. The club that outlawed alcohol was rare, and entertainment free of "spirituous liquors" seldom attracted press attention. In fact, the Olympic Club of Philadelphia expelled one of its members who argued too strenuously in favor of a ban on alcohol at club functions. As long as drinking was a part of other social activities, enclosed or controlled by recognized social forms, it called forth no denunciations. Reporters could even suggest that participants in a "muffin match," where beer seems to have been de rigueur, had overimbibed, and do so in a thoroughly good-natured manner. Once drinkers moved outside that kind of collective supervision, however, the same reporters saw the matter in a completely different light.[21]

Interpretations of a disturbance during a match between the Mutual and Irvington clubs in 1867 focused on drink and the lower classes:

> Just about this time the storm which had been brewing among the brutal elements of the assemblage, and which had previously manifested itself in sundry knock-downs and rows among the short-haired bruisers present, culminated in a regular battle, in which a party of Newark "roughs" and a delegation of their brethren from the Sixth Ward of New York, were the conspicuous actors, numerous draughts of "Jersey lightning," held for sale in booths on the ground, having had its due effect in arousing the predominant passions of the aforesaid "roughs" to the boiling point.

According to *Wilkes' Spirit of the Times*, "the disturbance was caused by four Newark rowdies who had imbibed from the liquor stands on the grounds. . . . For a time the scene was worthy of an Irish fight at a fair, about a dozen fellows being engaged in it, nearly all being of the bull-necked, low-browed, crop-haired brutes who degrade humanity so much in our cities." Order was restored through the efforts of the Mutuals and Irvingtons, who took up "clubs" (baseball bats?) and forced back the "rioters." Both papers argued that the way to prevent such disturbances was to hold all championship matches on enclosed grounds, where the police could bring *their* clubs to bear on the "roughs."[22]

The metaphor as well as the proposal of enclosure is noteworthy here. When drinking was enclosed (embedded) in social and class conventions, as in postgame entertainments and club meetings, the fraternity did not think twice about it. When it was not so enclosed, when it was public, open to all (but especially to lower and immigrant) classes, then it had "disorderly" potential. Similarly, when the game itself was so enclosed, the forces of order could be brought to bear on the aroused passions of those who refused to abide by the rules of the game. Enclosures, of course, could also exclude—and a common argument used in favor of fenced-in grounds was that admission fees could then be manipulated to screen out "undesirable" (that is to say, poorer) spectators.[23]

Ballplayers were participating in a culture that distinguished itself as much as possible—and sometimes by the wielding of clubs —from the "roughs," the poor and unskilled and "unrespectable." When Chadwick and other reporters used the language of youth to describe adults of the lower classes, when they used such charged language to characterize anyone outside the proper behavioral boundaries, they may have found their most receptive audience in these men. Even so, the game never lost its association with that center of working-class culture, the saloon, although those who kept up the association made up only a part of the baseball world, wheras they had once been the overwhelming majority. Increasingly, baseball "management" battled against player ("employee") drinking, while that drinking remained stubbornly and defensively central to the culture of professional baseball players and their fans. Baseball's relation to drinking furnishes an excellent example of a pattern that characterized many aspects of the game's history in the late nineteenth century, perhaps especially between the late 1850s and the early 1870s.[24]

This pattern may best be described as a series of divisions or unfoldings: divisions of complex roles and ideas into component parts;

unfoldings of tightly packed, dense tangles of relationships into more spread-out, scattered configurations. All of the possibilities of the future, in other words, were contained in the "original" manifestations of the game. At the beginning of this period men played baseball not as professionals or amateurs, but as both. These and other conflicting ideals—skillful play to win and play for fun, manly restraint and boyish excitement, partisanship and impartiality—could not be resolved by the people who represented them. They were experienced as inescapable tensions within the lives of players, of clubs, and even of the National Association, which was founded upon and caught between the twin desires to "improve, foster and perpetuate" the game and "the cultivation of kindly feelings among the different members of Base Ball Clubs."

The problem is that almost as soon as we identify these tensions, they threaten to fly apart. As they could not be resolved, each side moved to separate itself from the other in the hope, if not of eliminating the other, then at least of being able to ignore it. That is what was happening in the early 1860s, as clubs divided themselves (and were sorted by the press) into contenders for the championship and clubs that played for the fun of the thing. In a parallel manner, one means of resolving the conflict between men and boys was to separate organizations into senior and junior clubs. But as the history of the game makes quite clear, separation was an answer only to the most obvious expressions of the problem. Fourteen-year-olds and thirty-year-olds could each have their own clubs. That said and done, however, there remained the intense debate and, we must conclude, continuing anxiety within the senior fraternity over manly and boyish behavior, expressed in the conflict over the fly rule, the highly charged language of age and class, and the frequent divisions of senior clubs into veterans and juveniles. Similarly, even in highly competitive clubs some players took their play more seriously than others, some were more manly than others, some more professional and others more amateur.

All of these strains led to divisions in the game, many of which took place in the 1860s. But the process continued; the same tensions led to many subsequent divisions in baseball history. "Unfolding," then, may be the better word. The tendency for the game's unresolvable tensions to find expression through separation and further division, and at every level to reproduce themselves and divide again, has been the motive force of baseball history.

As baseball clubs sprang up everywhere and the center of the game migrated to what had been its periphery, baseball's older core was also changing. Activities and attitudes that had been contained within a single city, a club, or even a single ballplayer were finding expression in a multiplicity of cities, clubs, and ballplayers. Parts of the game that had been held together by the force of club fraternalism were now being represented increasingly by various "classes" of clubs and players. No longer, Chadwick feared, would ballplayers combine qualities of manliness, honor, skill, and self-control. In the future players would be either professionals or amateurs, and try as he might to think otherwise, Chadwick had to recognize that amateurs were not going to be as skillful as professionals, and that the new players were never again going to "play with the same kinds of feelings or for the same objects as they used to."

5

"Revolving" and Professionalism

The Decline of the National Association

As we observe the consequences of baseball's expansion, we must be wary of taking any one consciousness, such as Henry Chadwick's, as an exclusive guide to baseball's emotional or material world during these years. While Chadwick saw numerous forms of control over and within the game slipping (if not speeding) away, others saw these same changes as opportunities. Where Chadwick feared ruin, the most skillful players—the early professionals—were experiencing boom times.

By 1866 and 1867 it was well known that important clubs often paid some, if not all, of their first-nine players either salaries or shares of gate receipts. In order to put a winning team on the field, clubs were more than willing to break the National Association rule against compensating players. The press commonly referred to "professional clubs" in 1867, even though there were not supposed to be any in the National Association.

Clubs could pay salaries because admission to the most popular enclosed grounds in the New York area (the Union and Capitoline grounds) had risen from 10 to 25 cents. In addition, several clubs were charging admission to their own games, while many other clubs simply participated in what became known as the "gate-money system."

Most vividly representative of the changes affecting the game in the late 1860s were the "revolvers," players who moved from club to club with varying rates of frequency, in search of better positions, better salaries, or changes of scenery. Revolving did not appear abruptly as a full-fledged phenomenon in 1867; players had been leaving one club for another since the late fifties and early sixties. Money is known to have been involved in some of these movements, as in the cases of Al Reach and James Creighton. It is probably safe to assume that, although some clubs undoubtedly offered special inducements to attract certain players, other factors were usually at work. But as early as 1860 and 1861, player movements were a staple of baseball news.[1]

Clubs sought players primarily to strengthen their first nines. That is the way the press reported and analyzed club "acquisitions," as they were called long before contracts were involved. Since players almost never moved from strong clubs to weak ones, we can conclude that those who were willing to change did so to play on better teams. That desire clearly motivated Fred Waterman, Nat Jewett, and Alphonse C. (Phonny) Martin, who changed clubs twice as a group, first leaving the junior Irving Club of New York and joining the Empires in 1865, and then signing on with the Mutuals a year later.[2]

Although these movements were followed by the press, they drew very little criticism even when they must have raised some eyebrows, as when three top players on the Excelsiors joined the rival Atlantics late in the 1862 season, or when a player jumped from the Eckfords to the Atlantics and back, all within the space of six months. The explosive increase in such movements and the beginnings of substantial criticism of them came in 1866, the same year that the number of National Association clubs shot up from ninety-one to more than two hundred. Suddenly New York players were in demand all over the Northeast and Midwest. Within the baseball capital, too, as they lost players to Chicago, Washington, D.C., Baltimore, and Cincinnati, clubs competed for top players and nines altered rapidly. This state of affairs, as I have already suggested, both encouraged and distressed baseball commentators, especially those based in the New York area. On the one hand, "their" game was sweeping across the country, and "their" players dominated first-class play. On the other, the relative stability of local club nines had ended, New York and Brooklyn players had abandoned their ties to club and city, and New York–area nines could no longer count on ruling the baseball roost.[3]

The actions of the NABBP, as it tried to deal with the problems posed by the unprecedented expansion and commercialization of the game, both measured and contributed to the confusion over the best way to deal with these developments. None of the issues arising from these changes which came before the association in the late 1860s was resolved to the satisfaction of the association's membership or its larger constituency. As the centers of power in the game shifted, many of the "modernizers" of the early part of the decade became the "traditionalists" of the latter half, thus inaugurating a process of extremely rapid generational turnover destined to be repeated hundreds of times in baseball history.[4]

First, and apparently the most innocuous of these issues, was the question of club representation in the association. More than two hundred delegates attended the 1866 convention, most of them representing individual clubs, the others state associations. Over three hours were needed to call the roll, collect dues, and "decide upon the admissibility of delegates." In one room, then, the association faced the problem of the game's having become "truly national" (as its propagandists put it proudly and tirelessly). All of the Rules Committee's recommended amendments to the constitution had to do with admission of state associations, and a hybrid body emerged from the 1866 convention, made up of individual clubs and state associations. Individual clubs could choose to represent themselves or delegate that privilege to their state association, and the voting power of those bodies was directly proportional to the number of their member clubs. The following year, therefore, the convention was an odd mix of delegates representing state associations from the East and Midwest, and club delegates, nearly all from East Coast clubs. Such "mixed representation," Chadwick observed in the *Chronicle* a week later, was a "farce."[5]

This characterization rested not on some abstract notion of how the "true interests of the game" ought to have been served but on the fact that eleven delegates representing eight associations wielded more than two-thirds of the almost 700 votes in the convention, while the remaining votes were cast by more than 150 delegates. Nearly 300 votes were controlled by just four western associations—those of Illinois (110), Indiana (42), Ohio (88), and Wisconsin (52). The eastern delegates, particularly those who had been attending conventions for years, must have found it disconcerting to see so many clubs represented and votes cast by so few men, whom they could have known but briefly. On the other hand, when Dr. Jones, the Rules Committee chairman and longtime Excelsior delegate, proposed that the mixed representation system be continued, the majority of delegates objected, calling instead for a plan based on state representation only, and prompting Jones to resign his position. Chadwick then wrote the report on which the new plan was based. He claimed later that he had been "the originator of the plan of State Association representation." Why had he wanted to originate it? For one thing, he wanted the association to be national in scope, and feared that a system of individual club representation alone

> would have driven the four sections of the country into four distinct Associations, viz., Eastern, Western, Southern, and Northern, instead of a code of playing rules governing every reputable club throughout the land, we should have had four or five distinct styles of playing base ball, and the term "National Game" would have become a misnomer. Instead of this, however, we have . . . insured the establishment of one code of playing rules applicable to every club in the country, and a National Association that, in fact, as well as in name, is a national institution.[6]

The system of state representation, then, helped the association address the problem of geographic fragmentation and assert national control over the game, keeping it from lapsing into a variety of regional games, the very circumstances out of which organized baseball had emerged twenty years earlier. Since then, regional versions of the game—most notably the Massachusetts game in New England and town ball in Philadelphia—had been battled and defeated. Twenty years of "progress" were at stake.

There were hints, too, of other benefits to the new system. Mixed representation had made the convention "a discordant assemblage." Such language was usually used to describe unruly spectators at a match. Now there would be many fewer delegates. Had the system been in force in 1867, for example, only twenty-eight delegates could have attended. Such a small gathering was less likely to be carried away by "excitement," "passion," or confusion, and would be sufficient protection against democratic upsurges. No one addressed the possibility that a small convention could be much more easily dominated by a few delegates than a large one.

The only place in which such democratic excesses might have existed was the Nominating Committee, which waived all irregularities in club applications. Acknowledging that it had not been able to "ascertain the condition, character, and standing of all the clubs," the committee could "only assume" that the applications were "based on good faith." It nonetheless sought to reassure the convention on one important matter: "It is not presumed by your committee that any club who have applied are composed of persons of color, or any portion of them; and the recommendations of your committee in this report are based upon this view, and they unanimously report against the admission of any club which may be composed of one or more colored persons." The convention accepted the report, the object of which, according to Chadwick, was "to keep out of the Convention the discussion of any subject having a political bearing, as this undoubtedly had." Another account lamely agreed, claiming that the report was proposed "in the belief that if colored clubs were admitted, there would be in all probability, some division of feeling, whereas, by excluding them no injury could result to anybody, and the possibility of any rupture being created on political grounds would be avoided."[7]

There was in actuality "division of feeling" at this convention, even without the "political" question of race. It is interesting that, even in so politically insignificant a gathering as a convention of baseball players—fully ten years before the larger national spectacle of "reunion and reaction"—one presumed price of "national" (or organizational) unity was the exclusion of black people from membership. The gesture seems above all empty. It provoked no discussion in the convention (although the *New York Tribune* correspondent ridiculed it as "cowardly"), and there was no indication at the time than any black or interracial club had ever applied for membership.[8]

The principle of eligibility was not always employed so pointlessly. The National Association could not outlaw the playing of baseball for money, but it did bar professional players from participating in match games, and, in a stronger version added in 1866, threatened expulsion of any club that paid any of its players, as well as of any club that played against such a club. Even in the association, where sentiment appeared overwhelmingly opposed to professionalism, the rule lasted only two more years. According to M. J. Kelly of the *New York Herald*, "the leading clubs of the country violate it in the most bare-faced manner, and . . . [it] is a dead letter to a very great extent." By 1868, opinion had shifted substantially among both convention delegates and association officers. Presenting the re-

port of the Rules Committee, Chadwick acknowledged, first, the ob-
solescence of the statutory prohibition on professionalism ("merely a
dead letter"); second, the impossibility of framing a law that could
not be "evaded"; and third, "the lack of power to enforce it even if
such a law could be framed." In view of these no doubt depressing
facts, "the Committee had deemed it expedient to divide the fraternity
into two classes": professionals—"all players who play base ball for
money, or who shall at any time receive compensation for their services as players"—and amateurs—"all other players."[9]

But the most important part of the committee's report was the admission that the association lacked the power to do anything else.
The National Association, in other words, had lost the power to
shape the development of the game, and had been reduced to following it, with more or less reluctance from year to year, while trying to
preserve a semblance of control over a game that had acquired its
own momentum.

Nowhere was this momentum more obvious than in the increasing
amount of movement among players as they "revolved" from club to
club, a practice the association had tried to inhibit. The basic rule
against revolving required players to "have been regular members of
the club which they represent, and of no other club," for a specific
period of time before a match. Until 1868 that "probationary" period
continued to be thirty days, although the rule was made more restric-
tive in other ways. The first attempt to reduce player mobility was a
Rules Committee proposal in 1866 that the probationary period be
lengthened to sixty days; it was the only amendment to fail that year.
The difference of opinion within the association clearly indicated that
some clubs and players were benefiting from the shorter period. Players, after all, would hardly have revolved if there had been no place
to go.[10]

Complaints about revolving and eligibility were dealt with by the
Judiciary Committee, whose cases in 1866 and 1867 were another ba-
rometer of the tensions besetting the growing fraternity. In 1866, for
example, two clubs claimed that expelled players had been used ille-
gally, and a member of the Philadelphia Athletics charged that his
club was paying three players $20 a week for their baseball services.
Evidently loath to take action, the committee relied on technicalities
to dismiss or effectively ignore all three cases. The following year ten
of the dozen complaints before the committee charged clubs with

fielding nines containing ineligible players. In a complete turnaround, the committee held extensive hearings and made firm decisions in most cases, annulling games and censuring clubs and players for irregularities.[11]

The biggest case, however, stirred up such controversy that it had to be reargued before the entire 1867 convention. In organized baseball's first betting scandal, Thomas Devyr, William Wansley, and Edward Duffy, all of the New York Mutuals, had confessed to "selling" a game against the Eckfords in 1865. A little more than a year after Devyr was expelled from the Mutuals for his part in the fix, the club, evidently in need of a good shortstop, restored him to his position in the club's first nine. Two protests were lodged against the Mutuals for playing Devyr during the 1867 season. The first was dismissed for want of evidence other than "newspaper reports" and "mere idle rumors," but the second was sustained; the committee held that the Mutuals had violated the association's constitution in playing an expelled player, and declared the game in question null and void. This decision was very likely influenced by another complaint on the docket at the same meeting of the committee: a Fulton Club member's protest against his own club's admission of William Wansley, the ringleader in the 1865 fix. Devyr had more sympathy among the fraternity, but the committee could not easily have distinguished the two cases; it held that both former Mutuals should remain barred from baseball. The Mutuals, planning to appeal the decision to the entire convention, continued to play Devyr.

There was an anticipatory air as the National Association convened in Philadelphia on December 11. The Mutuals had done their homework. They circulated a printed explanation of their position, along with a long plea from Devyr that his case be looked on favorably. That evening the case was argued, as a debate, between the "plaintiff," a member of the Union Club, and the "counsel" for the Mutuals. Doubtless influenced by the Mutuals' circular, the convention voted overwhelmingly, 451 to 143, to reverse the Judiciary Committee's decision and allow Devyr's reinstatement. No serious effort was made to overturn the decision on Wansley. Devyr's skill and popularity may have played some part in the deliberations, but the key distinction was that between the Mutuals, the most influential club in the association in the late 1860s (and one of the strongest professional clubs in the country), and the relatively powerless Fulton Club.[12]

The ballplaying fraternity probably felt that Devyr had paid enough for his error. He had been, as he pointed out in his letter to the convention, only eighteen years old in 1865, "in very needy circumstances," and "not really . . . conscious of the enormity of the crime." Even Chadwick confessed himself to be "in favor of leniency in this case, in view of the lapse of time since commission of the offence, and the fact that the parties have been already severely punished by being so long debarred from play and social recognition among the reputable members of the community."[13] But many delegates also understood the Mutual Club's desire to field the strongest nine it could, and Devyr was known as a fine shortstop. Many clubs had become less concerned about the character of their players, and did not always want to be reminded of a player's past faults or less than spotless reputation.

Baseball history seems to have gotten very dense in 1867 and 1868, as conflicting ideals and organizational forms of the game became increasingly tangled, on the field, in clubrooms, in the pages of newspapers, and in the gatherings of players and club members in conventions. The game had reached the limits of its structure. It needed to expand, to divide and multiply, and the National Association of Base Ball Players was no longer an adequate framework. By the last years of the decade, it was satisfying no one, and interest in it declined precipitously.

Size alone would have been a serious problem. Ballplayers associated with one another first in clubs, then in an association of clubs. They thought of their organizations as fraternal, and put a high premium on sociability. By the late 1860s, however, club membership itself had become problematic; adversarial proceedings before the Judiciary Committee were needed to decide who belonged to which club when. The conflicts between clubs which the fraternity had hoped to keep on the field had entered what were supposed to be the more fraternal proceedings of the ballplaying community. Conventions, then, had become very different kinds of gatherings, at once larger, more anonymous, and more marked by conflict. Participants' concern that members of their fraternity all be of gentlemanly character was more difficult to satisfy in a large organization, especially one based on state representation. Reputations had come to depend almost entirely on newspapers and gradually were reduced to their most easily quantifiable element—the record of wins and losses.

Second, the association's image was not helped by its reinstatement not only of Thomas Devyr but of Edward Duffy—on the motion of a New York delegate in 1869—and, finally, of William Wansley, the original member of the 1865 conspiracy—on motion of John Wildey, president of the Mutuals, in 1870. Chadwick vented his disgust at the results of these two conventions in scathing remarks about the "unscrupulous clique" of professionals who had "captured" the association. Along the same lines, the 1869 convention eliminated the distinction between amateurs and professionals. "By this [change]," Chadwick argued, "not only are all clubs placed on the same level as regards playing strength, but, all that has been previously done to place professional ball-playing upon a reputable footing has been nullified." By acting as though professional ballplaying did not need even the justification implied by distinguishing it from amateur ball, the professionals had turned the tables on the amateurs (although, to be fair, they did not try to exclude amateur ballplaying).[14]

Third, as soon became obvious, when the game's center moved to Ohio and state representation was instituted, what resulted was not a reconstitution but a real fragmentation of the game—not in terms of rules (as Chadwick had feared) but in other ways, having to do with the relationships of professional and amateur play, of clubs and players, and between clubs. In the face of this fragmentation, what kind of "national unity" was being maintained, even formally, in the association? For size produced paradoxical problems. None of the conventions between 1868 and 1870 had more than thirty delegates. Even though they represented about two hundred clubs, the size of the gatherings must have recalled the meager war years of 1862 and 1863, the last conventions that so few had attended. And no convention after 1867 came close to representing the more than three hundred clubs of that year's convention.

Of what purpose, then, was a convention made up of a very small number of delegates representing hundreds, even thousands of clubs? The oddity of such a scheme was that the National Association actually did very little other than make rules. Even the Judiciary Committee was losing its importance as state committees took over the duties of deciding who was eligible to play with whom and when. So the association could have become simply a body of rulemakers (which might have satisfied Chadwick), but most participants in the conventions were at least as interested in the sociable aspects of the organization as in "perfecting" the rules. They also enjoyed personally arguing and voting on their clubs' positions on such matters as the fly rule and the issue of professional ball. When it was simply a matter of instructing a distant delegate how to count one club among the forty or fifty in a state association, baseball politics lost much of its appeal. And finally, in the last few years of the decade, the New York clubs, under the leadership—if not outright control—of the Mutuals, reasserted their former dominance of the association.[15]

Lacking a moral or cultural core, this collection of opposing ideals, desires, and forms could no longer be held together. Repressed conflicts broke through the restraints of "the best interests of the game." The fourteenth and final convention of the NABBP in 1870 was full of ironies. Confusion reigned all through the country over "revolvers," amateurs, and professionals, yet the Judiciary Committee had "nothing to report, as no dispute of any kind had been brought before their notice during the past year." John Wildey of the Mutuals, appropriately enough, was elected president of the association, which promptly and unanimously resolved "that no rules and regulations be recognized as authority in matters pertaining to base-ball other than those published in pamphlet form under the direction of the present session of the National Association." It could hardly have been lost on the delegates that the need (or desire) to make such a statement was itself the clearest evidence of the association's irrelevance. Never before—even in the early days of the organization, when its authority was in the process of being established—had the NABBP made such an impotent claim.

The same meeting that presided over the reinstatement of Wansley also witnessed the final attempt by traditionalists to halt the embrace of professionalism. One of the New York delegates (interestingly, this disagreement was played out among the nine members of the New York delegation) moved that "this Association regard the custom of publicly hiring men to play the game of base-ball as reprehensible and injurious to the best interests of the game." At the end of a long debate, the result of which was never in doubt, the motion lost, 17 to 9. True to form, *Wilkes' Spirit of the Times* blandly observed that "the resolutions and amendments passed by the above Convention will subserve in a high degree the best interests of our national game and from the interest taken in the meeting and its proceedings, there is every prospect that the next annual meeting will be even more numerously attended." The reporter was simply whistling in the wind. Much more accurately, Chadwick predicted that no amateur club would be represented at the next meeting, and that even the professionals would stay away in droves. The following year saw separate conventions, as amateurs and professionals formed separate associations.[16]

Baseball Capital and Baseball Labor

Another division in the fraternity ran at least as deep as that between professionals and amateurs and had fully as many consequences for the history of the game: that between clubs and their players. It had seemed only practical at first to sort members by skill into first, second, third, and "muffin" nines, but by the late 1860s the distinction between the first nine and the rest of the club had grown sharper and stronger. Even clubs that did not pay their players engaged in practices that accelerated the spin of the revolving door, thus helping to create a class of nomadic professional ballplayers.

One of these practices was exempting top players from payment of club dues and other fees. A form of payment (if very small), this exemption, which was used by amateur as well as professional clubs, loosened the ties between player and club, and made it easier both to join up and to move on. The following excerpt from the Judiciary Committee hearings on a dispute between the Union and Atlantic clubs over the status of one Shelley affords a revealing glimpse into the practices of clubs and the assumptions of the ballplaying fraternity. The "Witness" was Tull V. Sterry, secretary of the Union Club; Page was "counsel" for the Atlantics, Gifford for the Unions:

MR. PAGE (to the witness)—What do I understand you to mean by an exempt member?

WITNESS—We have three classes of members, honorary, active, and exempt.

MR. PAGE—I know all that; you have just explained that point. What I wish to know is what the duties or privileges of an exempt member are?

MR. GIFFORD—If the Committee please, I should like to know what the counsel are endeavoring to get at by this irrelevant questioning? I object to queries not bearing directly on this case; not that I fear any ventilation of the method our club has of doing business, but that time is wasted by entering upon these outside matters.

MR. PAGE—I would state to the Committee that in view of the fact that Mr. Shelley was elected an "exempt" member of the Union Club, and as I am not exactly posted as to the status of such a position in a club, I desire to be informed on the subject, and I claim that I have a right to question the witness on this subject.

CHAIRMAN (after some discussion)—Go on with your examination, Mr. Page.

MR. PAGE—Mr. Sterry, will you tell me where in the difference exists between an exempt member of your club and an active member?

WITNESS—Certainly, sir. An exempt member has no vote in the club, and no power to hold office. An active member does both, and pays dues.

MR. PAGE—Then exempt members do not pay dues. Is that it?

MR. GIFFORD—If the gentleman will allow me the remark, he must be aware that there are a class of members in every club who do the paying part of the business, and but little else, and—

MR. PAGE—The counsel on the other side will excuse me if I object to any interference with my cross-examination.

.   .   .

MR. PAGE— . . . Mr. Sterry, how many exempt members have you in your club?

WITNESS—About nine or ten. (Another general smile.)

MR. PAGE—About nine, you say. Can you name them?

WITNESS—Their names are on the books.

MR. PAGE—I presume so; but can you name them? Tell me one.

WITNESS—Mr. Balcom.

MR. PAGE—Who else?

WITNESS—Mr. Walker.

MR. PAGE—Is Mr. Birdsall an exempt member?

WITNESS—He is.

MR. PAGE—Is Mr. Pabor?

WITNESS—No, sir.

MR. PAGE—Is Mr. Martin?

WITNESS—No, sir.

CHAIRMAN—I would state, in regard to Mr. Birdsall, that he is an active member of the club, I myself being cognizant of the fact of his dues as such having been paid.

MR. PAGE—Then exempt members are those who, though they play in matches, do not pay dues, and are not entitled to vote or to hold office. Do I understand you rightly, Mr. Sterry?

WITNESS—Yes, sir.[17]

Both Gifford and Page were being at best disingenuous in the former's objection to "irrelevant questioning" and the latter's "desire to be informed" on the subject of exempt members. Gifford plainly wanted to avoid a "ventilation" of his club's "business" methods, and Page was well "posted" on what he was trying to establish. So, incidentally, was everyone else present, as the "general smile" indicated. "About nine or ten" clearly meant "the first nine" to those in attendance, although it turned out that Page was unable to show that the entire first nine consisted of exempt members.

Although revolving was usually discussed as if it were simply a phenomenon affecting players—the term, after all, refers to players' movements—clearly clubs were providing much of the incentive for ballplayers to revolve and forsake their current club loyalties. When Shelley took the stand at this hearing a few minutes later, he told of being approached by Dr. Bell of yet another club (the Eclectics), who urged him to play in one of its matches: "He said he didn't think he could," the *Chronicle* reported, "as he was a member of the Union Club. Dr. Bell then replied 'Nobody up here [in Hoboken] knows you, and that won't make any difference. The club we are to play with is pretty strong, and we want to win the game if we can.'" Bell was no newcomer to the fraternity. A relatively prominent member of New York baseball circles since the early 1860s, he was hardly unfamiliar with the customs of baseball clubs. And yet, in direct contravention of the letter and spirit of his club's and the association's rules, he solicited a member of another club (whom he knew only as a skilled player) to "join" his club for a match, and counted on the unlikelihood that he would be recognized. Previously, familiarity with one's fellow players had been felt to be one of the mainstays of this fraternal, club-based sport. If we look carefully here, we can see the beginning of the transformation of baseball club players into baseball workers; the creation, in effect, of a mobile labor force of skilled player-workers. Although revolving set club against club, its deeper impact was on the relationships between clubs and players.[18]

Before we proceed, one further point needs to be made about revolving. Everyone in the baseball fraternity thought that, as a matter of justice, every player (or member) ought to be able to change clubs if he wished. Even as he castigated "this 'revolving' business," Old Peto Brine maintained that "if a man don't get treated well after doing good service, and leaves his club for one where he can find pleasanter companions and better treatment, it is excusable." And as we have seen, player movements in the early 1860s were not treated by the press or the association as abuses of baseball ethics or as contrary to the best interests of the game. The problem with this justification for changing clubs was that it was thoroughly undermined by the practice of considering players as "special" or "exempt" members, in effect temporary, nonvoting "representatives" of the club— hardly the central participants in club life they had been five and ten years earlier.[19]

Revolving, then, was one of the key developments that made possible the full professionalization of the game. The necessary social and cultural foundations were all in place by the advent of the Cincinnati Red Stockings in 1869 and the National Association of Professional Base Ball Players in 1871. The separation of club and player took place eight to ten years before the National League of Professional Base Ball *Clubs* formalized the divide by explicitly constituting itself as an organization of clubs rather than players. Let us look at some of the implications of this division.

The nature of the business relationship between a player and his club was such that once begun, it was nearly impossible to limit. That relationship existed between the player and the club directors, while the rest of the club became spectators. In time, the club members merged with the rest of the game's fans, spectators both of the competition on the field and of the struggles between players and club directors over the gains of the rapidly growing baseball business. Imbalances between clubs and players gave this new business some of its most peculiar characteristics.

Baseball capital and baseball labor had different needs. For one thing, the capital was not nearly as mobile as its labor force. Clubs' often substantial investments in grounds and a clubhouse, as well as their growing involvement in local civic boosterism and urban rivalries and their profitable connections with local railroads and other transportation companies, worked to bind clubs to local settings. They could go on tours, as professional and amateur clubs did more and more often in the late 1860s, but it was understood that they represented their hometown. As the baseball world became national (or at least genuinely regional, covering the Northeast and Midwest), there were far more clubs than there were first-class players to fill their nines. Consequently, the scores in this period included some of the most lopsided in the history of the game. What else could be expected when a professional metropolitan nine met the pride and joy of a small town, or even a large city's frequently amateurish and recently organized ball club?[20]

The number of clubs and the intensity of urban boosterism gave a strong push to professional baseball. Players were in demand, and they became quite mobile. The irony was that boosters who sought prestige by fielding a strong "local" nine made lucrative offers to distant players, urging them to break any local ties they may have had, come to their city, and play for a new set of "loyalties." So an important, perhaps even necessary element of hypocrisy was injected into the game in the form of "club loyalty": the demands of the "home team" were used both to justify "importing" and paying players and to disguise these very financial relationships. If "hypocrisy" and "disguise" are too strong for this era, later in the nineteenth century and all through the twentieth, clubs and their press allies consciously and cynically manipulated "home team" images and feelings. Many club directors, other club members, even some players wanted to believe in these notions, so the disparity may be better understood as sincere wishful thinking, a mixing, as it were, of memory and desire.[21]

In making ballplaying into a form of paid and mobile labor, clubs opened up some extremely recalcitrant problems. On the one hand, as relatively immobile sources of capital, clubs wanted players to be free to move to them. On the other hand, these same clubs wanted to have some way of keeping players from revolving away from them as easily as they had come. Clubs also disagreed among themselves over the kinds of restraints they wanted, and the disparity in their approaches accounts for the contradictory pattern of the restrictions passed by the National Association in its last years. The same convention that recognized professionals in 1868 also acted to inhibit revolvers by doubling the probationary period to sixty days. John Wildey of the Mutuals, confident that his prosperous club could offer sufficient inducement to attract and hold any player it wanted, had proposed that it be reduced to ten days, a period that would have effectively eliminated all restraints on revolving. Poorer and nonprofessional amateur clubs naturally supported longer probationary periods—one delegate proposed ninety days—as a way of holding on to players increasingly likely to be tempted by attractive offers elsewhere.[22]

Rarely acknowledged in the midst of the intense emotion and equally intense practical scheming of these years was the fact that the players, as the sole possessors of skills very much in demand, held the balance of power in the baseball world. They, understandably, wanted no restrictions at all on their mobility, and ignored the sixty-day rule when they wished. Whether a club's match was eventually nullified by a judiciary committee, after all, bore very little on the arrangement between a player and "his" club. While clubs battled among themselves over the legality and legitimacy of their actions, players continued to play, be paid, and move on.

Over a period of ten to fifteen years, then, "first-class" competitive baseball was transformed from an avocation primarily of clerks and skilled craftsmen into a form of skilled work in its own right. The relative scarcity of baseball craftsmen earned them high wages and substantial freedom of movement. Their employers, as a matter of course, sought whenever possible to reduce the power of their employees. They began signing players to contracts more favorable to the club, usually for whole, but single, seasons. They also began to formulate and enforce rules to govern players' conduct off the field as well as on it. And in an abrupt and far-reaching innovation, clubs and the press began talking about baseball—clubs, players, and playing itself—in the language of management.

The vocabulary of management entered the baseball world suddenly, almost without warning, in 1867. If a reporter wanted to praise or criticize what previously would have been called the "direction" of a nine, he now talked about the "management" of a nine. Baseball reference books started running sections headed "How to Manage a Nine," and the harmony formerly attributed to players' familiarity with each other and many hours of practice began to be ascribed instead to the "management" of the captain. Similarly, club activities—administrative, financial, even social—received approval or censure on the basis of the skill with which they were "managed."[23]

This language, and the ideology it invoked, appeared in baseball at precisely the moment when many clubs were becoming small and medium-sized businesses, businesses whose employees were commanding relatively high salaries. Its effects were not only linguistic. Previously, most clubs had had officers known as directors. Now new boards of directors hired the players and employed team captains to manage them. From instruments of collective, fraternal, clubwide self-discipline, club rules became regulations for the players to follow and for the captains—backed up by the club—to enforce. So the ideology and practice of management became an important part of clubs' efforts to gain more control over their players.[24]

In the late 1860s baseball was separating into classes: directors (soon to be owners), managers (drawn from among the players, hired by the owners), and player-workers—a division that has persisted to the present day. These new classes, the products of the professionalization and fragmentation of the game during these years, battled for control of the baseball world throughout the latter nineteenth century. Profoundly distressed by these divisions and conflicts, baseball fans of the late 1860s were already taking refuge in the "good old days" of 1860, conveniently forgetting much of that tumultuous season and repressing the years in between. From these years on, baseball reminiscence takes on an aura of unreality, repeating the same denunciations of the present, displaying the same reverence for a past when things were different and better. The two histories of baseball—the emotional, generational, cyclical history and the organizational, chronological, linear history—split apart in the late 1860s, and the disappointed fan of that era is immediately recognizable as the modern fan lamenting the loss of his "good old days."

6

The National Game

Home and Away

The 1860s proved to be a momentous decade in the history of baseball. At the beginning of this short period the game was centered in the New York metropolitan area and embedded in the rich social life of fraternal clubs. Ten years later the game had escaped the confines of both New York and club fraternalism. Baseball's transformation from a local club sport into an association of "clubs" scattered over the Northeast and Midwest was encouraged by the very structure of the game's play and organization. More than any other American game, baseball was built on a geographical and psychological sense of localism—if we take localism to be simultaneously an attachment to one place and fear, antipathy, or competitiveness toward other places. There had always been a "home" club or nine and a "visiting" club or nine in baseball, and the action of the game alternated between the home and visiting sides. From the earliest days of the organized game, nearly every club had its own, home ground.[1]

Challengers were visitors from another neighborhood or town, strangers sometimes literally as well as figuratively. They were also frequently identified by the locales of their clubs. The Brooklyn Atlantics, for example, were named for Atlantic Avenue—one of the major thoroughfares of the city—and were known familiarly as the "Bedford boys," for the section of Brooklyn in which they played. Other Brooklyn clubs also bore the names of streets (Putnams, Clintons) or neighborhoods (Williamsburgh, Green Point). Far more than among New York–area cricket clubs, rivalry in baseball quickly assumed a territorial form and language. For a full decade after the

Fashion Course all-star matches in 1858 (and in the minds of some fans, for most of the following century), baseball's strongest rivalry remained that between New York and Brooklyn clubs.[2]

The game itself internalized the play of locale and loyalty. Many contemporary commentators, remarking on the differences between baseball and cricket, argued that baseball was a much faster game than its English counterpart—not only because it took a few hours instead of an entire day or two days to play one match, but because the game itself was livelier. Melvin Adelman has pointed to baseball's more rapid alternation of offense and defense as the key to this perception. But in a baseball game, offense and defense were not abstractions: they were the home club and the visitors, or our boys and the out-of-towners, or us and them. In each inning sides alternated in possession of territory (although territory itself was not the object of the struggle). The actual competition was over one side's passage through a field patrolled by the opposition. Players at bat began their would-be circuit in the safety of "home base" and ventured (if they were successful) out to the three points of "safety" in the entire field —the three bases—in the hope of completing the circuit and coming back "home" to score in safety.[3]

The game was a constant play of safety and danger, intensified by the need to get "home" both in order to be "safe" and in order to win. Such safety and danger depended on an imaginative rendering of the field which took "home" at least as seriously as the "real" club took its geographical home. The travel of the visitors was analogized into the necessary travel of all players through the territory of their adversaries, while the proud possession of the home club—their "ground"—was by turns not theirs at all, a region where they could be put "out" for the slightest error of skill or judgment. What local rivalry existed between neighborhoods, towns, or cities, then, received particular intensification and dramatization on the ballfield.

That dramatic focusing of local rivalries helps explain the excitement generated by the game, as well as the tendency of spectators to express dissatisfaction with umpires, the opposing club, or even their own club. It also provides a way of seeing the contradictions inherent in the attachment to a local club. For the desire for a winning nine could and did conflict strongly with the feelings of localism. The tension between these two sets of feelings, held in uneasy balance during the late 1850s and early 1860s, began to shift in favor of winning, as neighborhoods, followed by towns and cities, began to "import" players and claim them as their own.[4]

Numerous paradoxes attended this development, not the least of which was that the intensity of neighborhood (increasingly, urban) baseball rivalries in the late nineteenth century grew in inverse proportion to the local nativity of the home team. The more intense the rivalry, the more likely a club's ability to raise the sums necessary to attract a professional nine to "represent" the club. And by the late 1860s, the distance between "constituent" and "representative" was widening in baseball almost as rapidly as it was in politics. (That baseball remained closer to the people—at least in their imaginations—than politics is suggested by the eagerness with which politicians sought at the time, and have continued to seek, to associate themselves with baseball clubs.) As American cities began a period of unparalleled and accelerated growth, the local imagination was subjected to serious strains, which produced contradictory attitudes toward baseball "representatives."

The Birth of the Cincinnati Red Stockings

It is at this point, then, and in this context that we should approach the Cincinnati Red Stockings, known to fans and historians alike as the first "all-professional" club, or the first "all-salaried" professional club, or the first "admittedly" all-professional club.[5] However we choose to acknowledge their firstness, there can be no doubt that the Red Stockings marked a turning point in the history of the game.

Their legendary status is best explained by the fact that so many strands of baseball history came together in the relatively short history of the club. The most important of these threads may very well have been the career of Harry Wright. One of the truly dominant figures of the baseball world between the late 1860s and early 1880s, Wright carried a good portion of American sport history in his own life. Born in England in 1835, the son of the noted cricketer Sam Wright, Harry was brought to the United States as a baby. Like his father, Harry was engaged as a professional bowler by the St. George Cricket Club in 1856. (Although cricket professionals often played in matches, they resembled teaching pros in modern tennis and golf clubs.) The grounds of the St. George Cricket Club were at the Elysian Fields at this time, and there Harry began to play a different game with another occupant of the Fields, the Knickerbocker Base Ball Club. Joining the Knickerbockers in 1858, he quickly became one of their more valued players.[6]

In 1866 Wright moved to Cincinnati as the professional of the Union Cricket Club, hired at a salary of $1,200 a year. Later that year he was involved in organizing the Cincinnati Base Ball Club, which played its matches on the field owned by his employer. The new baseball club borrowed more than grounds. At least four members of the Union Cricket Club also played on the baseball club's first nine, including pitcher Harry Wright. Many more members of the cricket club doubtless belonged to the newer club.[7]

The relationship between cricket and baseball in Cincinnati recapitulated that between the two sports in New York, but more rapidly. At the end of the 1867 season Harry Wright switched games and went to work—at the same salary—for the Cincinnati Base Ball Club. This change, while it could not have seemed especially consequential at the time either for the clubs, for Harry Wright, or for the history of baseball and cricket, in fact constituted one of the most significant events in the history of all three. Wright, the English-born professional cricketer (who later referred to cricket as "my first love"), astutely shifted his paid allegiance from a sport that was gradually losing its popularity to the fast-growing, increasingly profitable game of baseball. The decision to play as a professional did not have to be made in the face of strong feelings in favor of amateur play—he and his father had been earning their livings from manly sports for years. Wright's skill and reputation meshed perfectly with the growing ambitions of the Cincinnati club.

In 1867 the club defeated all but one of its opponents. The exception, the Washington Nationals, walloped the Cincinnatis 53 to 10, partly as a result of the assistance of Harry Wright's younger brother George. That defeat by an eastern club seems to have determined the Cincinnati directors to begin employing professionals. So, interestingly, did the club's indebtedness. According to a later report, the club owed some $600 to $700 at the beginning of 1868, exclusive of what they still owed on the lease for the Union Grounds. For the 1868 season, accordingly, the club decided to fence in the grounds, charge admission, and employ some professional players. Thus, in order to get the club out of debt, the directors incurred larger liabilities in the form of players' salaries and improvements to the grounds.[8]

Urban rivalry and local attachments were important factors in this decision as well. The Buckeye Club, also of Cincinnati, was the Red Stockings' major local competitor; both clubs fielded semiprofessional nines in 1868. Henry Chadwick suggested in 1870 that this city rivalry had been the major force behind the professionalization of Cincinnati baseball. To challenge the Red Stockings, the Buckeyes engaged two professional players. The Red Stockings then procured two more (in addition to Harry Wright), whereupon the Buckeyes added four professionals, inducing the Cincinnatis to add two more, in addition to Charley Gould, who left the Buckeyes for the Red Stockings. When the Red Stockings won the first match, the Buckeyes promptly imported three players from Washington, D.C., for the next contest, though to no avail.

Having established their local superiority, the Cincinnatis broadened their sights. They traveled east to take on the best-known and most successful clubs in the fraternity, but without notable success. Victories over the Philadelphia Olympics and Washington Nationals and a split with the champion Morrisania Unions whetted the club's appetite for a better nine. Club members may have been pushing for a more successful *club*, too. In late 1868, the *Clipper* reported, the Union Cricket Club gave up the ghost and "resigned to the Cincinnati Base Ball Club all their rights, title and interests to and in the Union grounds and the improvements, provided the base ball club would guarantee to them the use of the grounds at certain times for practice, and assume all the indebtedness."[9]

According to the former president of the Cincinnati club, the grounds had been held under joint lease by the two clubs for eight years at $2,000 a year. Each club furnished half the outlay, "both being represented in the management by delegates to a Board of Directors." They also spent $10,000 in 1867 for buildings and other improvements. These figures, he asserted at the time, were "sufficiently heavy to warrant the statement that the clubs have exhibited considerable courage in pledging themselves to an undertaking of such magnitude." Evidently the cricketers had more courage than prudence. When they ceded their interest in the ground to their baseball partners, over $7,500 was still owed on the field alone. The baseball club formed a stock association with $15,000 capital and authorized the sale of $7,500 worth of stock in order to help meet the club's total indebtedness of "$8,500 or $9,000." Buyers were found for only about $3,000 worth, however, and the club began the 1869 season owing about $6,000. Or rather, it would have owed that much if it had not decided to undertake an even greater obligation and risk.[10]

Given the size of the club's debt, some of the members very likely argued against getting deeper into the baseball business. Others no doubt claimed that only investment in a first-class nine could make enough money to bring the club out of the red. Still others were probably unconcerned about the money the club owed. After all, the club counted 380 members in 1867, among whom were many men of considerable means. The elements were certainly there for a dispute between traditionalists and modernizers, although the only evidence that one took place lies in the resignation of an unpaid member of the 1868 nine who was unhappy with the mix of professionals and amateurs on the same team. The club directors may have shared the sentiment, but if so, they went in the opposite direction. "Still bent on obtaining a leading position as the most successful nine in the country," according to Chadwick, the club "went to work in a business-like manner, and got together the first *regularly trained* professional nine which had ever been placed in the field."[11]

Baseball histories sometimes give the impression that the Cincinnati club emerged full-blown and previously unknown to the baseball fraternity. This was hardly the case. Ohio baseball had grown strong enough to provide a National Association president in 1867, and city baseball clubs, particularly the Cincinnatis and the Buckeyes, received a good deal of press attention. Aaron B. Champion, president of the Cincinnati club, was also head of the Ohio State Base-Ball Association in 1868; he had, according to one account, "the reputation of having done as much toward advancing base-ball in the West as any other individual." The rivalry between the Buckeyes and Red Stockings was a matter of journalistic interest, and both clubs' professional additions in 1868 were covered in detail.[12]

But there is a more striking point in the interest taken in Cincinnati baseball. The dominance of New York teams was broken by the Red Stockings, who were only one of several teams, including the Philadelphia Athletics, that could have done the same thing. On the other hand, to say that "Cincinnati" dominated baseball implied the successful appropriation of baseball relationships by the ideology of urban boosterism. Fewer and fewer of the first-nine players of either the Buckeyes or the Cincinnatis were genuine residents of the city. As each club hired more players in turn, the two clubs became increasingly "represented" in the field by eastern (largely New York) players. So the eastern eyes watching the Cincinnati game were also focused on New York players who had relocated in the Midwest. Interest in baseball as a national game, then, depended in part on the nationalization of formerly regional ballplayers.

For all of locals fans' interest in the home club, the sporting press was creating a baseball public whose interest was acquiring national scope. This expansion was assisted by the mobility of ballplayers, the same ballplayers fans castigated as traitorous for revolving away from their home clubs. Spectators read about Cincinnati baseball not only to see how the game was progressing out West. The size of the coverage—and the amount of readers' interest—had more to do with the exploits of players already well known to eastern audiences. "The Cincinnatis have strengthened their nine with two first-class New York players," observed *Wilkes' Spirit of the Times* in early 1868, "Harry Wright, who pitched for them last year, and John Hatfield, late of the New York Mutuals." In another story on Cincinnati the next week the eastern origins of the professional Red Stockings and Buckeyes figured prominently. The new players came from the Mutuals, the Nationals, the Eurekas of Newark, the Irvingtons of New Jersey, and the West Philadelphia Club. When the Buckeyes met the Cincinnatis for the city championship, the spectators' excitement was attributed by one reporter to the fact "that these two clubs strengthened themselves for the contest by the introduction into their organizations of no less than seven first-class players from the Eastern States."[13]

Baseball fans, commentators, and promoters were caught, then, in a series of contradictions that admitted of resolution only in unsatisfactory ways. They chose by and large to ignore the fact (or repress the knowledge) that these were contradictions, and preferred to rail at one side or the other, nominally in service to the opposing ideal, in fact depending on a vision of the game free of difficulty and conflict. Desire to see the game as national conflicted with their strong attachment to the game as an expression of local environments and loyalties. Paradoxically, that very loyalty was strengthened by the widening scope of competition, but the geographic expansion of the competitive sphere seriously undermined the extent to which players themselves expressed those loyalties other than as, in effect, actors playing roles.

Uniform Identities

Baseball's nationalization in the late 1860s thus strained the localism that had sustained the game in its early years. Institutionalized revolving supported by widespread professionalism confused spectators, who were suspicious of players who could move so easily from club to club, city to city. If players could exchange one club's uniform for that of its rival from one season to the next, wondered fans, who were they?

The baseball uniform itself offers some clues. Even in the early 1860s reporters noticed particularly attractive or striking uniforms. Clubs whose members were lax about suiting up for games or practices came in for criticism. Club feeling and pride were at stake in the members' public appearance as club representatives. At such times, uniforms helped legitimate the game that these men were playing, by referring visually to the ritual dress of other manly fraternal organizations, such as fire companies and volunteer military companies. Uniforms helped enforce members' sense of comradeship—that they were all fellows in the same club—as well as a sense of apartness. Partial or mixed uniforms, then, broke the spell cast by such regalia. Reporters were sensitive to these issues, having a stake themselves in the creation and maintenance of distinctiveness on the ballfield. Like the fences around enclosed grounds, the ropes that kept back spectators, and the foul lines on the field, uniforms were boundaries between what was baseball and what was not, between who belonged on the playing field and who did not. Men inside the uniform belonged to a club. Men outside of it were onlookers.

"There is more importance attached to the selection of a regular uniform for a base ball club than the fraternity generally think there is," argued the indefatigable Chadwick, for whom the importance of everything in the baseball world was greater than "the fraternity generally think." Chadwick had two principal concerns: that "one of the last things a club should . . . do, is to change the colors or form of its uniform"; and that therefore when "a club is first organized," particular care should be taken to adopt a tasteful and appropriate uniform. That his first comment on the importance of uniforms emphasized the dangers of changing them suggests that Chadwick had revolving and the problem of local attachments very much on his mind. It was hard enough to keep track of players who moved from club to club. One of the anchors that made such movement bearable was a certain club continuity, the relative stability of clubs' names, in some cases their officers, and usually their uniforms. Even a spectator whose knowledge of team lineups was not fully up to date could tell which clubs were playing just by recognizing the uniforms. Club nicknames were often derived from club uniforms: aside from the Cincinnati Red Stockings and Chicago White Stockings, the Mutuals were commonly referred to as the Green Stockings, and the Olympics of Washington, D.C., as the Blue Stockings. Changes in uniforms—those of individual clubs as well as of the entire fraternity—have often produced commotion in the baseball world, much more than seems appropriate to a simple change of shirt or pants style. Fans' allegiance to particular insignia or styles was (and remains) a sign of the intensity with which the emotional pull of a desired stability has been felt throughout the history of the game.[14]

In the heyday of the baseball club, then, with its rituals, suppers, soirees, and winter balls, uniforms served as expressions of club sentiment, of fraternal feeling and pride. Deviations from the ideal were criticized for reflecting poorly on the club. *Wilkes' Spirit of the Times* complained in 1864 that "for a season or two past, . . . our ball clubs have grown negligent in regard to their appearance. . . . A reform is needed in this matter." The reporter went on to discuss the issue at length, making some important connections:

> One of the attractive features of a ball-ground on a match-day is the appropriate uniforms of the players; in fact, to see a nine come on the ground and play a regular match in their club suit, others in a portion of it only, and others again merely in their shirt sleeves, has the appearance of poverty in the club, not creditable to any respectable organization. There is nothing to prevent a base-ball player's uniform from being as well known as that of a United States soldier. It is only requisite that each club should have a distinct style of cap, the pants and shirt can be the same for all, blue and white being the desirable colors. . . . But whether these colors are chosen . . . is of secondary impor-

tance, so that each club own a distinctive uniform and, what is more, wears it at all times on the ball-field. . . . Get new uniforms, gentle-men, if you can afford it, and wear them whenever you play ball, if you want to look like ball-players.[15]

The keys here were a combination of consistency (in pants and shirts) and distinctiveness, so that players were identified first as members of the ballplaying fraternity ("if you want to look like ball-players") and second as members of a particular club. Although taste was an is-sue, it was not nearly so important as the fact of having uniforms.

Specifically, uniforms were one of the means by which a "respect-able organization" established its distance from the "appearance of poverty." Ever concerned to solidify baseball's position in the world of respectability, the reporter clearly identified the world he feared (poverty) even as he acknowledged its proximity in his final admoni-tion: "Get new uniforms, gentlemen, if you can afford it."

The reportorial advice about uniforms, then, drew on a powerful set of fears and antagonisms by suggesting that sloppy, incomplete, or nonexistent uniforms gave the "appearance of poverty." Uniforms served the seekers after respectability quite well as they sought to dis-tinguish themselves from the poor and the roughs—men, boys, and would-be gentlemen who could not afford uniforms.[16]

But if uniforms began as measures and badges of club (and overall fraternal) identification, by the late 1860s and 1870s they had ac-quired a new function. Now, it was hoped, they would provide ball-players and clubs with an outward sign of the identity that appeared to be lacking in so many areas. Even though the horses had escaped, Chadwick was still trying to close the barn door. By concentrating on uniforms, commentators were adopting a device from the theater. Uniforms came off just as easily as they went on. But if distinctive dress could not change the players, it could give the anxious spectator something to grasp. It would not be the last time in baseball history that this illusion was fostered by baseball's promoters and seized upon by a confused public.

Chadwick's second point about uniforms, "that particular care should be taken to adopt a tasteful and appropriate uniform," was likewise revealing. He mentioned four possible styles, the last of which was "the mixed, circus-style of dress, generally worn by junior

clubs and country village organizations, in which bright red is a conspicuous color." Clearly he hoped to distinguish the more "manly,"
or more mature and advanced, organizations from the relatively unso-
phisticated junior and country clubs.

Here we can see the beginnings of an otherwise curious phenomenon in baseball history: the cultural prejudice against the country.
Baseball myth, after all, is firmly rural. Yet players from the country,
or from small towns, have been considered hicks, yokels, or hay-
seeds since the 1860s. Recall that, according to Chadwick in 1867, it
was mainly the insufficiently self-controlled "country" spectators who
still hooted at umpires. The "villagers" of Louisville, Kentucky, had
been the most partisan and least "well-bred" of all the audiences en-
countered by the Washington Nationals on their tour that year. This
development is partially explained by the fact that New York was the
center of the baseball world during these years. The rest of the explanation lies in the way professional baseball grew: nearly always in
larger towns and cities with populations large enough to support an
entertainment business based on gate receipts, but drawing players
from the entire surrounding region, or even (occasionally) from
across the country. So the very fact that a disproportionate number of
professional ballplayers had come from rural areas to play on teams
based in cities produced prejudice against the country boy.

In the metropolis itself, the "conspicuous color" of the fire company uniforms was a very bright red. It was fire company runners,
like the baseball club followers, who were the most visible representatives of the city's "untrained" residents. This chain of associations
was less extended for nineteenth-century urban residents than it may
seem over a hundred years later. Uniforms were more remarkable
then than now; volunteer fire companies had been prominent sources
of "disorder" in the 1840s and 1850s; and their uniforms were a distinctive red. Associating juvenile, lower-class partisanship with
bumpkins and the "untrained," all dressed in flaming red, was easy
and natural for Chadwick and his readers. George Wilkes's reporter
had recommended the adoption of blue and white. The taste and propriety of baseball uniforms, then, were meant to anchor the increasingly drifting identity of ballplayers, and to strengthen the permeable
barrier between the respectable game and the bawdier aspects of urban recreational culture.[17]

Management, Triumph, and Defeat:
The Red Stockings of 1869 and 1870

By an interesting coincidence, the first issue of *Beadle's Dime Base-Ball Player* to carry Chadwick's advice about uniforms appeared in 1869, the year of the team known for its uniform, for its first-rate eastern ballplayers, and for its extraordinary season-long string of victories. Let us look closely at the Red Stockings of that year and try to see what converged in this team full of firsts.

Perhaps most important of all, the Red Stockings were, in Chadwick's words, the first "regularly trained" all-professional club. For if the language and ideology of management had come to organized baseball in 1867, its first triumph was Harry Wright's management of the Cincinnati club. Wright offered a model of baseball management that was matched by few (if any) others. What we understand today as a team manager was the team "captain" in the 1860s and 1870s — the player responsible for making tactical decisions about the game on the field. The "manager" of the club in these years was its business manager, the club official — often the corresponding secretary — in charge of making arrangements with other clubs for games, handling travel plans, reserving hotel rooms for the players, and the like. It is important to remember that all through this period clubs did not have prearranged playing schedules the way nearly all clubs (even Little League teams) do today. As a result, the conscientious manager spent an enormous amount of time writing letters and sending telegrams to his counterparts in other clubs just to arrange matches. It fell on Wright to arrange club tours that were filled not only with games but with contests that would pay enough to make the trip worthwhile. He performed this task for the Cincinnati club better than it had ever been done before by anyone, for any club. The Red Stockings' 1869 tour was the most extensive ever undertaken, and the club ended up turning a profit.[18]

Though largely unheralded, Wright's business management was an outstanding contribution to Cincinnati's success and ought to be listed in the catalogue of firsts. His efforts to subject an extremely irregular and unpredictable set of encounters (baseball games) to the systematic supervision of business management carved out new territory in the material history of the game.

Some people besides members of the Cincinnati club must have been aware of Wright's tireless work in these matters. Baseball men knew how difficult it was to arrange such a lengthy tour as the one announced in the papers in early 1869. They were also the recipients of his letters. But most of the praise that came his way—and there was a substantial amount during and after that season—centered on his management of the nine itself, on his captaincy of his men on and off the field. That is what Chadwick meant when he said that the Red Stockings were the first "regularly trained" professional nine. Harry Wright was more involved in the lives of his players than any previous captain had ever been. He directed and supervised their practices, decided who played where and when, maintained morale, and kept an eye on their eating, drinking, and sleeping habits. He was, in effect, the first modern baseball manager.[19]

This point has been understood only partially by students of the game. Emphasis has fallen primarily on Wright simply as baseball's "first professional manager," or on his "zeal as a field manager and trainer." But the key to Wright's importance as baseball's first real manager was the way he altered relations among the nine, firmly establishing his authority over the players in every aspect of the game. Wright negotiated contracts with them, and he ordered them about on the ballfield and off. His control over the players' lives off the field was never as complete as he would have liked, but he did establish the *principle* of that authority.[20]

Backed by the directors of the club and his years of experience in the game, Wright's authority partook simultaneously of a variety of hierarchical relationships. First, although not strictly an employer, he acted as the employer's representative. Whether or not a player actually worked—that is, played—was up to Wright. Second, he was the club provider: by arranging games, Wright put bread on the table for everyone. So in dealing with a particular player or group of players, he spoke for the welfare of the club as a whole.

Finally, Wright was thirty-four in 1869, almost twelve years older than the average Red Stocking. All but one of the other players were between twenty and twenty-three years old, and the oldest, Asa Brainard, was twenty-seven. When Wright referred to the nine as "the boys," he may have been including himself as well, but the term had more force as an acknowledgment of age difference that implicitly asserted a form of paternal authority. Wright's managerial style was firmly rooted in the complex of emotions generated by the tensions between men and boys, or imagined tensions between manliness and boyishness. His paternalism may have been strengthened further by the presence of his much younger brother George. Only twenty-two years old in 1869, George Wright was already widely known as one of the finest shortstops, batters, and all-round players in the game. That Harry traced his lineage back to the professional cricketer Sam Wright and forward to his brother George (and later his even younger brother Sam, Jr.) gave his voice the added force of the sporting past.[21]

If the Red Stockings represented a departure in some areas, they were firmly within baseball tradition in others. The first nine consisted for the most part of well-known players who came from the ranks of skilled artisans and clerks, including two "in insurance," one bookkeeper, two hatters, a marble cutter, a pianomaker, a jeweler, and an engraver. (The last two were Harry and George Wright, who, although they made their livings from baseball, also had trades.) Their salaries were discussed in the press, and deserve some attention. "Captain Harry" received $1,200. George Wright was the team's highest paid player, at $1,400. Asa Brainard, the pitcher, and Fred Waterman, the third baseman, were paid $1,100 and $1,000, respectively. The five remaining starters got $800 apiece, while the substitute was paid either $600 or $800.[22]

Such figures are not very informative, however, unless they are put in the context of the work world of the late 1860s and early 1870s. Because the fluctuations of the economy could radically affect the number of days worked and wage rates, the income of skilled workers varied widely—from around $525 a year at the lower end of the scale to as much as $750 at the upper end. Since the lowest-paid of the regular players on the Cincinnatis earned $800—and that on a contract that ran for only eight months (March 15 to November 15) —it is clear that professional ballplayers were doing quite well. Yet with the exception of George Wright, who earned nearly twice as much as most of his teammates, the Red Stockings did not make so much more than their fellow artisans as to be considered wealthy. The five or six at $800 made in eight months what it took the best-paid and most regularly employed skilled craftsman a year to earn. Nevertheless, the potential clearly existed to make considerably more than even a very well-paid artisan. The four best-paid Red Stockings, for example, earned from 15 to about 70 percent more than the top craftsman's wage.[23]

These salaries, though noted in the press in June, excited less comment than the remarkable play of the Red Stockings. The momentous eastern tour began on May 31, and the club's first big victory came a week later, when the Cincinnatis beat the surprised Troy Haymakers. They then made their way into the metropolis, the lion's den for any western or country ball club. Taking on the "champion" New York Mutuals, Cincinnati squeaked out a 4-to-2 win, an extremely close game by the standards of the time and "the best-played game ever witnessed," according to the *Spirit of the Times*. Doubtless buoyed by this stunning victory, the Cincinnatis proceeded to administer a "crushing defeat" to the Atlantics (32 to 10) the next day, and an even more lopsided whipping to the Eckfords the day after. At this point the club vaulted into new prominence, exciting the admiration and envy of the baseball world. The "marvelous" Red Stockings, enthused one reporter, "are the only true exponents of the game to-day. Full of courage, free from intemperance, they have conducted themselves in every city they visited in a manner to challenge admiration, and their exhibitions of skill in the art of handling both ball and bat call for unexampled praise. Their present tour has done more to elevate the game than any trip of the kind ever before known." Although New York was the equal of Cincinnati "in manly, courageous, and gentlemanly players," the story continued, "our own clubs will profit by the example set them by the Red Stockings in the matter of playing and organizing a nine."[24]

This theme appeared repeatedly in game stories and editorials. Even though the club was "composed almost entirely of Eastern *materiel*," according to one account, it was only "by the most assiduous training, and under the management of the first, best, and only trainer of a club nine—Harry Wright—[that] the men were brought to a degree of perfection—physically and otherwise—never before witnessed." Audiences in Buffalo were impressed by another aspect of this training: except for their captain, none of the Red Stockings uttered a word on the field. The "lesson" taught New York was "that steady, temperate habits and constant training are all conditions precedent to a first-class organization."[25]

The *Spirit of the Times* directly addressed the question of Cincinnati's right to the championship in an editorial following the club's New York victories. "CINCINNATI THE CHAMPION CITY," ran the headline, an honor that could not "fairly be abated by the fact that many of the players went to the West from New York." Even though the players might have come from the New York area, their "capital play is mainly to be attributed to their organization, and, as that originated and was perfected in Cincinnati, that city is fully entitled to credit therefor."[26]

This assertion ratified the nationalizing of players and the game. On the one hand, players "from" New York populated the other clubs, so that the spread of New York players across the Northeast and Midwest reenacted the spread of the "New York game" across the same areas on the road to become the "national game." Yet writers were apparently willing to give up their claims to departed players, ascribing loyalties and granting claiming rights to the player's new "home" club or city. In return, of course, any player who revolved into New York baseball circles could be considered a New Yorker by virtue of playing on a New York nine. Such a reformulation of player citizenship, although never quite completed, helped local fans accommodate themselves emotionally to the growing irrelevance of players' cities of origin.

One could turn this observation around and argue that the stress on an urban "home" occasioned by the nationalization of the players and clubs more accurately resembled propaganda designed to disguise real developments in the game, and thus contributed to the beginning of the mythmaking that has characterized so much baseball reporting and commentary ever since. Of course, even the notion of an urban home rested on social quicksand. Forty percent of New York's population in 1850 was foreign-born. And the well-documented furious pace of geographical mobility among city residents in the mid–nineteenth century meant that anyone's hold on a particular "hometown" had to be tenuous. These analyses need not be mutually exclusive. What to some was an emotional accommodation to a changing reality was for others (or even to the same people) a more or less deliberate refusal to look at the changes head on.

In any event, such accommodation or refusal has continued to structure fans' attitudes toward the problem of locality in baseball. Each fan, it seems, must, in the course of his or her private loss of baseball innocence, see a favorite player depart, a hometown boy traded, a quintessential Yankee or Dodger or Cardinal suddenly move to another team, don another uniform, and appear to forget his previous home. That movement is painful for a fan to watch, and it causes pain each time it happens, at least partly because, as we have seen,

the game internalizes that very problem—home and away, at bat or
in the field, our boys and the visitors. Only by remaining immune to
the emotional pull of the game could its followers not be affected by
apparent violations of this impulse to claim a home territory and
home players. In other words, for fans little was to be gained by seeing the fraternity of professional ballplayers as they were: potentially,
universally interchangeable. Rather than face the complete industrialization of the game, a development for which there was little emotional support, it was far easier to participate in a fictive process of
hometown identification.

Cincinnati's dominance of the baseball world turned out to be
short-lived. Although the season of 1870 began with much promise,
the club's undefeated streak finally came to an end in New York, as
the Atlantics narrowly beat the champions in an eleven-inning contest. That game broke the Cincinnati spell over the rest of the baseball world. Suddenly the Red Stockings became just another first-
class club that could be beaten now and then. Five more defeats
followed during the season, still an excellent record, but hometown
enthusiasm was beginning to fall off.[27]

Pleading the "claims of their private business," the president and
secretary of the club resigned in August. Although they (and Harry
Wright) had pulled the Cincinnatis out of debt, their final financial
report predicted no profit, and when the year was over the balance
sheet showed that the club had just broken even. More serious
changes followed the close of the season. Amid reports that the club
would be "thoroughly reorganized" for the next season to eliminate
the "growlers and shirkers of the present nine," as well as those who
would "not contract to abstain from the use of intoxicating beverages
at all times unless prescribed by a physician in good standing," the
club leadership went a step further and resolved to abandon the professional arena altogether.[28]

The circular with which the club directors announced their decision
touched on so many aspects of the club that it is worth a close look.
Apparently intending at first to continue the course of the past two
seasons, the board had been in "communication with many of the
leading professional ball players throughout the country, as well as
with the various members of our former nine." Unfortunately, they
concluded, paying the "enormous salaries" now demanded by professional players would "plunge our club deeply in debt." The past two

years had shown that a nine with a payroll in excess of $6,000 to $8,000 "cannot, even with the strictest economy, be self-sustaining." With current salary demands, the "maximum sum . . . would be very nearly doubled." To avoid backruptcy the club would have to impose a "heavy levy" on its members to make up the difference.[29]

Not that the club had refused to call on its members in the past. In fact, the members had "year after year contributed liberally for the liquidation of the expenses incurred in the employment of players." This year, however, the directors did "not feel justified in calling on them again." Money—that is, meeting the salaries of a professional nine—was an issue, but not the only one. The recipients of the salaries had failed to live up to expected standards. "Payment of large salaries causes jealousy," argued the directors, not making it clear whether they meant jealousy among players or between players and other club members, "and leads to extravagance and dissipation on the part of the players." Such behavior, "injurious to them," was also "destructive of the subordination and good feeling necessary to the success of a nine."

Whether these charges accurately described the 1869 and 1870 Red Stockings is another matter. Jealousy, extravagance, and dissipation notwithstanding, the club lost no games in 1869 and only six the following year. While some of the players were apparently given to occasional nighttime sprees, there is very little evidence to suggest widespread dissipation. Wright, while not tyrannical, did not look kindly upon flagrantly unrespectable behavior.[30]

The circular can be read more usefully as a statement (if a belated one) about the transformation of baseball from a fraternal club sport into an entertainment business. Even its language was mixed, dominated by turns by a concern for business accounting and by the spirit of club fraternalism. This confusion was particularly evident in the claim that high salaries had destroyed "that subordination and good feeling necessary to the success of a nine." Three or four years earlier the word "subordination" would not have been used. "Harmony and good feeling" might have been, or perhaps "discipline"—understood as *self*-discipline—and "good feeling," but not "subordination." The directors were talking about their employees' failure to behave as subordinates, and in so far as they were serious about the good feeling, they were talking about the club members, and about the bygone days of genuinely fraternal clubs.[31]

It was to that prior state of grace that the directors made their concluding appeal, expressed in the new language of amateurism: "We believe that there will be a development of the amateur talent of our club, such as has not been displayed since we employed paid professionals, and that we will still enjoy the pleasure of witnessing many exciting contests on our grounds."

Inasmuch as the club had employed professionals almost since its founding, the reference to its early amateur days must be taken with a grain of salt. The club, evidently frustrated by its failure to make money even with an outstanding championship club, was blaming its problems on the uppity players—jealous, extravagant, dissipated, and insubordinate—and retreating from the heartless world of professional baseball into the sheltered glen of amateurism. Although the directors appealed to the club's experience of "good feeling," the circular indicated their major focus: dollars, cents, and the management of their player-employees.

Their appeal to amateurism, and to its supposed affinity with the simpler fraternal days of the game, could be made only disingenuously. They had tried something very different, and when it failed to satisfy the club in either emotional or material terms, they recoiled from professionalism like lovers scorned, wrapping themselves in the cloak of amateurism. Even so, the circular concluded with gestures in another direction. The club and its grounds, the directors pointed out proudly, were "entirely free from debt." Despite their best efforts to reclaim baseball "tradition," the club directors had been so greatly influenced by their experience as pioneers that they could speak only in the language of baseball's modernity. Lest anyone think that withdrawal from the professional arena would diminish the quality of Cincinnati baseball, they expressed confidence in the "many exciting contests" sure to follow.

7

Amateurs in Rebellion

The Amateurist Critique of
Professional Baseball

The Cincinnati Red Stockings' abrupt and public withdrawal from the professional game apparently resonated widely in the baseball world. For only after the Red Stocking leadership announced its decision to embrace amateur play did the *Spirit of the Times* deal at length with what it suddenly called the "very costly and very unsatisfactory" system of "pay[ing] nine players to travel about the country and represent the real club, which was all the time at home." All at once the paper seems to have discovered that professional players "were not, in very truth, members of these clubs at all, but only hired assistants." This argument was directed not against the existence of professional players but against "putting . . . [them] forward . . . as *bona-fide* members of the clubs." The integrity of the club was at stake. Victories by the Red Stocking nine "only made the poor play of the real club at home more glaring by the strong contrast, and thus discouraged the young men and striplings who played upon their home grounds." Ordinary club members had been reduced to the status of paying onlookers, as the division within the club paralleled the split in the larger baseball world between players and spectators. The suggested remedy was to "confine the club solely to paying members, to the total exclusion of payees," and for the club to refuse matches with any club that fielded a professional player in its nine.[1]

What is striking about this editorial is not its analysis of a professional nine's effect on a club (which was almost entirely accurate) but that the most influential sporting paper of the time was reversing the course it had helped to pioneer. Press concentration on "first-class matches" between the most highly skilled players for the "championship" had been the distinguishing feature of baseball journalism for the better part of a decade. Now that the Cincinnati club had decided to abandon baseball professionalism, the *Spirit of the Times* discovered this "strange" and "vicious" system.

What was the source of this disgust? The usual bugbears—gamblers and "roughs"—were not even invoked. Over and over the editorial returned to the theme that professional players "were not, in truth, members of these clubs at all, but only hired assistants." This was an odd way of referring to the professional players, who were universally recognized as the outstanding exponents of the game. In fact, the writer was at pains to point out that "excellence as players is not to be attributed to any superior insight or to any special method. It results only from physical aptitude and long practice. That is all there is about it." Even though the substance of the observation— that practice was the key element of baseball skill—was widely understood, the dismissive tone ("no superior insight," "That is all there is about it") was new and unusual. Professional players were, in effect, being demoted. Even their teaching role (which seems to have existed more in theory than in fact) was of no value: "There is nothing in the game to make the instruction of a professional player needful."

Professionalism had kept the "real members," the "amateurs," from becoming skilled players, under a system "simply calculated to benefit nobody but those who chose to make a regular trade of that which can never be to millions anything but a sport and a recreation." Here was the nub of the problem, and it is important that we recognize the novel language with which it was stated. Though the debate over baseball professionalization was vigorous and widespread, the opponents of play for pay had rarely, if ever, evidenced such outright scorn not only for the ballplayer who earned a livelihood from the game—made it his "regular trade"—but for the very activity of a regular trade. The hostility directed at "hired assistants" smacked less of a principled opposition to wage labor (an opposition still very much alive in the United States during these years) than of a straightforward expression of class condescension toward those who made their livings at regular trades.

The alliance of respectable artisans, clerks, small proprietors, and the sporting middle class which had been responsible for the culture of early baseball clubs was unraveling. To be sure, the game was marked by vexing developments. Clubs in the older sense of the term were not surviving the changes brought by professionalism. But the editorial might have opposed professionalism in the name of (or in the hope of) resuscitating the fraternalism that had characterized such clubs. Instead, respect for craft and its practitioners, whether in the shop or on the ballfield, had all but disappeared. Casting its lot higher up the class ladder, George Wilkes's paper cut itself off from the culture in which baseball had been nourished and steadily decreased its coverage of the professional game.

Significantly, this privileging of amateur play was accompanied by one of the earliest references in baseball literature to the game's character as "a sport and recreation." In one sentence the writer managed to stake out almost entirely new territory in the history of the game's consciousness: those few who made baseball a "regular trade" were participating in a "vicious system," while the game could "never be to the millions anything but a sport and recreation." The different parts of the baseball world which the sentence described—the highly skilled top-flight players and the less skilled, less well-trained second-, third-, and muffin-nine players—had existed for some time. The appeal to a separate world of "sport and recreation" as the source of the game's legitimacy, however, was unprecedented, and all the more so because it was opposed to baseball as a "regular trade." The notion of sport as pure recreation, of leisure activity as pure play, could arise only after baseball play had also become baseball work. "Pure recreation" and the assertion of its superiority over "professional play," then, originated as a critique of playing for pay.

In other words, the real movement in the first few decades of baseball history is best understood not as the corruption of pure play by the desire for victory or the subsequent effort to make money from the game. Pure sport was unknown during these early decades, except as the idea of it surfaced in the company of its opposite, play taken seriously enough to demand practice and discipline. The eventual division of the players into professionals and amateurs, though it could not eliminate this tension, at least separated the leading tendencies. And only when professional baseball seemed to have reached a truly dominant position in the baseball world did the concept of pure sport and recreation receive formulation and attract champions. If originality or priority is taken as the measure of purity, then it would be more accurate to say that sport and recreation corrupted baseball, by introducing standards and values quite foreign to the culture of the game as it had been played by its most skillful practitioners for fifteen years. Suddenly the game was challenged in the name of those who played it badly, less frequently, for exercise, and principally as sport and recreation. Which was the corruption of the game?

This argument would have persuaded few commentators in the baseball world of the late 1860s and early 1870s. Far more widespread was the view expressed by the *Boston Herald*, that it was "the business feature of the game that [was] bringing it into disrepute."[2] Squabbles over gate receipts, covered in the sporting press, had become a staple of baseball's new commercial culture. The *Spirit of the Times* and the *Herald* were not alone in their opposition to this culture. Many members of the fraternity also thought it alien to the values they sought in the baseball community and on the playing field.

Accordingly, some of these men, led by Dr. Jones of the Excelsiors and representatives of several of the game's oldest clubs—the Knickerbocker, Eagle, and Gotham clubs of New York, among others—called in early 1871 for a convention of delegates from amateur clubs "for the purpose of organizing a national association of amateur base ball players." Jones's call, in the form of an address to amateur clubs, had something of the character of a manifesto; since it came at a crucial moment in the history of the game, it is worth examining closely.

First of all, Jones, a physician, focused on the "great want of physical out door culture in this country," a fact "so apparent that argument . . . is rendered superfluous." Baseball, he believed, was healthier than any other sport. The physical benefits it provided rivaled the list of moral and physical attributes Henry Chadwick had listed in the 1860 *Beadle's Dime Base-Ball Player*. "As a recreative exercise," Jones maintained, "it brings into play every muscle of the system, expands the chest, improves the breathing capacity of the lungs, and thereby purifies the blood, strengthens the nervous system and exhilarates the mind, and secures to its devotees sound and refreshing sleep." When "these facts became known" a "few years ago," he claimed, the game became popular. Jones then drew an extraordinary picture of those years:

Employers willingly and cheerfully gave their employees time to play base ball, and in many instances accompanied and participated in the pastime with them. All classes of society, the mechanic, the merchant, the professional classes, the school children, the collegiates, the aged and the young, the church member and minister, the public official, the private affluent member of society, all joined in the sport, either as a player or member of some base ball club, and hundreds upon hundreds of wives, mothers, sisters and daughters graced the ball field by their presence. Everything seemed to indicate that an American national out door pastime, fraught with influences the most beneficial and desirable, had been established, and so indeed it had.[3]

This account is most remarkable for its overall vision of unity and harmony. Unbounded by class lines, baseball time was "willingly and cheerfully" granted employees by their employers, who went even further and "participated in the pastime with them." Not only did the game ignore distinctions between workers and employers, it suffused the entire society equally: "all classes of society . . . joined in the sport." The significance of this fantasy lies in the conflicts it explicitly denies and in the extravagance of its assertion of a harmony that never existed. Though Jones lived in a city aboil with ethnic and class violence, turbulent politics, draft riots, and battles between street gangs, he depicted class and cultural harmony. In so doing he edited out the special importance of artisans and clerks in the culture and play of competitive baseball. The observation that "all classes" contributed equally to the game was in reality a claim that the middle and upper classes had dominated baseball's development: "the merchant, the professional classes, . . . the collegiates, . . . the . . . minister, the public official, the private affluent member of society."

Not content merely to have brought all the classes together in his vision of baseball's past, Jones insisted that this state of grace had also been blessed by union between males and females under the shelter of the family. "Wives, mothers, sisters and daughters"— women all securely enclosed in families—brought their happy influence to the ballfield. Class harmony and domestic bliss prevailed, thus establishing an "American" pastime "fraught" only "with influences the most beneficial and desirable." The total absence of conflict, of competitive emotion, of sex distinctions and class divisions marks this "history" as the clearest example of Edenic fantasy in the baseball world during these years. This garden, though, had peculiarly American and Victorian qualities: the escape from class structure and the compensatory reliance on the metaphor of the family.

Its corruption, therefore, and unsurprisingly, came at the hands of the Old World. Having established the "American national out door pastime," Jones continued: "The influence of the habits of the Old World soon manifested itself. England and other places had what they called professional cricket players, who made a living by playing cricket, a national sport of England. Why should not America have a professional class of ball players; there was money in it; why not secure it?"[4] Chief among the Old World demons, then, was the "professional class of ball players," whose principle was to make money where money was to be made. This unsavory class then "induced" the National Association "to hold its annual convention in other places besides New York." To Jones and his colleagues (nearly all of whom represented clubs in the New York metropolitan area) New York was the seat of baseball virtue, and the move even to Philadelphia opened the game up to the influence of money-seekers and Old World vice. At the 1867 convention, they lamented, the "Constitution . . . was ignored, and foundation laid to bring the game into disrepute, by allowing the Association to be controlled by professionals. . . . Friends of the national game," they concluded, "we appeal to you to aid us in our attempt to restore this pastime to its former high status." The proposed amateur convention would work to eradicate the "evils" fostered by the "machinations of the unprincipled, ambitious, or the money-seekers," principally by "discountenanc[ing] the playing of the game for money, or as a business pursuit."[5]

The clubs behind this appeal had been out of the baseball mainstream for some time. Neither the Excelsiors, Knickerbockers, Eagles, nor Gothams had been important competitors or leading members of the fraternity for a half-dozen years. Feeling their own marginality in the era of professional baseball, they tried to recreate a bygone arena in which their voices would be heard and their play respected. That is one key to their appeal, and to the ideology of amateurism generally: the assertion of the game's original purity (that is, before the advent of money and business) and the attempt to "restore" the game to that lost state. They ignored the reasons why professionals had come into the game, why baseball was played for money, and why it had become a "business pursuit." These amateurists were propelled by a vision of a genteel, harmonious world of sport, in which all classes and all ages and both sexes came together in healthful recreation under the governance of manly middle- and upper-class men.[6] That this world had never existed helped to ensure that their effort to recreate it would fail.

And fail it did. Since the effort has been undertaken so many times in baseball (and other sporting) history without success, the essence of amateurism may very well be the effort itself. For a restorative movement provides an opportunity for those not in the mainstream to declare their loyalty to original goals, primary values, and opposition to the prevailing values and organization of the game. Even though they do not succeed in "reestablishing" what they think of as the world they have lost, the chance to breathe in the emotional atmosphere of that world serves, at least for a time, as its own reward. But let us look at the sincere efforts of the first group of men in baseball history who tried "to restore this pastime to its former high status."

"Restoring" the Pastime

In response to the amateurist call, twenty-six clubs met in New York in March 1871 and formed the National Association of Amateur Base Ball Players. The rules of the new association were, except for strictures against professionalism, essentially those of the previous one. Even among the amateurs, however, money was an issue. There was strong sentiment at the convention, probably among clubs with wealthier members, against allowing clubs to charge admission to their games. Resisting this trend, the prominent Star Club, which had been selling tickets for years, threatened to withdraw unless admission fees were allowed, and won the right to continue the practice. The apparent contradiction earned the new association the sarcasm of the *Spirit of the Times*, which found it peculiar that clubs were to be allowed "to take gate-money and yet not be considered in a great measure professional clubs."[7] But the real significance of the conflict lay in the fact that even when the amateur clubs went off by themselves to "restore" the game, to erect barriers between "their" game and the mainstream, between the "real" game and its "vice-ridden" counterpart, the very tensions that had led the amateurs to withdraw surfaced immediately in their own convention.

Although gate receipts were certainly an issue, the most commonly articulated and widely held notion of the difference between professional and amateur baseball focused on the question whether or not players were paid—employed—to play the game. We may look at this dividing line as the boundary between a club and a business. Clubs paid outsiders for services to the club, such as mowing the grass and cleaning the clubhouse. Richer members subsidized their poorer fellows, but that relationship, if not exactly disguised, was not advertised outside of the club. A business, on the other hand, was characterized not only by its desire to earn money but by the fact that it employed workers. And if a club employed its own members—or rather, if some of its members employed other members—its fraternal character was, at the very least, in jeopardy. The division within a club between employers and employees may have been unsettling to members who did remember days when "all classes" in a club participated in the game, and there was no class that was employed by the others.

Yet if these speculations are correct, they address only part of the problem felt by the amateur activists. For however attractive they may have found the thought of restoring the truly fraternal "old days," they also spoke of current professional *players* in terms suggesting that it was not merely the soul of the club that bothered them; equally worrisome were the "character," "habits," and class status of the professional players.

In the late 1850s and early 1860s many baseball clubs had been an amalgam of merchants and professionals, clerks and shopkeepers, and skilled craftsmen. When professional opportunity beckoned, it was mainly artisans and clerks who responded, and these same clubs divided along their class axes. Many simply disbanded; in others one side won out and the dissenters left. The pattern of division and unfolding was very much at work in the late 1860s and early 1870s as clubs felt the twin pressures of potential financial stakes and player employment. In 1867 and 1868, the fraternity had dealt with these questions by changing or enforcing NABBP rules. Two years later the emphasis on rules was overshadowed by a concern for class.

The Mutuals attempted to deal with the problem in an imaginative fashion: they formed an amateur nine alongside their professional nine. The *Spirit of the Times* recommended this course to the other prominent professional clubs. Drawing on the vocabulary of cricket, the paper referred to the different nines as the "players" and the "gentlemen," thus aiding the movement toward class distinctions within the game and in individual clubs. Formerly in the baseball world, the term "gentleman" had conveyed the manly qualities that could be attained by self-controlled Victorian artisans. Now, incorporating distinctions in employment (gentlemen did not "work" at baseball, players did), the term became far more divisive, marking class distinctions more than blurring them. "Gentlemen" became the mainstay of amateur ideology. An account of an amateur contest between the Knickerbockers and Stars in 1872 put the matter quite bluntly: "It is true that amateurs cannot devote the same time to practice that men who make it a profession can spare; but the advantages of education and superior intelligence ought in a very great measure to make up for this disadvantage."[8]

An emphasis on college baseball signaled the class dimensions of the amateur movement. Although college matches had been covered occasionally in the sporting press during the 1860s, they had generally been considered novelties. Now, in contrast, *The Base-Ball Guide* predicted that "it is to the college matches each season . . . that the admirers of the game will have to look for the finest displays of the beauties of the game and the most exciting contests of each season." Since this statement was so much at variance with obvious fact, the writer admitted that the professional clubs had the "material . . . to make the best displays," but that the "evil influences" associated with some nines cast doubt on the extent to which the players "will exert themselves to their utmost to win." No such doubt could taint college matches, "for the *esprit de corps* and the natural rivalry between leading colleges to carry off the palm of their Alma Mater must necessarily lead to legitimate efforts to win in every instance."[9]

Here, too, the image of the mother country was invoked, as the writer expected to see American college competition on the baseball field "made as interesting and exciting as are the cricket matches between the elevens of Oxford and Cambridge and Eton and Rugby in England." It is instructive to compare this use of England with that made by Jones in his address to the amateurs. Jones used the specter of Old World class divisions, particularly the bad habits of the working classes, as a yardstick with which to measure the degradation of American baseball, while the *Guide*'s writer appealed directly to the most upper-class English institutions as models for American baseball. In both cases England was characterized by its division into classes. While baseball had earlier prided itself on not being structured in the same way, as clubs themselves split into classes and each class tried to isolate and control the version of the game it most enjoyed, amateurists appealed directly to the class-divided English sporting world both to strengthen their arguments and to provide models for the kind of sport they sought.

At the same time that professional baseball was expanding most rapidly, then, exponents of amateurism were organizing a form of resistance—at the very least an enclave protected from the professional touch, at most a base from which they could begin to mount a transforming attack on the professional game. In the process, they infused their cause with class snobbery and concentrated on the exploits of college baseball clubs, which they elevated to the status of the cutting edge of the amateur movement. In fact, it was fortunate for the amateurs that the college clubs existed, for without them the amateur organization would have folded even earlier than it did. As it was, the association met only infrequently and died from lack of interest within a few years.

In the sense that the amateur movement represented a form of baseball traditionalism, it was ill suited to engage in the kind of organizational initiative that had always been the province of baseball's modernizers. Amateurs had no trouble forming their own clubs, but anything larger than a city or state organization appears to have been beyond their abilities or interest. Essentially a defensive, inward-looking impulse and ideology, amateurism arose in reaction to the dominant influence of the professional players and "clubs." Declarations like that of the Beacon Club of Boston—"The club is endeavoring to interest all lovers of genuine amateur playing who give their time to the national game from pure love of the sport, and not for any pecuniary benefit"—became necessary only as a defensive effort to legitimate the kind of baseball its members liked to play. It nevertheless spoke to the sporting desires of large numbers of people. The Beacon Club doubled its membership in a week, from thirty to sixty, and the amateur Staten Island Club listed two hundred members at the end of 1873. In 1873 and 1874, amateur baseball began to get more press attention than it ever had before. Brooklyn's Prospect Park became the scene of regular amateur contests that drew thousands of fans.[10]

Almost as soon as the amateur arena started to grow in importance, very familiar structures began to appear within its boundaries. Despite the Beacon Club's profession of "pure love of the sport," its members discussed an amateur championship of Massachusetts and appointed a committee to sound out other clubs on the idea. The irony of this undertaking is now obvious. What had distinguished the Knickerbocker Club of the early 1860s from most of its contemporaries was its refusal to compete for the championship. It was that decision that had prompted *Wilkes' Spirit of the Times* to describe the club as playing "purely for sport." A decade later, championships had become so ingrained in baseball thinking that even self-conscious, self-proclaimed amateurists considered them a natural part of the game.

Amateur clubs also followed the patterns set by the professionals in putting together tours. In 1874, for example, the Flyaways of New York City went on a three-week tour through central New York State, and the western tour of the Staten Island nine included stops in Cincinnati; St. Louis; Keokuk, Iowa; Springfield, Illinois; Jackson, Michigan; and Guelph and Toronto in Canada.

Though reporters emphasized the presence of women at amateur matches (something they had ceased to do in regard to professional games), amateurs showed they could display just as much "ill-feeling" and inappropriate behavior on the field as their less gentlemanly professional brethren. The St. Louis Red Stockings, for instance, convinced that their hosts, the Keokuk Westerns, had provided an umpire with a hometown bias, simply walked off the field. Two explanations surfaced: (1) the Westerns were attempting to win the game unfairly, and (2) the Red Stockings left the field for insufficient reasons. Whichever story one accepts, at least one of these gentlemanly amateur nines was behaving according to a standard not noticeably higher or purer than that upheld by professional nines. And when the Arlington Club of New York visited the Graftons of Worcester, they ended up having to pay for their transportation to and from the grounds, as well as for advertisements that never appeared. Describing their experience in a sarcastic letter to the papers, they concluded by acknowledging "another little delicate attention extended by the Graftons, viz., the umpire, under whose rulings it would be impossible for any visiting club to win." [11]

So clubs' interactions under the banner of amateurism had all the earmarks of those in the professional arena. Within clubs, too, amateur status seems not to have impeded the development of structures common to professional clubs. Of the Staten Island Club's more than two hundred members in 1873, only twenty-eight (14 percent) played in any of the club's twenty-five matches. Nearly half of the twenty-eight played in fewer than five matches. Eighty-five percent of the club members, in other words, played in no matches at all, while the regular players accounted for less than 10 percent of the members. This was more participation than there would have been if the club had employed a professional nine, and it is conceivable that the possibility of playing in a match was perceived as genuine by the regular members. The structure of the club, however, in terms of who did the playing and who did the watching, was a far cry from the amateurist ideal of universal participation, and was much closer to that of a professional club. Other amateur clubs were organized similarly. The Resolutes of Fall River, Massachusetts, reported sixty members at the close of the 1873 season, but only fourteen had participated in any of the club's games, and of those only nine or ten could be considered regulars. Boston's active Beacon Club played twenty-six matches that year, but averages were listed for just fourteen players. When they were not proclaiming the beauties of amateur baseball, reporters wrote about top amateur clubs as though they were professionals. "Accessions to their playing strength" had helped the Staten Island Club in 1873, while the Nameless Club (of Brooklyn) came in for criticism the following year for fielding a light-hitting shortstop when better men could have been found: "the directors of the club will be derelict in their duty if they fail in this important matter"; the entire "infield needs a thorough overhauling." [12]

Had such grandiose claims not been made for the purifying nature of amateur ball, there would be little point in scrutinizing its results. But the amateurists both expressed and drew upon powerful emotions. That very intensity of feeling calls for a close look at what organized amateurism was able to produce. And its product strongly resembled the better clubs of the early 1860s, such clubs as the Mutuals, Excelsiors, and Athletics. All of these clubs carefully assembled "first-class" nines, practiced assiduously, and eagerly pursued ballfield victories (including the "championship") with little interest in the "pure love of sport"—a category reserved precisely for those clubs that did not "acquire" players or practice regularly, and did not (and could not) compete for the championship.

Let us conclude this chapter with two versions of amateurism that pointedly illustrate its difficulties. The *Spirit of the Times* of November 14, 1874, carried the record of the amateur Easton Base-Ball Club for the season just concluded, a record "unsurpassed by any amateur club in the arena." Between May 6 and October 28 the club had played forty-two games, often playing twice a week, sometimes every other day, and during one week four times. Overall the club won most of its games (thirty-three), but it did not play only amateurs: in its contests with professional clubs, it lost five of eight. Despite the charged language often used to describe the vices of professional baseball, amateur clubs did not completely seal off their arenas from the activities of professional clubs. Nor did the Easton Club look very different from its professional counterparts. Ten players accounted for all but a handful of the club's runs (675 of 704, or 96 percent), and the Eastons' success was attributed to its president, vice-president, and "captain, [who] has had full management of the doings of the club for the past three seasons, arranging all games and doing all the correspondence. That he did his work thoroughly, the club record will tell."[13]

In what sense was the Easton Club amateur? Its nonprofessional status could have consisted only in the nonpayment of its playing nine. Even so, the club played frequently enough and "visited" far enough afield to raise questions about whether players were being paid. As I have suggested, that single boundary may have been the most important of all to ballplayers of the time. And yet, short of an explicit paycheck, the social relations of playing ball on the Easton nine resembled much more than they differed from those of a genuinely professional team. In both cases, the nines were playing for keeps.

In the next version of amateurism we can see that an attempt to move backward in cultural time imported more from the present than was realized by those who made the attempt. The Brooklyn Excelsiors, a powerhouse of metropolitan baseball in the early 1860s which had since declined, went up the Hudson River to Peekskill on July 4, 1870. It was, in effect, a trip back in time, as they went "to avail themselves of passing the Fourth pleasantly in the country, and on a ball field where the surroundings would remind them of the good old times when games were played for the pleasure and excitement incident to the sport." This was an unusual way to describe the Excelsiors, the club that began paying the young James Creighton under the table as early as 1860. But even during this idyllic visit ten years later, when the Excelsiors found that the "villagers" had taken the lead, their captain "roused" them "to the necessity of doing earnest work." The players responded to the call and "carried the enemy's works by storm."[14]

Here we see the emotions to which baseball commentators appealed, as well as the vocabulary (and ideology) that crept into efforts to describe an era that no longer existed, if indeed it ever had. The reporter's knowledge of the game in 1870 betrayed his attempt to re-create the lost world of the good old times. Whether or not the Excelsiors had all this in mind, of course, is another question. However eager they may have been to pass the Fourth "pleasantly in the country," they may not have been trying to recapture old times, nor need they have thought of their efforts to win as "work." They did, however, respond to the call of their captain and play hard enough to make a comeback. The reporter's effort to cast the event as a journey into the good old days was a failure, just as amateurism itself failed to recreate a golden past. Even the partisans of the amateur movement—such as the reporter—undermined their cause, and the world of the amateur ended up looking (as it does today) very much like the world of the professional, encased in the structures of work.

8

Professional Leagues and the Baseball Workplace

"Baseball Is Business Now"

If the events of 1870 led some members of the baseball fraternity to forsake professional baseball altogether in the name of a newly discovered ideology of amateurism, they led others to plunge further into organizing the professional game. Following the 1870 convention of the National Association of Base Ball Players, it was widely assumed that the professional clubs would form their own association. When professional representatives met in March 1871 and founded the National Association of Professional Base Ball Players, therefore, their action caused no special excitement. Historians, in retrospect, have called this association baseball's first professional league, the first attempt to structure the baseball business. Because it was in name an association of players rather than clubs, historians have tended to assume that during its five-year lifespan, professional players themselves controlled the organization of the game. The brief interlude of "workers' control" came to an end, in this view, when the National League of Professional Base Ball *Clubs* was established in 1876 and placed control firmly in the hands of baseball's businessmen. Albert Spalding gave credence to this version when, thirty-five years later, he described the founding of the National League:

The idea was as old as the hills; but its application to Base Ball had not yet been made. It was, in fact, the irrepressible conflict between Labor and Capital asserting itself under a new guise. . . . Like every other form of business enterprise, Base Ball depends for results on two interdependent divisions, the one to have absolute control and direction of the system, and the other to engage—always under the executive branch—the actual work of production.[1]

In point of fact, the two organizations were more alike than has been supposed. Players did not run the first professional association. The only active player at its founding meeting was Harry Wright, who by then had transferred his managerial abilities and loyalties to the new Boston Red Stockings. Conventions of the association consisted of but one delegate from each of the member clubs (the number varied between eight and thirteen). Other than Wright, only two or perhaps three other active players ever attended these meetings. Along with Wright, the most prominent player in the NAPBBP was Captain Robert Ferguson (of the New York Mutuals, Brooklyn Atlantics, and Hartfords), whose two terms as president of the association have misled historians into overestimating the players' influence. But Ferguson himself acknowledged the effective division between players and management just after his election: "On taking the chair he thanked the Convention for the honor conferred on him, which he looked upon not only as an honor to him, but to the *playing class*." Ferguson's presidency was an "honor," a completely ceremonial position indicating the minimal power players actually had in the association's affairs.[2]

The NAPBBP dealt with three basic issues—establishing a recognized championship, rules changes, and the enforcement of player contracts—and did so with moderate success. Although the "whip pennant" awarded to its most successful club did not put an end to disputes between other would-be champions, the association did rationalize the competition so as to produce one "Champion of the United States." And its authority over the rules of the game went unchallenged.

It was not, however, much of a business organization. Clubs could enter the lists for the championship merely by paying a $10 entry fee, but it seems to have been difficult for the baseball public to support more than eight or nine professional clubs at a time. Five of the eleven entries in 1872 failed to finish the season. Two of nine dropped out in 1873, and four of the thirteen starters in 1875 withdrew after running up dismal records. Only one complete set of starters finished a season—the eight clubs of 1874.[3] Revolving was an equally serious problem. Not only an issue between clubs, it was also an indication of changed relations between clubs and their player "representatives," now employees. The baseball businessmen of the NAPBBP recognized this fact, and their most important achievement may very well have been their success in converting the problem of revolving membership into a question of employee contracts.[4]

Important developments in baseball history can be observed in the language as well as the structure of the game. Almost as abruptly as the vocabulary of management had entered the baseball lexicon to stay in 1867, the term "business-like" began to be used widely only four years later. In stories about the upcoming 1871 season, for example, player contracts were big news. One Ned Cuthbert had agreed to leave the Philadelphia Athletics for the Chicago White Stockings on the condition that "the consent of his family could be obtained to reside in Chicago." He (or the White Stockings) failed to get the family's approval, and the two clubs quarreled over the player each claimed. According to a reporter who disapproved of the entire proceeding, "the only conclusion to be arrived at, is that a more unbusiness-like transaction could scarcely be imagined." What was "unbusiness-like" about the transaction, of course, was that Cuthbert did not sign as a free actor in the market, and combined a personal consideration with what, to the reporter, ought to have been a simple labor contract. In commercial, "business-like" baseball, players were to be treated as completely mobile, unfettered individuals free to contract with any club independently of familial, geographical, or fraternal considerations.

Assessments of players began to emphasize "business-like" behavior, a combination of qualities grouped around silence and steadiness on the ballfield. Charles Mills of the Mutuals, for instance, was "quiet and business-like on the field," like his teammate, the "quiet, steady" Joe Start. On this remarkable team, the third baseman was "quiet, steady, and well-behaved," the right fielder not only a "sure catch" but a "hard, steady worker," and the center fielder "steady, cool, and quiet." Not all of these characteristics, it should be noted, were just being discovered. Players had been commended for their coolness and self-control ever since the late 1850s. But "quiet" was a new form of praise, and in combination with "steady" it described the ideal conduct of paid labor. Quietness and steadiness were qualities that meshed perfectly with the managerial demands of the Mutuals' Captain Robert Ferguson, who, it was predicted, would "insist upon implicit obedience from his men."[5]

Clubs, too, found their behavior and play judged in these terms. When the Stars arrived late for a game with the Olympics, they were enjoined to "remember that it is not only discourteous but thoroughly unbusiness-like to keep their opponents, and maybe a couple of thousand people, waiting their pleasure." Later that week the Bostons and Olympics played a game "with greater quietness and business-like purpose" than the reporter had ever seen. While objecting to umpires' decisions had always been frowned upon, and "growling" among players had frequently drawn criticism from reporters and commentators, quietness itself had rarely been touted as so desirable. Similarly, steadiness, while always appreciated as a virtue, took on new importance as the game was reordered.[6]

The biggest problem for baseball's businessmen and their supporters was that the game plainly was not, and could not be made into, a predictable, rationalized commodity easily managed by business principles. Outcomes of baseball games were, and remain, notoriously difficult to predict, and even the best clubs have bad days. Off days became more frequent in the late 1860s and early 1870s, when clubs began to play fifty or more games in a season. Because the lifeblood of professional baseball—gate receipts—depended on spectators and the weather, scheduling was a major issue.

The NAPBBP had no fixed schedule, so it fell to Harry Wright, as secretary of the Boston Base Ball Association, to make all his scheduling and financial arrangements with other clubs. This was an extremely time-consuming process, often requiring extensive negotiation. Fully 90 percent of Wright's correspondence from 1871 to 1875 consisted of inquiries or responses to inquiries about possible games. Wright understood that a schedule had to be adapted to the habits of potential spectators, so he tried to space out games in a particular city and avoid saturating the market. He also wrote dozens of letters arranging games for July 4 and other holidays, when especially large attendance could be expected.[7]

Watching Wright struggle to put together a profitable schedule, we can see his attempts to subordinate all his feelings about the game and his fellow players—friends as well as enemies—to the goal of constructing a stable, ongoing business concern. Although Wright had been making a living in sport since the early 1860s, and in baseball since 1867, he was still powerfully affected by the fraternal pull of the game. Occasionally he reminisced about the "Old Red Stockings" in purely personal terms, while he was perfectly able to turn that sentiment into a money-making proposal that played on the public interest in the champions of 1869. Four players from that team were on the Bostons, and the other five were on the Washington Olympics; Wright proposed splitting up the nines so as to play "the 'Red Stocking Nine' vs. Olympic and Boston," if the ground proprietor "will make us a respectable offer."[8]

Wright was not alone in his strong emotions about the game. He did stand out, however, in his relatively successful attempts to control that emotion, or to direct it into profitable channels. Upon receiving a letter from his friend Nick Young (of the Olympics), Wright tried to soothe Young's distress at Wright's scheduling a game with the rival Washington Nationals. "I am very sorry there is so much feeling existing between your two clubs," he wrote. "I made the game with the Nationals first, because my experience has taught me that the [Boston] nine play a better game when they play the weaker club first. Again, we could not ignore the Nationals, as they are an old club, and playing them the last game would be about as much. I look on our game with your nine as certain to draw a large crowd if it was the last of half a dozen games." Young's displeasure was a combination of the insult he felt he had sustained at the hands of his friend Harry, anger at being scheduled last, and worry that the final game would not draw as big a crowd as the first. Wright tried to please all parties, but was especially interested in keeping clubs inside the fold. He tried to ensure that association membership remained stable, that each club stayed happy enough with the scheduling to complete a full complement of championship contests. No one else in the new league seems to have taken on this burden, and yet it was essential that these principles be observed if the league were to survive—or rather, if the member clubs were to survive as moneymaking concerns and remain in the professional association. As Wright put it to Young with unusual clarity and self-consciousness, "Base ball is business now, Nick, and I am trying to arrange our games to make them successful and make them pay, irrespective of my feelings, and to the best of my ability. If I should fail, then I will try and do better next time."[9]

This statement is revealing in two ways. First, Wright needed to make clear the extent to which the principle he enunciated was a departure from previous practices, and poorly understood by his colleagues. Second, it illustrated the conflict between feelings and business that existed in Wright himself as well as between clubs. Having participated in the baseball fraternity for up to fifteen years, many club officials found it difficult to subordinate fraternal feelings (including conflicts) to the demands of the baseball marketplace. Wright's own resolution of the conflict in favor of business principles was far from complete, as he explicitly acknowledged ("if I should fail"). Further showing the strain of his effort, Wright concluded the letter fraternally: "I am pleased to see the kindly feelings expressed in your letter, and I can assure you of the same being fully returned when you visit our city. Trusting that we will have a pleasant game, and more of them . . ."

Because winning teams drew more spectators and gate money than losing ones, manager-captains—with the backing of boards of directors—tried to fashion a productive process that maximized championship victories. First, they sought to make their own authority absolute, to ensure that they could train, position, and supervise their labor force as they wished. This authority, which they considered justified by their need for an obedient, disciplined work force, extended far beyond the confines of the baseball workplace—the ballfield—to players' social and drinking habits, their living arrangements, even the time they went to bed.

Accordingly, club directors formulated new rules to govern players' conduct. From instruments of collective, fraternal, clubwide self-discipline, club rules became regulations for the players to follow and for the captains and the club to enforce. If only the 1872 regulations for the Cleveland Forest City Club were "stringently enforced," predicted the *Spirit of the Times*, the club would be favored to win the championship. These measures were clearly intended as guidelines for labor discipline, even though they continued to hold to the fiction that the players were "members" and not employees of the "club." The captain, they asserted, had "full control" over and total responsibility for the "discipline of the club." He was to "require the members to practice each day" except match days and Sundays and to report "absentees" and "misconduct" to the board of directors; he was empowered to suspend any player for "disobedience of orders, intoxication, or conduct unbecoming a gentleman." A player's unapproved absence entitled the board to cancel his contract, and any "refusal to obey the captain in the exercise of his lawful authority" rendered him liable to a fine or expulsion. Perhaps the sternest of a severe set of

regulations—and one all but inconceivable a mere ten years earlier
—was the following:

> *Fourth.*—During the playing season every member of the club is *re-*
> *quired* to abstain from the use of intoxicating liquors in any shape, and
> from keeping late hours. And if, at any time during the season, any
> member of the club becomes intoxicated or incapacitated and unable
> to play base-ball from the effects of dissipation or disease brought on
> by the same, the Board may suspend, fine, or expel him on the charge
> being proven.

Had these rules been "strictly enforced," observed Chadwick after the
season, "the nine would not have been disbanded as they were." [10]

Ballfield victories proved so difficult to guarantee that club officials strove to control factors outside the game which could affect
players' performance. Harry Wright instituted preseason training for
his teams, and his contracts required players to report up to a month
before the opening of the season. Even as the professional association
was holding its organizing meeting in New York City, the Red Stockings were "busily at work training themselves in the Tremont Gymna-
sium," which the *Spirit of the Times* reported was "splendidly fitted
up with every convenience and appliance that a hard-working ath-
lete could ask for." When they were not "working," the Boston players were "all under the watchful eye of the astute Harry. George
[Wright], Harry, and Gould live together, and the other seven 'boys'
live next door in a private house, so they are all under Harry's wing."
This kind of living arrangement was standard for the Boston players,
who, like those of other clubs, traveled together and stayed in the
same hotels when away from "home." Harry Wright exercised fatherly and managerial authority over his players. Paternalistic as well
as contractual, baseball's labor relations resembled those of an early-
nineteenth-century workshop in which journeymen lived under the
same roof as their master. [11]

Wright's system appears to have aroused little objection, at least
partly because it fitted so well into the emotional patterns that had
prevailed as long as the game had been organized. Men and boys,
veterans and rookies, old-timers and juveniles, seniors and juniors,
metaphorical fathers and sons had been inextricably linked on the
playing field, in baseball organizations, and in the consciousnesses of

players, reporters, and fans from baseball's earliest days. Periodic attempts to purify either the adult or children's realm had failed without exception.

Nor were these relationships only emotional. New players always came from the ranks of youth; in 1871 the average age of the eighty-three professional players listed in *Beadle's* was between twenty-four and twenty-five. Only six of these players were thirty or older (and two were just thirty). Without these six players, the average age of the remaining seventy-seven players was just over twenty-three and a half. Few were married, so their position in the baseball family was clearly that of sons.[12]

When Harry Wright referred to his players as "the boys," as he did frequently, he was fairly accurate. The term nevertheless illustrated the peculiarities of his relation to his players, in which his managerial authority was enhanced by his emotional involvement with them. On the other hand, that very closeness occasionally allowed him to forget his paternal role and relax as one of the boys. The pull to do so must have been irresistible at times. One evening during spring training in 1872, for example, he finished a letter with a reference to his newest player, Andrew Leonard: "Andy is now in the parlor singing to an accompaniment on the piano. He is quite an addition to our band (of brothers)."[13]

In dealings with his players, especially when he was negotiating contracts or trying to persuade them to accept a difficult situation, Wright could cajole and flatter in a way that relied heavily on the personal relationships he had established. Attempting to get second-baseman Ross Barnes to sign with the club for another season, Wright told him how exciting it would be to announce Barnes's return at a club meeting that week:

> I should be pleased to announce, proclaim, enunciate, inform those assembled . . . that you have . . . *consented*, condescended, to travel with when necessary, *stay* with when wanted, and play with the Champion nine for the season of 1873. See what *Eclat* that will give us. "Ross Barnes going to play with the Boston nine again." Hurrah! Rah! Rah! Rah! (Echo in the streets.) Hurrah! You want to play with us, of that I am certain.[14]

Although he could be corny and patronizing, Wright was a shrewd businessman who insisted that ballplayers take all of the risks in a contract. He was also extremely scrupulous as a business manager, probably much more so than most of his counterparts. When the Red Stockings fell short one year and could not pay the players their full salaries, Wright did not try to hide the fact, but made sure that the amounts owed were paid the following year. When a player was so dissatisfied with a club policy that he threatened to abrogate his contract, Wright—in a firm and fatherly manner—attempted to show him that the policy was necessary, that breaking his contract was foolish and would injure his "future prospects," and offered to give him his "honorable release" if "you are dissatisfied with our management . . . and would prefer to try your future with some other nine."[15] Wright struggled, in other words, to preserve the emotional context of the game as he had known it for many years, at the same time that he worked long hours to make it a successful business.

The Origins of Baseball Statistics

In their search for predictable victories, baseball directors and captains developed new methods of evaluating their players. As employees of stock companies, players were considered to be potential subordinates as well as practitioners of baseball skills. That Robert Ferguson's players did what they were told and "went about their business quietly" became as important as the quality of their field play. Similarly, Harry Wright's evaluations of players were not simply assessments of skill but analyses of player-*workers* as well. His advice to a manager about to hire Asa Brainard, Wright's pitcher on the Cincinnati Red Stockings, was characteristic. Brainard, Wright observed, was a "hard worker in games, especially first class ones," and played a "good uphill game." His baseball talents were outstanding, but any agreement with him should be "*all* on *paper*, and properly signed and witnessed." He would "shirk practice" from time to time and get "notions in his head, but a little plain talk, play or no pay, is usually effective." Wright figured that "his experience for the last two seasons, and his being a married man," would have so "improved him" that he was a "good investment, for this season and the next also." After being something of a troublemaker, in short, Brainard had settled down.[16]

But getting the game and its players to settle down and become predictable was finally an impossible job, no matter how hard Wright tried. Occasionally his exasperation burst out, as it did in a revealing letter to Henry Chadwick. Ross Barnes needed "driving" more than any other player, Wright complained, because of both his "careless and indifferent play" and his constant "finding fault with his accommodations." James O'Rourke's "thinking of 'the girl I left behind'" and his "stubborn disposition" nearly got him thrown off the field, while Cal McVey responded to a suggestion by a stand-in captain by telling him "to go to h—." "Stubbornness," daydreaming, and "odd notions" were the same sorts of problems in players that unreliability was in the scheduling of games between clubs. Irregularity, unreliability, bad weather, injuries, slumps—all compounded the difficulties of running a baseball business.[17]

Players' ballfield performance, the key to club victories, remained one of the least predictable ingredients of baseball success. Many of Harry Wright's colleagues lacked his eye for baseball talent. Moreover, the sheer geographical spread of the game by this time made it impossible for any one person to observe all of the potentially first-rate ballplayers. As a result, the late 1860s and early 1870s saw the development of a highly sophisticated means of evaluating players: baseball statistics.

Almost everyone who has written about the history or significance of baseball has remarked upon or celebrated the importance of the game's statistics. Only Allen Guttmann, in his attempt to discover "why baseball was our national game," has seen "the tendency of baseball toward extremes of quantification" as fundamental to the game's preeminence in the nineteenth century. Guttmann's insightful and elegant essay demonstrates that baseball statistics have figured prominently in the best fiction written about the game, as well as in reporters' and fans' analyses and experiences of baseball. This "wealth of quantified information," Guttmann argues, is a mark of baseball's "modernity," and he asks whether "baseball's special attraction"

lies in its primitive-pastoral elements and simultaneously in its extraordinary modernity, in its closeness to the seasonal rhythms of nature and, at the same time, in the rarified realm of numbers? I assume that we have here not a contradiction but a complexity, a paradoxical situation in which the special, carefully bounded and regulated conditions of a game enable us to have our cake and eat it too, to calculate the chances of a fastball or a successful bunt and, at the same time, to luxuriate in the warm sunshine of an April afternoon.[18]

Even if true, these lyrical speculations do not explain why the game was quantified in the way it was and when it was. Nor do they address the prior question: Why baseball statistics at all? The principal answer is that baseball statistics were developed, employed, and promoted as measures of players' productivity on the ballfield. As baseball players became baseball workers employed by baseball businesses, statistics multiplied and became radically more sophisticated. They were touted explicitly as the only way of truly measuring players' performance over the course of an entire season, in a manner that would permit an objective assessment of their value to their clubs.

Some statistics existed before the game became openly professional, so it was not only the primacy of business principles that led to such measurements. Cricket, after all, had fairly extensive statistics, and baseball reporters clearly borrowed from the English game, however reluctant they may have been to admit the fact later on.

As early as 1864, Henry Chadwick had argued that the averages he listed in *Beadle's* "must be regarded as the only fair criterion of a player's skill, in the matter of batting, at any rate." He continued in words well ahead of their time:

Many a dashing general player, who carries off a great deal of *eclat* in prominent matches, has all "the gilt taken off the gingerbread," as the saying is, by these matter-of-fact figures, given at the close of the season; and we are frequently surprised to find that the modest but efficient worker, who has played earnestly and steadily through the season, apparently unnoticed, has come in, at the close of the race, the real victor.[19]

This observation, which by invoking the "efficient worker" anticipates the game's development into a business, Chadwick repeated in his annual guides through the late 1860s. He remained a partisan of the steady, efficient worker as he gave advice on "captaining a nine." The "steady earnest workers" were worth "two of your dashing, brilliant players, who shine one day, and play listlessly the next."

For this reason Chadwick opposed the practice of giving prizes for home runs, because (in a pattern we recognize today) the batters who hit the most "generally [had] the poorest average of bases on hits." A reporter in early 1868 made a similar observation in the course of praising the play of the veteran Dickey Pearce:

> The fact is, players who engage in matches frequently have learned the value of economizing their strength, and I specially commend the judgment shown by Pearce in contenting himself with securing his first-base easily rather than in exhausting his strength in extra efforts for more bases on hits. Long hits are showy, but they do not pay in the long run. Sharp grounders assuring the first-base certain, and sometimes the second-base easily, are worth all the hits made for home-runs which players can strive for. Take the average of heavy hitters, and you will find that those who go in for the Pearce style possess the best record at the close of the season.[20]

Here we see standards of productivity being developed and applied to baseball players. Even more, these baseball standards were consciously being adapted to the predictable rhythms of industrial work imposed by many nineteenth-century employers. The effort to bring regularity to baseball work and steadiness to baseball's workers was extended to the play of entire clubs. The Atlantics' "spasmodic" play instead of steady, persevering work, warned one reporter, would hurt the club's financial prospects.[21]

Despite Chadwick's early efforts, the game's statistics remained rudimentary before the emergence of open professional ball in the late 1860s. Until 1869, season totals usually consisted of figures, by player, for the total and average (per game) outs made and runs scored. Some clubs compiled much more extensive records of their nines' play, but the "averages" were mathematically quite primitive. Only in 1869 did statisticians start to publish "averages of bases on hits" (that is, the average number of times per game a batter reached first base on a base hit), according to Chadwick "the only true criterion of a batsman's skill." That same year Chadwick introduced his "latest and improved system of scoring," which would "provide correct and reliable data for a true estimate of the skill of each player at the bat and in the field in a game." The following year saw the beginning of genuine decimal averages in the record books, and the averages given in the 1871 *Beadle's* for the professionals of the previous season began to resemble the form that baseball batting averages have had for nearly a century.[22]

These numerical indices furnished an objective yardstick by which employers could measure the abilities of players they had never seen. As professional baseball expanded geographically, statistics became increasingly important to managers. In the absence of personal contact, Harry Wright relied on statistics to evaluate unknown players. "James White is not here," he wrote to a Pennsylvania hopeful, "so I can learn nothing from him in regard to your playing abilities, but if you will send me the record of your play this season . . . I can form a good idea."[23] It is only by looking at baseball as work, then, and not as play, that we can understand this characteristic—and otherwise seemingly paradoxical—feature of the national game.

The National Association of Professional Base Ball Players lasted only five years. Because it had no screening mechanism, it could not ensure that member clubs were, for example, located near a large pool of potential spectators, or that they could rely on an adequate amount of invested capital. Relatively high player salaries, which the association was unable to curb, contributed to clubs' financial problems. In the unstable situation generated by so many club failures, the commercially successful clubs—such as the Red Stockings and Athletics—could dominate association play, and Harry Wright's team won four of the five NAPBBP pennants. (The Athletics won the first.) Finally, by 1875 powerful antagonisms had arisen between the Athletics and a number of other clubs, including Boston and Chicago. This combination of financial weakness and club conflict paved the way for what one historian has called, accurately, the "National League coup."[24]

The most important changes in baseball during these years took place at the level of the professional clubs, where baseball play was being transformed from a self-disciplined, fraternal craft into baseball labor, a form of work organized, directed, and disciplined by a management accountable to a board of directors. The new baseball player-workers, predominantly young men from the artisanal and clerical worlds, were apparently happy to trade independence for the high salaries of the baseball "club," while baseball's new businessmen struggled, with only modest success, to rationalize the game into a paying concern.

The National League

While baseball clubs were competitors in the search for players and on the ballfield, they also had a mutual interest in making the game as a whole into a stable, profitable enterprise. Whereas Gilded Age industrial corporations had gobbled up competitors and tried to establish monopolies before creating cartels, baseball's most farsighted businessmen saw the need to order their competitive relationships much more quickly. After all, they were in the business of selling first-rate competition. If the competitors disappeared, so did the business. But ball clubs were not entirely unlike other corporations. They competed over markets and, in a sense, raw materials. (Baseball players may be conceptualized as both the raw materials and the labor of the baseball business.) It is not surprising, then, that the provisional solutions to their problems adopted by baseball owners resembled those developed by large industrial corporations.

William Hulbert of the Chicago White Stockings hatched a plan for a new baseball association based on territorial monopolies and a restricted number of strong, financially healthy clubs. Such a core group, he reasoned, could afford the unity that would be necessary to limit competition for players and reduce salaries. This new association, explicitly an organization of clubs—not players—would replace the National Association outright. Hulbert probably could not have carried off his scheme without the backing of Harry Wright, the most prestigious figure in the game; but Wright was so incensed by the Athletics and the association's inability to challenge them that he gave Hulbert his full support. At a conference of four eastern clubs called by Hulbert at New York's Central Hotel on February 2, 1876, the National League of Professional Base Ball Clubs was born. Hulbert wisely invited only the strongest clubs, so the National League was able flatly to replace the NAPBBP. It remained organized baseball's dominant institution until the turn of the twentieth century.[25]

An account of the National League's success in the frequently chaotic world of late-nineteenth-century professional baseball lies beyond the scope of this book. Shrewd, tough-minded business leadership certainly played an important role in the story. So did the growing size of the baseball business and the larger pocketbooks of the league's club owners. Still, it is worth pointing briefly to the ways in which the National League dealt with a few of the important issues raised during the previous twenty years of baseball history.

First, the league screened its members, requiring that clubs be based in cities with populations greater than 75,000 and admitting just one club in each such city, thus granting it a territorial monopoly. Second, in order to "regulate the baseball championship of the United States" and to guarantee each member club a certain number of playing dates with well-known clubs, the league instituted a playing schedule for all of its clubs before the 1877 season.

Third and most important, the league intervened decisively in the baseball workplace. Although such actions were sometimes justified as efforts to protect players from unscrupulous owners, the new league abandoned all pretense of being an association of players. Its constitution maintained that professional clubs and professional players had "mutual interests," but dealt with players as club subordinates. The league guaranteed to each club "the right to regulate its own affairs, to make its own contracts, to establish its own rules, and to discipline and punish its own players." Intending to unite its members against the market power of the ballplayers, it prohibited league clubs from employing anyone "who has been discharged, dismissed, or expelled from any club belonging to this League." Sanctions against offenders were harsh. Any club found to be in violation of this provision "shall be at once considered as having forfeited its membership in the League, and all other League clubs must and shall, under penalty of the forfeiture of their membership in the League, abstain from playing any such club for the remainder of the season."[26]

In some ways the baseball labor market of the 1870s resembled that of the mid-1970s immediately after the beginning of free agency: in both cases professional clubs felt compelled to pay the relatively high salaries demanded by the best players in the hope of attracting more spectators to watch winning baseball. But there were no tax advantages to operating a baseball business in the 1870s. Even the best-managed (and winningest) clubs rarely made much money. On receipts of almost $38,000 in 1875, for example, the Boston Red

Stockings cleared $3,261. The previous year the club had cleared $833. The Philadelphia Athletics cleared less than $10 for the two years 1871 and 1872. (Their $5,000 profit in 1872—on $26,000 in receipts—went to pay off the debts of the previous year.)[27]

One look at a club balance sheet was all it took to see the largest single expense. Players' salaries ran from $15,000 to $20,000 per club during these years, and club directors determined to bring them down. Their solution, first introduced in partial form in 1879 and expanded in 1883, was the reserve clause, the centerpiece of baseball's labor relations for nearly a century. This clause, added to every player's contract, made him eligible to play professional baseball only with his current club, and gave that club the right to "reserve" his baseball services (that is, reserve them from the market) for the following year. The club could exercise this right indefinitely, unless it traded or sold the player's contract to another club, which then could exercise the same right, or unless the club "released" him. No other club that was a party to the reserve rule could sign a player who wanted to ignore the rule, under penalty of expulsion from the National League. This rule, which in effect converted player-employees into club property, gave club owners extraordinary power over their employees' lives within organized baseball.

President Abraham Mills of the National League firmly believed that the reserve rule, by bringing stability to the baseball labor market, served players as well as clubs. He wrote to a colleague in 1883, as he was arguing for the rule's extension to cover eleven players instead of five:

> The course of professional base-ball playing in this country is strewn with the wrecks of clubs which have undertaken to carry a salary list they were utterly unequal to, resulting, of course, in the high priced players being stranded in mid-season, with considerable amounts due them by such clubs, which they have never yet received. This result is directly chargeable either to the unrestricted competition which prevailed when professional base-ball was inaugurated, or to the limited system attempted in more recent years, which the League has certainly given a fair trial.

Before the institution of the reserve rule (and the 1883 agreement by which three professional leagues agreed to respect each other's contracts), Mills claimed later, these conditions "render[ed] the disci-

pline requisite to the proper exhibition of the game on its merits prac-
tically impossible."[28]

The National League had performed a remarkable feat. Faced with
a high-priced work force, it had managed to convert each employee
into an indentured servant or, as the leader of the players' union
wrote a few years later, "a chattel." In the name of baseball progress
and stability, baseball's businessmen had imported a labor system
from the past (although the Emancipation Proclamation was only
twenty years old in 1883). They governed this system, however, with
the sanctions and labor practices of other Gilded Age industrial corporations. The National League kept a "black list" of particularly
troublesome players, while individual clubs enforced labor discipline
with fines, suspensions, temperance oaths, salary limitations and re-
ductions, demotions, and bed checks. Spalding even hired Pinkertons
to see if his men honored their pledge to abstain from alcohol.[29]

The league and its practices did not go unchallenged. Rival leagues
came and went; the National League bested some and reached accommodations with others. Sometimes the competition was over territory,
sometimes over players, sometimes over Sunday baseball, ballpark
drinking, or admission fees. But it was the struggle for the baseball
workplace that produced the most bitter battle between baseball
leagues in the history of the game: the 1890 "war" between the
National League and the Players' League—the latter founded by
the Brotherhood of Professional Base Ball Players, the players'
union. For players and owners alike the main issue was the National
League's labor practices, the most important of which was the reserve rule. The players lost their fight to regain control of the baseball workplace, and remained ever more firmly the property of their
employers. Nevertheless, claimed Albert Spalding, leader of the National League's "War Committee" in 1890, "the genius of our institutions is democratic; Base Ball is a democratic game." But the democracy of the national pastime could be celebrated only by those who
did not play the game and therefore *could* experience the ballpark exclusively as an arena of play. For those who worked there, the experience of the ballpark more closely resembled that of a benign planta-
tion, or perhaps a comfortable company town.[30]

Epilogue

Playing for Keeps

How did baseball players so quickly lose the power they had in the late 1860s and early 1870s? First, what they enjoyed in the earliest professional years is characterized more appropriately as individual marketplace freedom than as collective power. Only rarely did ballplayers negotiate with clubs as a group; the Brotherhood of Professional Base Ball Players was not organized until 1885. During the years when it counted the most, then, players only exercised their freedom—they did nothing to structure or protect it. Second, playing baseball well demanded skill, self-discipline, and practice, but few ballplayers seem to have shown much interest in using those qualities to manage the baseball business. Those who did—Albert Spalding, Harry Wright, Al Reach—quickly shifted their allegiance to the difficult business of making baseball pay. Third, the very size of player payrolls brought relatively wealthy businessmen into the game, men whose resources and experience made them formidable adversaries. And finally, players were young men in their early twenties, frequently unprepared for the world of contracts and corporations.

It is difficult to know how much Harry Wright's paternalistic management of the various Red Stockings served as a model for future club directors and managers. It is certain, however, that a similar paternalism became institutionalized in professional baseball, and still pervades the relationships between players and managers. What began as a kind of fraternal self-identification among ballplayers as "the boys" (even as they sought to distinguish themselves from the literal and figurative world invoked by "boys") gradually became part of managers', directors', and owners' ideological arsenal as they battled players over the structure of the baseball business in the late nineteenth century. The paternalism of the baseball world, like the continued use of the term "club," was plainly anachronistic. But it was not (and is not) an anachronism without purpose. Baseball owners, officials, and propagandists benefited enormously from their insistence that players were boys in the man's world of salaries, contracts, lawyers, and big business. These men have nearly always discussed baseball's labor relations in terms of parents and children.

The persistence of that strategy has been due in part to the variation in the lengths of baseball's many cycles. For it is not only the generational turnover among fans that produces the repetitive similarity of baseball's emotional history. A far more rapid rate of change governs the movement of players in and out of the game. Young players constantly take the place of their elders, and the process accelerated in the 1870s.

In the early years of the decade, most club captains were also players. By the latter 1870s and 1880s the playing captain was on the way out. Players remained roughly the same age, then, as their managers grew older. Managers had broken out of the player's short generational cycle into a longer one—they often saw many generations of players pass through their clubs. If these men treated their players, even veteran players, as children, their attitude is at least understandable.

As a managerial strategy too it was likely to be effective, personalizing an employer–employee relationship and invoking paternal authority in a situation that had genuine familial elements. The popularity of the nickname "Pops" for baseball managers and coaches suggests the quasi-filial attitude held by thousands of players toward their managers over the years. But "Pops," of course, could be used ironically and sarcastically as well, and when players rebelled against managerial authority, they did so frequently as errant boys: staying out late, running off without telling the manager, sulking over real or imagined poor treatment, objecting to being treated as children.

Club directors and owners have absorbed the metaphors and habits of thought of this father–son relationship with considerably less of the experience that would have given it life. Although generally they have treated their employees as employees, they have commonly used images of paternity to describe their feelings for their players, both positive and negative. Firmly anchored in the material structure of the game, more so than any other participants in the baseball world, they have constantly exploited the game's emotional language. The only real businessmen in clubs, they prefer to see themselves as benevolent baseball fathers. This self-image has led them to broadcast the "hurt" they feel when their "charges" seek control over their own salaries, working conditions, or freedom in the marketplace. Reacting with irrational force, owners have vigorously rejected nearly every attempt by players to organize, combine, and negotiate with them as equals. Rather than appeal to the ideology of capitalist business, owners have appealed to familial feeling, and acted as though their paternal care were being scorned. Baseball's peculiar labor practices led to even more peculiar emotions, for these reactions were less characteristic of corporate directors than of former slaveholders, emotionally distressed when their freed slaves chose not to continue in service to their erstwhile masters.

In those feelings they have usually been joined by fans, who also manage to fantasize a familial relation with the club, and who have always resented players' pursuit of their own individual or collective interests. Both owners and fans, after all, have had longer relationships with given clubs than the great majority of players. These two groups, therefore, have been in the odd position of seeing the short cycles revolve with what appears to be unseemly speed. That tension alone has tended to strengthen their attachment to the club and its long-term fortunes, an attitude that makes any one player (or manager) expendable. The player, of course, considers the interest of any one team expendable in the (to him) larger effort to further his own career, financial security, or postbaseball life.

One of the things that has made baseball history interesting in the last fifteen years is the fact that for the first time in nearly a century, the power relations between players and owners are changing substantially in the players' favor. Very few players, owners, administrators, or fans have known quite what to make of these changes, partly because their thinking still runs in the well-worn grooves I have been discussing. Despite the booming financial prosperity of the game, huge numbers of writers, fans, club and league officials, and even some players are profoundly disturbed by what they see as the spectacle of the kids taking over the candy store—a candy store that is now worth hundreds of millions of dollars. What they still cannot see is that the kids have not even raised the question of owning the store, though they have been quite adamant about getting a larger percentage on the candy they help to sell. Owners splutter and fulminate, aging sportswriters thunder about the salaries of utility players, veteran players mutter about the expectations of rookies, but the real changes have to do with the players' exercise of marketplace power in this imagined club and familial environment—a power they have not had since the 1870s. And because the players are now organized into a union—and one that has had extremely sophisticated leadership, a strong record of success, and a high degree of commitment from its members—the players' collective power is greater now than it has been at any earlier point since the 1890 season, when it looked for a brief time as though the Players' League might supplant the National League.

By bringing this power to bear on a set of relationships no longer insulated from the marketplace by the reserve rule, ballplayers are widely seen as violating the baseball equivalent of the family circle—an emotional haven in the heartless world of big business and hard-nosed money dealings. Linear history has invaded the cyclical history, and few observers, fans, or participants are entirely immune to the anxiety produced by the crossing of this boundary. For many, in fact, the categories collapsed into each other during the 1981 players' strike, and they simply could not or would not look directly at this upsetting, even painful phenomenon. Others responded by spraying vitriol over the sports pages and airwaves in an attempt to injure those responsible for the collapse.[1]

It is difficult to see what new structures—emotional or material —might arise to contain these developments. What can be predicted with some confidence is that as owners remain fixated on forcing players to accept some new version of the reserve rule, and as players resist their efforts with the strength born of collective victories, the baseball workplace will remain the chief battleground of baseball's near future. With the departure of Marvin Miller (the former director of the players' union) from the baseball scene, there is no truly imaginative leader in the game—no one even interested in exploring what baseball's future might look like.[2]

In the late 1850s organized baseball was a club-based fraternal sport thriving in the cultures of respectable artisans, clerks, shopkeepers, and middle-class sportsmen. Two decades later it had become an entertainment business run by owners, boards of directors, and managers, its exhibitions performed by player-employees. When baseball was most like what we tend to think of as play—when fraternal good cheer instead of salaries sustained its players—it was in fact quite close to the urban workplace. Artisans and clerks dominated first-rate play, and the language of the game was barely distinguishable from the language of productive labor. Better clubs took their play seriously, practicing regularly and specializing players' skills at one or two positions. Even clubs that did not strive for match victories, such as the Knickerbockers, struggled to make their game truly manly and respectable. During those years most of the basic emotional tensions of the game—manliness and boyishness, desire for victory and love of true sport, self-control and excitement, respectable and low behavior—were held together by the force of club fraternalism.

With the advent of widespread professionalism in the late 1860s, these tensions began to divide clubs, baseball associations, commentators, and fans, only to reproduce themselves anew at every level of the game. Two distinct kinds of baseball history appeared: one cyclical, repetitive, and emotional, the other linear, chronological, and material. The latter celebrated baseball's "progress" and "perfection," while the former became obsessed by an effort to recapture the good old days. Surviving until today, these competing histories have helped obscure the game's simultaneous development into an arena of play for spectators and work for players.

The point is not that baseball was destined (or doomed) to become just another business. It is rather that the experience of baseball play cannot be understood apart from the experience of work—inside as well as outside the game. Baseball play, whether self-disciplined in fraternal clubs or managed in paternalistic corporations, was nearly always serious. Baseball became the national game not simply because it was fun to play and watch but because it was played for keeps.

Notes

PROLOGUE

1. *American Chronicle of Sports and Pastimes,* January 9, 1868, p. 10. The author of the column used the pseudonym "Old Peto Brine," a play on the name of Peter O'Brien, one of the best-known baseball players of the early 1860s.

2. The first approach is taken by Harold Seymour, *Baseball,* 2 vols. (New York: Oxford University Press, 1960–1971), and by Steven A. Riess, *Touching Base: Professional Baseball and American Culture in the Progressive Era* (Westport, Conn.: Greenwood Press, 1980). The best such account of baseball's earliest years is Melvin L. Adelman, *A Sporting Time: New York City and the Rise of Modern Athletics, 1820–1870* (Urbana: University of Illinois Press, 1986). The best of the second genre is still Roger Kahn, *The Boys of Summer* (New York: New American Library, 1973). Baseball's oral histories also belong in this category. See especially Lawrence S. Ritter, *The Glory of Their Times: The Story of the Early Days of Baseball Told by the Men Who Played It* (New York: Macmillan, 1966); and John Holway, *Voices from the Great Black Baseball Leagues* (New York: Dodd, Mead, 1975).

3. Roger Angell calls this phenomenon "the web of the game." See his *Late Innings: A Baseball Companion* (New York: Simon & Schuster, 1982), pp. 361–379.

4. See Angell's pieces on the 1981 baseball strike grouped as "The Silence," in ibid., pp. 380–390. The irony is that Jackson himself really did play more for fun than for money, and not only because his salary was so low. On Jackson, see Donald Gropman, *Say It Ain't So, Joe! The Story of Shoeless Joe Jackson* (Boston: Little, Brown, 1979), and the fine review essay by Ronald Story, "The Greening of Sport: Jackson, Dempsey, and Industrial America," *Reviews in American History* 8 (September 1980): 386–392.

5. Melvin Adelman has made the best effort to date to compile these data on New York and Brooklyn club members and ballplayers between 1845 and 1870. I have relied heavily on Adelman's findings. See Adelman, *A Sporting Time,* chaps. 6–7. More recently, Stephen Freedman and George Kirsch have unearthed such information on ballplayers in Chicago and New Jersey. See Stephen Freedman, "The Baseball Fad in Chicago, 1865–1870: An Exploration of the Role of Sport in the Nineteenth-Century City," *Journal of Sport History* 5 (Summer 1978): 42–64; and George B. Kirsch, "The Rise of Modern Sports: New Jersey Cricketers, Baseball Players, and Clubs, 1845–1860," *New Jersey History* 101 (Spring–Summer 1983): 53–84. George B. Kirsch, *The Creation of American Team Sports: Baseball and Cricket, 1838–1872* (Urbana: University of Illinois Press, 1989), came to my attention as this book was going to press.

6. On nineteenth-century journalism, see Dan Schiller, *Objectivity and the News: The Public and the Rise of Commercial Journalism* (Philadelphia: University of Pennsylvania Press, 1981).

7. "George Wilkes," *Dictionary of American Biography* (New York, 1936), 20:218; Schiller, *Objectivity and the News*, p. 97. See also Alexander Saxton, "George Wilkes: The Disintegration of a Radical Ideology," paper presented to the Conference on Labor History, Walter Reuther Library of Labor and Urban Affairs and History Department, Wayne State University, October 1979. Iver Bernstein very kindly brought this paper to my attention before it was published in *American Quarterly* 33 (Fall 1981). On the competing *Spirits*, see Frank Luther Mott, *A History of American Magazines*, 5 vols. (Cambridge: Harvard University Press, 1957), 1:479–481, 2:202–204.

8. *Wilkes' Spirit of the Times*, May 11, 1861, p. 153; Saxton, "George Wilkes," pp. 15–16.

9. See Mott, *History of American Magazines*, 2:203, 3:208–209.

10. "Henry Chadwick," *Dictionary of American Biography* (New York, 1929), 3:587.

11. The earliest known description of "base-ball" is found in *A Pretty Little Pocket-Book* (London, 1744). Jane Austen's *Northanger Abbey*, published in 1818, includes a reference to the game. See Seymour, *Baseball*, 1:5–6; John A. Lucas and Ronald A. Smith, *Saga of American Sport* (Philadelphia: Lea & Febiger, 1978), p. 96.

12. This geneology was established definitively by Robert W. Henderson in his *Ball, Bat, and Bishop: The Origin of Ball Games* (New York: Rockport Press, 1947). The base-ball writer Henry Chadwick made the same point in the first edition of *Beadle's Dime Base-Ball Player* (New York, 1860), pp. 5–6. On Spalding, see Peter Levine, *A. G. Spalding and the Rise of Baseball: The Promise of American Sport* (New York: Oxford University Press, 1985).

13. Quoted in Frank G. Menke, *The Encyclopedia of Sports*, 3d rev. ed. (New York: A. S. Barnes, 1963), p. 66; Albert G. Spalding, *America's National Game* (New York, 1911), p. 20.

14. Efforts at debunking are seen most notably in Seymour, *Baseball*, 1:4–12; David Quentin Voigt, *American Baseball*, 2 vols. (Norman: University of Oklahoma Press, 1966–1970), 1:5–6.

15. Adelman found evidence of an earlier club—the New York Club—that disbanded after a few years, leaving no records. See his *Sporting Time*, p. 122.

16. Charles A. Peverelly, *The Book of American Pastimes* (New York, 1866), pp. 339–349, 357–358, 365–366, 371–372.

17. Ibid., pp. 472–474. Chadwick, ed., *Beadle's* (1860), pp. 31–35, describes and gives a brief history of the Massachusetts game and of the Massachusetts Association of Base-Ball Players.

18. The Knickerbocker rules are reproduced in Peverelly, *Book of American Pastimes*, pp. 347–348; and in Chadwick, ed., *Beadle's* (1860), p. 7.

1. THE BASE BALL FRATERNITY

1. *Constitution and By-Laws with Rules and Regulations of the Detroit Base-Ball Club, of Detroit, Mich.* (Detroit, 1868), p. 17.

2. "Muffin" was the term for an unskilled player, and "muffin play" indicated poor play. The baseball term "muff," meaning "error" or "to make an error," had its origin in "muffin." Throughout this period what we now call a team or a starting lineup was called a "nine," a term clearly influenced by cricket's "eleven."

3. That is, the first contest would be on one club's home field, the return match on the other's; if a third game was necessary, it would be played on "neutral" ground.

4. Dozens of such balls from the 1850s and 1860s are on display in the National Baseball Hall of Fame and Museum, Cooperstown, N.Y.

5. *Wilkes' Spirit of the Times*, September 27, 1862, p. 52, and October 25, 1862, p. 116; *New York Clipper*, November 3, 1860, p. 229. See also *Porter's Spirit of the Times*, November 22, 1856, p. 197, and May 14, 1857, p. 180.

6. *New York Clipper*, October 6, 1860, pp. 197, 195.

7. Ibid., February 2, 1861, p. 330. That same winter the Atlantics gave eight "invitation 'hops'" as well as a lavish third annual ball, which received equally lavish coverage in the sporting press. Expectations ran especially high for the balls of the Tammany-connected Mutual Club, which attracted prominent sportsmen and New York City politicians: *Wilkes' Spirit of the Times*, January 26, 1861, p. 324; February 9, 1861, p. 357; January 28, 1865, p. 343; March 24, 1866, p. 71. On the Mutuals and Tammany Hall, see Melvin L. Adelman, *A Sporting Time: New York City and the Rise of Modern Athletics, 1820–1870* (Urbana: University of Illinois Press, 1986), pp. 164–165. For a comprehensive treatment of baseball's political connections in the late nineteenth and early twentieth centuries, see Steven A. Riess, *Touching Base: Professional Baseball and American Culture in the Progressive Era* (Westport, Conn.: Greenwood Press, 1980), pp. 49–84.

8. *New York Clipper*, January 12, 1861, p. 306; December 29, 1860, p. 290. See also *Wilkes' Spirit of the Times*, December 24, 1859, p. 245; January 14, 1860, p. 294.

9. *New York Clipper*, August 27, 1859, p. 147, and July 28, 1860, p. 116; *Wilkes' Spirit of the Times*, May 23, 1863, p. 179. See also *Wilkes' Spirit of the Times*, October 4, 1862, p. 67; June 20, 1863, p. 243; May 13, 1865, p. 172.

10. *Wilkes' Spirit of the Times*, June 24, 1865, p. 259; April 30, 1864, p. 132; July 11, 1863, p. 292 (quoting *Providence Journal*); May 5, 1866, p. 147. See also ibid., June 20, 1863, p. 243; April 30, 1864, p. 132; May 14, 1864, p. 164; *New York Clipper*, October 6, 1860, p. 195; October 27, 1860, p. 221; February 2, 1861, p. 332; August 24, 1861, p. 146; August 31, 1861, p. 155.

11. *Wilkes' Spirit of the Times*, June 18, 1864, p. 242; May 6, 1865, p. 149; May 19, 1866, p. 178.

12. *New York Clipper*, May 26, 1860, p. 43; *Wilkes' Spirit of the Times*, October 15, 1859, p. 84.

13. *New York Clipper*, May 19, 1860, p. 37, and October 6, 1860, p. 195; *Wilkes' Spirit of the Times*, August 18, 1860, p. 379.

14. *Wilkes' Spirit of the Times*, October 6, 1860, p. 69; May 19, 1866, p. 178.

15. *New York Clipper*, July 9, 1859, p. 95; *Wilkes' Spirit of the Times*, January 28, 1865, p. 343. Also see *Wilkes' Spirit of the Times*, October 26, 1861, p. 116, and November 18, 1865, p. 188; *New York Clipper*, September 3, 1859, p. 160; November 17, 1860, p. 244, August 3, 1861, p. 124.

16. Harold Seymour, *Baseball*, vol. 1 (New York: Oxford University Press, 1960), pp. 23–24; Adelman, *A Sporting Time*, pp. 138–142.

17. This discussion is based on the extensive and pioneering research of Melvin L. Adelman in *A Sporting Time*. In particular, see the tables on pp. 126, 138–140, 155–156, 175–177. Adelman divided occupations into four general categories: professional and high white collar; low white collar–proprietor; skilled craftsman; and unskilled worker.

18. Stephen Freedman, "The Baseball Fad in Chicago, 1865–1870: An Exploration of the Role of Sport in the Nineteenth-Century City," *Journal of Sport History* 5 (Summer 1978): 56. These figures are based on the quarter of Chicago ballplayers during this period whom Freedman was able to locate in city directories. As is nearly always the case with such populations, their very "findability" pushes them up the class ladder. On New Jersey ballplayers, see George B. Kirsch, "The Rise of Modern Sports: New Jersey Crick-

eters, Baseball Players, and Clubs, 1845–1860," *New Jersey History* 101 (Spring–Summer 1983): 63. Almost a fifth of the ballplayers Kirsch found were students (10%), unskilled workers (4%), or semiskilled workers (4%).

19. One story did indicate that the formation of a baseball club had resulted from a game between the compositors of two Brooklyn papers, the *Eagle* and the *Union*, but that club and the *New-York Herald* Base Ball Club seem to have been exceptional: *Wilkes' Spirit of the Times*, May 19, 1866, p. 178. See also ibid., September 23, 1865, p. 54; November 18, 1865, p. 188; September 1, 1866, p. 12.

20. Ibid., November 30, 1861, p. 196; January 11, 1862, p. 293; September 23, 1865, p. 54; December 23, 1865, p. 259. For others see ibid., August 29, 1863, p. 403; October 3, 1863, p. 67; September 2, 1865, p. 13; September 9, 1865, p. 19; September 16, 1865, pp. 44, 45; October 21, 1865, p. 119; October 28, 1865, p. 140; June 2, 1866, p. 214. Freedman points out that most artisan ballplaying in Chicago during the late 1860s took place on what he calls "company clubs." His argument that companies sponsored these teams appears to be based on several famously (and unusually) paternalistic firms: the dry goods firms of John V. Farwell and Marshall Field, along with the Pullman Palace Car Co.: Freedman, "Baseball Fad in Chicago," pp. 54–55. Eastern workplace nines may have been sponsored by firm owners and managers, but I have seen no direct contemporary evidence of such relationships. Notices of such games in the sporting press implied that workers themselves organized the matches.

21. *New York Clipper*, October 6, 1860, p. 197; *Wilkes' Spirit of the Times*, December 8, 1866, p. 235. The Typographical Club of Philadelphia did attend the 1868 Philadelphia convention of the National Association: M. J. Kelly, *The Base-Ball Guide for 1868* (New York, 1868), p. 83. On typographers, see David Montgomery, *Beyond Equality: Labor and the Radical Republicans, 1862–1872* (New York: Random House, 1967), pp. 93–94, 172; George A. Stevens, *New York Typographical Union No. 6: Study of a Modern Trade Union and Its Predecessors* (Albany: New York State Department of Labor, 1913).

22. On the comparatively privileged position of New York City printers, see Sean Wilentz, *Chants Democratic: New York City and the Rise of the American Working Class, 1788–1850* (New York: Oxford University Press, 1984), pp. 130–131. On butchers, see ibid., pp. 137–139, but more especially Peter George Buckley, "To the Opera House: Culture and Society in New York City, 1820–1860" (Ph.D. diss., State University of New York at Stony Brook, 1984), pp. 343–344. On shipbuilders, see Adelman, *A Sporting Time*, pp. 125–126, and Wilentz, *Chants Democratic*, pp. 134–137.

23. "The Tompkins Blues, for example, were drawn from the ranks of Engine Company No. 30 and the butchers of Centre Market, attended the Chatham Theatre, and were known to be Tammany Hall Regulars. The Bowery [Theatre] had its own militia—the Hamblin guards—led by the stage manager John Stevens, that used the orchestra as a martial band for parades. The Star Volunteers, a military offshoot of Hose Company No. 34, used the Apollo Rooms for their semi-annual balls": Buckley, "To the Opera House," pp. 345–346.

24. Wilentz, *Chants Democratic*, p. 270.

25. No comprehensive list of fire companies or of baseball clubs exists, but the evidence I have been able to assemble suggests an overlap in the neighborhood of 80% to 90%. The discussion of volunteer fire companies relies on the following: Arlen R. Dykstra, "Rowdyism and Rivalism in the St. Louis Fire Department, 1850–1857," *Missouri Historical Review* 69 (October 1974): 48–64; Kathleen J. Kiefer, "Flying Sparks and Hooves: Prologue," *Cincinnati Historical Society Bulletin* 28 (Summer 1970): 83–107; Bruce Laurie, "Fire Companies and Gangs in Southwark: The 1840s," in *The*

Peoples of Philadelphia: A History of Ethnic Groups and Lower-Class Life, 1790–1940, ed. Allen F. Davis and Mark H. Haller (Philadelphia: Temple University Press, 1973), pp. 71–88; Rebecca Zurier, "The Volunteer Fire Station in Its Heyday, 1825–1865," chap. 2 of an unpublished study of fire-station architecture. For another analysis emphasizing the early game's relationship to volunteer fire companies, see Ian Tyrrell, "The Emergence of Modern Baseball, c. 1850–1880," in *Sport in History: The Making of Modern Sporting History,* ed. Richard Cashman and Michael McKernan (Brisbane: University of Queensland Press, 1979), pp. 205–226.

26. Zurier, "Volunteer Fire Station," p. 16.

27. In the case of the New York Mutuals, this symbol was a large green Gothic letter *M*; the Brooklyn Excelsiors carried a Gothic *E*. Later in the decade the Cincinnati Red Stockings sported a large red Gothic *C* on the breast of their uniform. Firemen, whose shirts were usually bright red, also wore identifying shirt fronts, sometimes displaying the number of their company and at times a crossed hook and ladder. For fine illustrations of Peck & Snyder's colorful line of baseball and other sports attire, see the advertisements reproduced in Janet S. Byrne, *American Ephemera* (New York: Metropolitan Museum of Art, n.d.), and the widely reproduced "New York Fashions," an 1869 lithograph by Ino Schuller, in Wells Twombly, *Two Hundred Years of Sport in America: A Pageant of a Nation at Play* (New York: McGraw-Hill, 1976), p. 78.

28. Theodore G. Gronert, "The First National Pastime in the Middle West," *Indiana Magazine of History* 29 (September 1933): 171–186. On the volunteer militia, see also Marcus Cunliffe, *Soldiers and Civilians: The Martial Spirit in America, 1775–1865* (Boston: Little, Brown, 1968), pp. 223–235, 247–251; Robert Ernst, *Immigrant Life in New York City, 1825–1863* (Port Washington, N.Y.: Ira J. Friedman, 1949), pp. 127–129; Susan E. Hirsch, *The Roots of the American Working Class: The Industrialization of Crafts in Newark, 1800–1860* (Philadelphia: University of Pennsylvania Press, 1978), pp. 99–101.

29. Elliott J. Gorn, *The Manly Art: Bare-Knuckle Prize Fighting in America* (Ithaca: Cornell University Press, 1986), pp. 49–50. Peter Levine argues that middle-class reformers' "ambivalence about their own society" led them to explore sport as a means of developing "values and character traits necessary for success." Physical and moral toughening could provide "relief from the rigors of the pursuit of material wealth—allowing the individual to reenter the battle with new energy": "The Promise of Sport in Ante-Bellum America," *Journal of American Culture* 2 (Winter 1980): 633–634. Benjamin Rader places "the conversion of mainstream Protestants to sports in the late nineteenth and twentieth centuries," but the key changes appear to have begun in the 1840s and 1850s, when sport was also justified "in terms of its utilitarian potentialities, its capacities to nurture better morals or to renew the mind and body for work": "Modern Sports: In Search of Interpretations," *Journal of Social History* 13 (Winter 1979): 318–319. E. Anthony Rotundo argues that a profound change in "the basis for masculine ideals—the shift from manhood of the soul to manhood of the body"—took place among northern white middle-class men in the first half of the nineteenth century: "Body and Soul: Changing Ideals of American Middle-Class Manhood, 1770–1920," *Journal of Social History* 16 (Summer 1983): 23–38. This brief summary of Victorian attitudes toward sport may be supplemented by John Rickard Betts, "American Medical Thought on Exercise as the Road to Health, 1820–1860," *Bulletin of the History of Medicine* 45 (March–April 1971): 138–145, and "Mind and Body in Early American Thought," *Journal of American History* 54 (March 1968): 790–801; Guy M. Lewis, "The Muscular Christianity Movement," *Journal of Health, Physical Education, and Recreation* 37 (May 1966): 27–28, 42; Walter E. Houghton, *The Victorian Frame of Mind, 1830–1870* (New Haven: Yale Univer-

sity Press, 1957), pp. 201–206; John A. Lucas and Ronald A. Smith, *Saga of American Sport* (Philadelphia: Lea & Febiger, 1978), pp. 108–115; Foster Rhea Dulles, *A History of Recreation: America Learns to Play*, 2d ed. (New York: Appleton-Century-Crofts, 1965), pp. 183–185.

30. Henry Chadwick, ed., *Beadle's Dime Base-Ball Player* (New York, 1860), p. 5. And see *Wilkes' Spirit of the Times*, February 14, 1863, p. 380, and December 17, 1864, p. 244; *New York Clipper*, August 20, 1859, p. 141, and June 1, 1861, p. 53. The best single discussion of Victorian health ideology and its relation to sport and physical education is found in Gorn, *Manly Art*, pp. 179–206.

2. EXCITEMENT AND SELF-CONTROL

1. *New York Clipper*, March 3, 1860, p. 364; *Wilkes' Spirit of the Times*, January 19, 1861, p. 308.

2. Frederick K. Boughton, secretary of the Atlantic Base Ball Club, to the editor of the *New York Daily News*, August 31, 1860; reprinted in *Wilkes' Spirit of the Times*, September 8, 1860, p. 5.

3. *New York Sunday Mercury*, August 9, 1863, in Henry Chadwick Scrapbooks, 1:7, in Albert G. Spalding Collection, New York Public Library; *New York Clipper*, August 15, 1863, p. 141; *Wilkes' Spirit of the Times*, August 15, 1863, p. 371.

4. *New York Sunday Mercury*, August 9, 1863.

5. Opposition to gambling on baseball games—on the part of fans as well as players—ought to be seen in the light of this powerful concern about the difficulty of self-control. It required "considerable moral self-control," thought Henry Chadwick, for a man who had bet heavily on a game to keep "from interfering in one way or another with the proceedings": Chadwick, ed., *Beadle's Dime Base-Ball Player* (New York, 1861), pp. 53–54.

6. Ibid. (1860), pp. 38–39. A number of commentators have focused on the importance of military language in early baseball. Steven M. Gelber in particular argues that, like military companies, baseball put a premium on discipline and machinelike cooperation, qualities that were most important in the new world of bureaucratizing business. "Both the real and the imagined link between war and baseball reinforce the interpretation of the game as one that appealed to men used to highly organized, bureaucratized, collective activity in which success and failure could occur at both the individual and the corporate levels": "Working at Playing: The Culture of the Workplace and the Rise of Baseball," *Journal of Social History* 16 (Summer 1983): 3–22. In my own view, Gelber radically overstates the importance of "bureaucratization" in the work world of the late 1850s and 1860s. The level and scale of corporate organization he describes existed in very few places until the rise of the large industrial corporations much later in the century. At this time, very few workers labored in such enterprises. In New York and Brooklyn, ballplayers were disproportionately concentrated in precisely those trades less affected by such developments. Melvin Adelman kindly showed me his unpublished critique of Gelber's argument, titled "Baseball, Business, and the Workplace: Gelber's Thesis Reexamined."

7. *Constitution and By-Laws with Rules and Regulations of the Detroit Base-Ball Club, of Detroit, Mich.* (Detroit, 1868), p. 17; *Revised Constitution, By-Laws, and Rules of the Hamilton Base Ball Club, Adopted 1858* (Jersey City, 1858), pp. 8–9; *By-Laws of the Harlem Base Ball Club, Embracing the Rules of Order* (New York, 1859), pp. 5–8;

Constitution, By-Laws, and Rules of the "M. M. Van Dyke" Base Ball Club (New York, 1865), p. 6; *By-Laws, Regulations, and Rules of the New York Base Ball Club of New York* (New York, 1861), pp. 10–12; Chadwick, *Beadle's* (1860), p. 39.

8. There were exceptions. The Harlem Club imposed 10-cent fines for all field offenses except swearing, which cost 50 cents for the first instance and merited expulsion for the second. One of the few clubs even to mention drinking in its by-laws, the club provided for immediate expulsion of a member "inebriated" at a meeting or practice, and forbade "spirituous liquors" at any game or entertainment of the club or its members. *By-Laws of the Harlem Base Ball Club*, p. 10. The Social Base Ball Club punished drunkenness a little less seriously, imposing a $1 fine for being "inebriated" at a club meeting or at field practice: Harold Seymour, *Baseball*, vol. 1 (New York: Oxford University Press, 1960), p. 20.

9. Chadwick, ed., *Beadle's* (1860), pp. 28, 30.

10. Not that players have ever been happy with the umpire's interpretive freedom. Among the arguments adduced to support an amendment to the rules in 1864 was that it would free the pitcher "entirely from any liability to the caprice of an umpire in reference to his interpretation of unfair balls," while taking "from the umpire that discretionary power which last season proved such a source of dissatisfaction, from the latitude it gave to an umpire to decide in favor of one club at the cost of another": *Wilkes' Spirit of the Times*, December 10, 1864, p. 229. Closer to home, umpires' vigorous enforcement of the balk rule in the 1988 season drew a huge outcry from players, fans, managers, and reporters.

11. Chadwick, ed., *Beadle's* (1860), pp. 30, 16; *New York Clipper*, November 9, 1861, p. 236. For criticism of "the waiting game," as it was called, see *New York Clipper*, July 12, 1862, p. 99; August 9, 1862, p. 130.

12. Chadwick, ed., *Beadle's* (1860), pp. 28–29; *Constitution and By-Laws of the National Association of Base Ball Players, with the Rules and Regulations of the Game of Base Ball* (New York, 1859), sect. 33, pp. 28–29.

13. "In all cases of players being touched on the bases, [the umpire] must decide for himself, no statements being worthy of credence, as no player can rightly judge in the matter": *New York Clipper*, July 12, 1862, p. 99.

14. *Wilkes' Spirit of the Times*, October 1, 1859, p. 52; *New York Clipper*, July 7, 1860, p. 93, and June 23, 1860, p. 74; emphasis in original.

15. See, for instance, *Wilkes' Spirit of the Times*, May 17, 1862, p. 173; August 22, 1863, p. 387; July 22, 1865, p. 332; October 21, 1865, p. 119; June 9, 1866, p. 231; *New York Clipper*, August 13, 1859, p. 132; June 23, 1860, p. 76; July 21, 1860, p. 107; March 29, 1862, p. 395; April 5, 1862, p. 403; June 28, 1862, p. 83; August 6, 1862, p. 122; *Wilkes' Spirit of the Times*, September 8, 1860, p. 5; October 6, 1860, p. 69; February 2, 1861, p. 340.

16. *New York Clipper*, May 14, 1859, p. 28; September 8, 1860, p. 164; emphasis in original.

17. Elliott J. Gorn, *The Manly Art: Bare-Knuckle Prize Fighting in America* (Ithaca: Cornell University Press, 1986), pp. 140–141.

18. *Wilkes' Spirit of the Times*, June 24, 1865, p. 259; *New York Clipper*, 8 November 24, 1860, p. 250. See also *New York Clipper*, December 8, 1860, p. 271.

19. *Wilkes' Spirit of the Times*, July 9, 1864, p. 292. Similar difficulties among New Jersey clubs are described in George B. Kirsch, "The Rise of Modern Sports: New Jersey Cricketers, Baseball Players, and Clubs, 1845–1860," *New Jersey History* 101 (Spring–Summer 1983): 77–80.

20. *Wilkes' Spirit of the Times*, June 9, 1866, p. 231.

3. THE "MANLY PASTIME"

1. See, for example, *Wilkes' Spirit of the Times*, January 7, 1860, p. 274.

2. Henry Chadwick, ed., *Beadle's Dime Base-Ball Player* (New York, 1860), p. 6.

3. *Constitution and By-Laws of the National Association of Base Ball Players, with the Rules and Regulations of the Game of Base Ball* (New York, 1859), p. 8. On the Junior Convention, see Chadwick, ed., *Beadle's* (1861), p. 52. During the years before the junior clubs formed their own association, they simply followed the senior association's rules of play and "concurred in its amendments from time to time": *Wilkes' Spirit of the Times*, December 28, 1861, p. 259.

4. It is possible to view the extensive press coverage of the junior clubs as compensation for the guilt that very likely accompanied their exclusion. After all, the senior players were turning not only against their own recent past but against some of their friends and younger brothers as well. Moreover, many of the seniors were only a year or two older than the juniors. Though this coverage was explicitly compensatory—junior clubs "may be, at times, undervalued by the Press and the senior associations, but we look upon and esteem them as the foundation of our 'national game'"—it employed language that served only to fortify the barriers, as in the following: "We have ever been disposed to regard the junior clubs as the true nursery and cradle of base ball, [where] we are to look for early development of skill and promise": *Wilkes' Spirit of the Times*, December 28, 1861, p. 259. See also ibid., March 21, 1863, p. 45.

5. "Few words enjoyed more popularity in the nineteenth century than this honorific ['manly'], with all its connotations of dignity, respectability, defiant egalitarianism, and patriarchal male supremacy": David Montgomery, *Workers' Control in America: Studies in the History of Work, Technology, and Labor Struggles* (Cambridge: Cambridge University Press, 1979), p. 13.

6. *New York Clipper* November 9, 1861, p. 234; *Wilkes' Spirit of the Times*, October 18, 1862, p. 100; Chadwick, ed., *Beadle's* (1861), p. 50. See also *New York Clipper*, October 18, 1862, p. 213, for the "insulting remarks of a crowd of blackguard boys at the match."

7. The most celebrated of such players was James Creighton, the young but eminent pitcher for the Brooklyn Excelsiors, who died of injuries received and aggravated while playing cricket and baseball at the age of twenty. On the ages of ballplayers, see Melvin L. Adelman, *A Sporting Time: New York City and the Rise of Modern Athletics, 1820–1870* (Urbana: University of Illinois Press, 1986), p. 169.

8. *New York Clipper*, September 22, 1860, p. 180; July 7, 1860, p. 89; emphasis in original. Umpires were rarely criticized in the press, and then only for ignorance or lax enforcement of the rules, or for failure to speak loudly enough to be heard.

9. *Wilkes' Spirit of the Times*, June 28, 1862, p. 269. And see *New York Clipper*, June 25, 1859, p. 75; September 24, 1859, p. 178; April 28, 1860, p. 13; August 4, 1860, p. 125; June 30, 1860, p. 83.

10. *Constitution of the National Association of Base Ball Players* (1859), p. 24. At the time, the "fly rule" was proposed only for catches in fair territory; "bound catches" in foul territory would still be outs. Nor would the fly rule affect the usual ways of putting runners out at the bases.

11. *New York Clipper*, March 24, 1860, p. 387. A number of baseball players joined cricket clubs in the 1850s and 1860s; fewer cricket players joined baseball clubs. On the relationship between cricket and baseball see Adelman, *A Sporting Time*, chaps. 5–6.

12. Chadwick, ed., *Beadle's* (1860), pp. 26–27.

13. *Porter's Spirit of the Times*, August 10, 1859, p. 388.

14. *Wilkes' Spirit of the Times*, June 4, 1864, p. 211; *New York Clipper*, November 10, 1860, p. 233; Chadwick, ed., *Beadle's* (1860), p. 27.

15. *Wilkes' Spirit of the Times*, September 24, 1859, p. 37.

16. *New York Clipper*, July 2, 1859, p. 87; July 9, 1859, p. 95; August 13, 1859, p. 132.

17. Ibid., August 27, 1859, p. 147; *Spirit of the Times*, May 28, 1859, p. 186; *Wilkes' Spirit of the Times*, May 28, 1864, p. 196, and June 11, 1864, p. 228. The correspondence of the Knickerbocker Base Ball Club is available at the New York Public Library.

18. *Porter's Spirit of the Times*, March 7, 1857, p. 5; *New York Clipper*, June 30, 1862, p. 82, and December 22, 1860, p. 284; Chadwick, ed., *Beadle's* (1861), p. 48.

19. *New York Clipper*, March 24, 1860, p. 387, and December 19, 1863, p. 287; *Wilkes' Spirit of the Times*, December 19, 1863, p. 243; *Beadle's* (1864), p. 35.

20. These conclusions are based on an analysis of votes at NABBP conventions, reported in *Wilkes' Spirit of the Times*, the *New York Clipper*, and successive editions of *Beadle's*.

21. *New York Clipper*, November 28, 1863, p. 258.

22. Chadwick, ed., *Beadle's* (1861), p. 58. "In order to obtain an accurate estimate of a player's skill, an analysis, both of his play at the bat and in the field, should be made, inclusive of the way in which he was put out; and that this may be done, it is requisite that all first nine contests should be recorded in a uniform manner, and to facilitate matters we give below a copy of the blank form . . ." (ibid.). Chadwick tabulated, by player, the number of matches played, the total and average number of outs made and of runs scored, the highest score made in an inning (probably borrowed from cricket statistics), the most and least outs made in a game, the number of matches in which a player was not put out (also a cricket statistic), home runs, and strikeouts. In a discussion of each team, he listed the number of runs made by each club and its opponents, and several of the individual players' statistics were aggregated into team figures. Times of games were given in several cases as well: shortest and longest games and the average game time. For example, the Atlantics' shortest game in 1860 was 1:30 (in five innings), the longest was 3:20, and the average of their sixteen games was 2:20: ibid., pp. 59–76.

23. Ibid. (1860), pp. 10, 38. I use the term "modernizing" to describe the efforts of those within the baseball world who wished to reform the game, to "perfect" it by eliminating its older features—not to invoke the "great transformation" by another name.

24. *New York Clipper*, November 10, 1860, p. 234; "Report of the Committee on Rules and Regulations," December 1860, cited in Chadwick, ed., *Beadle's* (1861), p. 44. Such travel evoked earlier patterns of baseball—or sporting—sociability, while the baseball culture of the metropolis focused increasingly on high-level competition, victory, and, by the end of the decade, gate money.

25. Chadwick, ed., *Beadle's* (1860), pp. 7, 9. The first rules are reprinted on p. 8. Chadwick was supported in this analysis by *Porter's Spirit of the Times*: "The Knickerbocker Club, having played the game for many years at the Elysian fields, Hoboken, were desirous of changing the rules of the game . . . ; and with that view, called a convention of all the clubs, to discuss the revision of the rules" (March 7, 1857, p. 5). See also *Porter's*, December 20, 1856, p. 262 (for the call), and March 7, 1857, p. 5. Contrary to some historians' claims that the Knickerbockers were "deposed" from the leadership of the organization they helped found, the Knickerbockers' David L. Adams, after serving as president of the NABBP in 1857, chaired its rules committee until he resigned from the Knickerbockers in 1862: Adelman, *A Sporting Time*, pp. 127–128. For the view that the Knickerbockers were deposed, see David Quentin Voigt, *American Baseball*, vol. 1 (Norman: University of Oklahoma Press, 1966), pp. 8–9.

26. *New York Clipper*, September 8, 1860, p. 165.

27. *Wilkes' Spirit of the Times*, May 14, 1864, p. 164; May 19, 1866, p. 178.

28. *New York Clipper*, October 10, 1863, p. 202, and October 24, 1863, p. 223; *Wilkes' Spirit of the Times*, May 19, 1866, p. 178.

29. *Wilkes' Spirit of the Times*, November 29, 1862, p. 196; March 21, 1863, p. 45. In addition, the Resolutes were planning to occupy the season of 1866 "with pleasure matches and practice games, rather than contests for the championship" (ibid., May 5, 1866, pp. 147–148).

30. Ibid., May 14, 1864, p. 164. See also ibid., June 18, 1864, p. 242.

31. *New York Clipper*, November 3, 1860, p. 228; *Wilkes' Spirit of the Times*, March 11, 1865, p. 23.

32. *New York Clipper*, October 21, 1860, p. 213.

33. Ibid., November 3, 1860, p. 228. Art. 2 of the NABBP's constitution reads: "The objects of this Association shall be to improve, foster, and perpetuate the American game of Base Ball, and the cultivation of kindly feelings among the different members of Base Ball Clubs." The tension in the game was written into this article, since its "improvement" turned out to be a rather different objective than the cultivation of "kindly feelings."

34. *New York Clipper*, April 6, 1861, p. 404.

35. Ibid., February 2, 1861, p. 332; September 28, 1861, p. 191; October 5, 1861, p. 194; October 12, 1861, p. 202; October 19, 1861, p. 210; October 26, 1861, p. 218; November 2, 1861, pp. 226, 228.

36. Ibid., May 3, 1862, p. 19.

37. Ibid., May 9, 1863, p. 26.

38. Ibid., November 3, 1860, p. 228.

4. GROWTH, DIVISION, AND "DISORDER"

1. *Ball Players' Chronicle*, October 3, 1867, pp. 8, 6.

2. This approach could present problems, however. Chadwick, as we have seen, was not really interested in the pre-Knickerbocker history of the game at all, except to dismiss it as child's play. Even his golden age was a construct that depended on the repression of an earlier period.

3. *Ball Players' Chronicle*, July 18, 1867, p. 3.

4. Some of Chadwick's reprintings of his own stories may be seen in ibid., December 12, 1867, pp. 2–3; December 26, 1867, p. 2.

5. *Wilkes' Spirit of the Times*, April 25, 1868, p. 148; May 2, 1868, p. 168; May 30, 1868, p. 252; April 24, 1869, p. 146.

6. *New York Clipper*, October 22, 1859, p. 211. The Excelsior Club of Upton, Mass., met its rival, the Union Club of Medway, Mass., in a match for $500; the following year they played for $1,000: ibid., July 21, 1860, p. 107; August 25, 1860, p. 148. Also see "Games in Massachusetts in 1859–1860 between Medway, Worcester, Upton [and] the $1,000 Ball Game," scrapbook in National Baseball Library, Cooperstown, N.Y. Clubs held fund-raising matches for the Brooklyn Sanitary Commission during the Civil War: *Wilkes' Spirit of the Times*, July 19, 1862, p. 308; July 26, 1862, p. 333; August 2, 1862, p. 340; *New York Clipper*, August 2, 1862, p. 123.

7. Harold Seymour, *Baseball*, vol. 1 (New York: Oxford University Press, 1960), p. 25; *Wilkes' Spirit of the Times*, October 22, 1864, p. 116, and December 3, 1864, p. 212; *New York Clipper*, November 9, 1861, p. 234, and November 16, 1861, p. 247; Melvin

L. Adelman, *A Sporting Time: New York City and the Rise of Modern Athletics, 1820–1870* (Urbana: University of Illinois Press, 1986), p. 151.

8. *Wilkes' Spirit of the Times*, November 11, 1865, p. 166. The Knickerbockers moved to the Elysian Fields of Hoboken precisely so they could secure—for $75 a season—a regular ground, and not have to depend on the gradually disappearing vacant lots of lower Manhattan: Adelman, *A Sporting Time*, pp. 121–122. See also *Wilkes' Spirit of the Times*, March 28, 1863, p. 59.

9. *Wilkes' Spirit of the Times*, August 12, 1865, p. 381.

10. *New York Sunday Mercury*, August 3 and 24, 1862, in Henry Chadwick Scrapbooks, 1:5–6, in Albert G. Spalding Collection, New York Public Library. An example of this language may be seen in *New York Clipper*, August 17, 1861, p. 143.

11. *Ball Players' Chronicle*, November 14, 1867, p. 5.

12. Ibid., August 1, 1867, p. 5; December 19, 1867, p. 3. Both of these westerners represented cities in the process of becoming baseball powers. Rockford was the hometown of Albert G. Spalding, the young star pitcher for the Forest City Club, the only team to beat the Washington Nationals on their western tour in 1867; George Sands belonged to the Buckeye Club of Cincinnati, which tried briefly and unsuccessfully in the late 1860s to rival the Red Stockings as the champions of the West. The playing strength of a delegate's club had much to do with its (and his) influence in the convention during these years. The association now liked its officers to be winners.

13. Ibid., June 13, 1867, p. 4; July 11, 1867, p. 4.

14. Steven A. Riess has furnished the best analysis of this ideology. See his *Touching Base: Professional Baseball and American Culture in the Progressive Era* (Westport, Conn.: Greenwood Press, 1980), esp. pp. 3–18, 31–39, 221–233. The irony is much stronger, of course, if one also takes into account the difference between the rhetoric of democracy and the game's treatment of its players.

15. *New York Clipper*, February 2, 1861, p. 332, and November 23, 1861, p. 251; *Wilkes' Spirit of the Times*, July 6, 1867, p. 347, and August 24, 1867, p. 6; *Ball Players' Chronicle*, June 13, 1867, p. 1; July 25, 1867, pp. 1–2; August 15, 1867, p. 2; August 22, 1867, pp. 3, 6. On the Eckfords, see *New York Clipper*, June 23, 1860, p. 76, and June 2, 1860, p. 51; *Wilkes' Spirit of the Times*, October 18, 1862, pp. 100–101.

16. *New York Clipper*, September 22, 1860, p. 180. As Adelman astutely observes, the club has stood out to historians mostly because they have "grossly exaggerated" the social distance between the Eckfords and other clubs such as the Knickerbockers: *A Sporting Time*, p. 125.

17. *New York Clipper*, September 1, 1860, p. 154; September 8, 1860, p. 163.

18. Ibid., September 8, 1860, p. 164. Note that these lower classes or immigrants "indulged" their passions rather than controlling them.

19. Sean Wilentz, *Chants Democratic: New York City and the Rise of the American Working Class, 1788–1850* (New York: Oxford University Press, 1984), p. 300–301. On the use of boys as unskilled substitutes for skilled workers, see pp. 33–34, 124, 126. For the single best analysis of the Bowery B'hoy, see Peter George Buckley, "To the Opera House: Culture and Society in New York City, 1820–1860" (Ph.D. diss., State University of New York at Stony Brook, 1984), pp. 317–323, 351ff.

20. Eric Hobsbawm, *The Age of Capital, 1848–1875* (New York: New American Library, 1979), pp. 246, 249–250.

21. *Wilkes' Spirit of the Times*, December 16, 1865, p. 252. An 1865 plan called for delegates from "country clubs" to assemble first at Dunham's saloon, where the fraternity would "give the visiting delegates a hearty reception before the convention": ibid., December 23, 1865, p. 259. On The Study, see ibid., March 23, 1867, p. 55. For a club

that served "nothing stronger than coffee," see *Ball Players' Chronicle*, November 28, 1867, p. 1. On the fight within the Philadelphia Olympics, see *New York Clipper*, May 31, 1862, p. 51. For a more relaxed attitude toward drinking, see, e.g., *Ball Players' Chronicle*, June 20, 1867, p. 2; August 8, 1867, p. 8; August 15, 1867, p. 7; Joseph M. Overfield, "Baseball in Buffalo—1865 to 1870: Heyday of the Niagaras," *Niagara Frontier* 47 (1965): 6; *New York Clipper*, November 3, 1860, p. 229.

22. *Ball Players' Chronicle*, July 4, 1867, p. 2, and August 22, 1867, p. 6; *Wilkes' Spirit of the Times*, July 6, 1867, p. 347.

23. Overfield, "Baseball in Buffalo," p. 8.

24. We are accustomed to thinking of nineteenth-century Victorian culture as insufferably earnest on the subject of proper morality, but the sports pages and airwaves of our own era are filled with equally pious pronouncements about athletes, alcohol, and drugs.

5. "REVOLVING" AND PROFESSIONALISM

1. The "no show" job was one of the most common monetary lures. Albert Spalding's first baseball employment was just such a job in a Chicago dry goods house, and Tammany Hall had put many of the Mutuals on the city payroll by 1866 or 1867. On player movements, see, e.g., *New York Clipper*, March 31, 1860, p. 396; April 21, 1860, p. 4; May 26, 1860, p. 43; July 20, 1861, p. 111; August 17, 1861, p. 143; *Wilkes' Spirit of the Times*, November 7, 1863, p. 147.

2. *Wilkes' Spirit of the Times*, May 9, 1863, p. 155; October 17, 1863, p. 100; Alphonse C. Martin Scrapbooks, National Baseball Library, Cooperstown, N.Y.

3. *Wilkes' Spirit of the Times*, October 4, 1862, p. 68; November 7, 1863, p. 147; April 30, 1864, p. 132.

4. Despite his clear emotional attachment to the "old days," Henry Chadwick was never far from the modernizing frontier of the game in these years. He argued in 1867 that "the objection to any amendments to the rules, or changes in the game, on the old-fashioned plea that 'what was good enough for our ancestors is good enough for us,' is an argument too puerile to have influence with any intelligent or progressive members of the fraternity": *Ball Players' Chronicle*, December 5, 1867, p. 4.

5. *Wilkes' Spirit of the Times*, December 22, 1866, p. 266; *Ball Players' Chronicle*, December 19, 1867, p. 4.

6. *Ball Players' Chronicle*, December 19, 1867, p. 4.

7. Ibid., p. 2; M. J. Kelly, *The Base-Ball Guide for 1868* (New York, 1868), p. 85.

8. Cited in *Ball Players' Chronicle*, December 26, 1867, p. 2. There were black clubs at this time, and their activities were occasionally mentioned in the press. It appears that they played mainly among themselves, although the white umpires in two games suggest that there was some contact between white and black ballplayers. See ibid., October 3, 1867, p. 6; October 10, 1867, p. 2; October 31, 1867, p. 3.

9. Kelly, *Base-Ball Guide for 1868*, p. 43; Henry Chadwick, ed., *Beadle's Dime Base-Ball Player* (New York, 1869), p. 48.

10. Chadwick, ed., *Beadle's* (1864), p. 16. In 1865, for example, the term "other club" was defined explicitly as a club "either in or out of the National Association." It was also meant specifically to exclude members of junior clubs from senior matches. In a move that anticipated the much more imperial practices of the professional leagues of the later nineteenth century, the association was in effect claiming control over parts of the game that did not acknowledge the NABBP's leadership. See Chadwick, ed., *Beadle's*

(1866), p. 17. For the practices of the professional leagues, see Harold Seymour, *Baseball*, vol. 1 (New York: Oxford University Press, 1960), chaps. 13–15, 18–22, 24–25; David Quentin Voigt, *American Baseball*, vol. 1 (Norman: University of Oklahoma Press, 1966), chaps. 8–9, 12–13, 15; *Wilkes' Spirit of the Times*, December 22, 1866, p. 267.

11. These hearings were covered in great detail in *Ball Players' Chronicle*, October 10, 1867, pp. 3, 6; October 24, 1867, pp. 1–2; October 31, 1867, p. 4; November 7, 1867, pp. 3, 6.

12. Ibid., December 19, 1867, pp. 2–3.

13. Ibid., October 10, 1867, p. 6.

14. Chadwick, ed., *Beadle's* (1870), pp. 45–51; ibid. (1872), pp. 40–41. As usual, George Wilkes' paper was more matter-of-fact. See *Wilkes' Spirit of the Times*, December 3, 1870, p. 234. The Mutuals had reinstated Duffy themselves in 1868. At its annual meeting that year the New York State association first sustained its judiciary committee and expelled the Mutuals, and then immediately voted to reinstate the club, "with but one dissenting vote": *Wilkes' Spirit of the Times*, November 14, 1868, p. 199. When the rule classifying players into professionals and amateurs was first passed, commentary focused on the precise point at which a club became professional; that is, it could have a "teaching professional" in its nine and still be counted among the amateurs, but if he played in a match, his club would need "the consent of the opposing nine, unless they, too, [had] a professional in their nine." If the majority of the nine consisted of professional players, the club was defined as professional: Henry Chadwick, ed., *The Base-Ball Guide* (New York, 1869), p. 24.

15. The argument might even be reversed: the increasing dominance of the Mutuals probably contributed to the lessening influence of the NABBP over the baseball world. The club had a widespread reputation for involvement in shady deals, betting conspiracies, and, given its close connections with Tammany Hall, corrupt politics. Boss Tweed was a member of the Mutuals' board of trustees from 1866 on, and a number of city officials, including Coroner John Wildey, were officers of the club. At the 1870 convention, in an exchange about Boss Tweed's alleged $7,500 contribution to the club, a delegate "stated that he gave 'the Boss' credit for too much judgment to suppose that he would give $7,500 unless he saw his way clear to get it back in some shape or another": *Wilkes' Spirit of the Times*, December 3, 1870, p. 244. Melvin Adelman has effectively challenged the easy equation of reputation and reality, but the fact remains that whether or not they deserved it, the Mutual Club did have the worst reputation in such matters of any club in the country, and it still continued to grow in influence. For a perceptive discussion of the Mutuals, see Melvin L. Adelman, *A Sporting Time: New York City and the Rise of Modern Athletics, 1820–1870* (Urbana: University of Illinois Press, 1986), pp. 164–165.

16. *Wilkes' Spirit of the Times*, December 3, 1870, p. 244; Chadwick, ed., *Beadle's* (1871), p. 91.

17. *Ball Players' Chronicle*, October 31, 1867, p. 4. Pabor, Martin, and Birdsall were all well-known first-nine players, and apparently genuine members of the clubs they played for. For another example of this practice, see Thomas H. Callan, recording secretary of the Jefferson Base Ball Club, to Jacob [John Hadley] Doyle, April 29, 1868, in John Hadley Doyle Scrapbooks, vol. 1, National Baseball Library, Cooperstown, N.Y. The letter notified Doyle that he had been "elected an active member and exempted from the payment of all dues, fees, and other assessments to the Club."

18. *Ball Players' Chronicle*, October 31, 1867, p. 4.

19. *American Chronicle of Sports and Pastimes*, January 9, 1868, p. 11.

20. Although the Nationals did lose one game on their western tour, they won games by scores of 53–10, 88–12, 82–21, 106–21, 113–26, 53–26, and 49–4: *Ball Players' Chronicle*, July 25, 1867, pp. 1–2; August 1, 1867, pp. 1–2; August 8, 1867, p. 2.

21. For a fascinating example of this process, see Gregg Lee Carter, "Baseball in St. Louis, 1867–1875: An Historical Case Study in Civic Pride," *Missouri Historical Society Bulletin* 31 (July 1975): 253–263.

22. That the association was of a divided mind on these related questions is further indicated by the exemption of college and junior clubs from the sixty-day rule. Junior or college club players could be inserted into the lineup of a senior club at will, as long as they did not belong to another senior club. Thus, while the mobility of senior players was reduced, the previously untouchable college and junior players became exploitable resources for all of the senior clubs, professional and amateur alike. See Chadwick, ed., *Base-Ball Guide* (1869), pp. 21–22.

23. *Wilkes' Spirit of the Times*, August 24, 1867, p. 7; November 2, 1867, p. 213; May 9, 1868, p. 196; May 23, 1868, p. 232; June 19, 1869, p. 281; *Ball Players' Chronicle*, June 20, 1867, p. 4; June 27, 1867, p. 4; July 4, 1867, p. 3; July 18, 1867, p. 2; August 15, 1867, p. 6; August 22, 1867, p. 6; November 7, 1867, p. 3.

24. Seymour, *Baseball*, 1:56–57. The payroll of the 1869 Cincinnati Red Stockings was over $9,000.

6. The National Game

1. So, of course, did cricket clubs, but cricketers commonly belonged to more than one club at a time. The attempt to restrict cricketers to one club was a relatively late development in cricket's American history, attributable mostly to the effort to Americanize the game. It failed. From nearly the beginning of the NABBP, however, the association insisted that membership could be held in only one club. For an excellent discussion of cricket in America, see Melvin L. Adelman, *A Sporting Time: New York City and the Rise of Modern Athletics, 1820–1870* (Urbana: University of Illinois Press, 1986), chap. 5.

2. The baseball world was not alone in identifying its favorites by their home territory. Politicians, for example, frequently had nicknames drawn from their hometowns or states. Others in the world of amusement carried such badges, both to allow hometown identification and to indicate a certain exoticism. Prizefighters in particular often carried the names of their hometowns: the Benicia Boy, the Manassa Mauler. Cricket clubs outside of New York frequently took the names of their towns or counties. Within the metropolitan area, however, clubs seem not to have sought local identifications, preferring instead a national label of origin. Nor did the most prominent eastern cricket clubs adopt neighborhood names, apparently preferring names of cities or ungrounded names: New York, St. George, Satellite, American. Moreover, the important conflicts in American cricket took place over national and international issues. First, the sport drew much criticism as being too "English"—not because it originated in England but because most of the best players were English immigrants. This dispute led to the founding of the American Cricket Club, an explicit attempt to encourage native American cricketers. Second, the major event of each cricket season was a series of "international matches" with a representative eleven from Canada, or, as in 1859, the visit of the All-England Eleven.

Less rooted in metropolitan neighborhoods or particular workplaces, the clubs relied on a broader, more geographically dispersed public of a somewhat higher class. One reason, then, that baseball was able to supplant cricket in the late 1850s and early 1860s was that the proliferation of local clubs in New York and Brooklyn tapped just those sources of support—in a purposeful and direct manner—that cricket clubs overlooked. See George B. Kirsch, "The Rise of Modern Sports: New Jersey Cricketers, Baseball Players, and Clubs, 1845–1860," *New Jersey History* 101 (Spring–Summer 1983): 53–84; and his "American Cricket: Players and Clubs before the Civil War," *Journal of Sport History* 11 (Spring 1984): 28–49.

3. In a cricket "innings," every player but one on each side must bat until he is put out. A team comes to the bat only after the entire other side has been put out. A game thus consists of just two full innings, and matches commonly take more than a day to complete. Baseball, by contrast, consists of nine innings, but only three players on each side need be put out in each inning, and the defense has more advantages than in cricket. In 1860 baseball games usually took from two and a half to three and a half hours.

4. The wide use of the term "import" indicates the extent of baseball's convergence with the world of commerce.

5. On the Cincinnati Red Stockings, see Harold Seymour, *Baseball*, vol. 1 (New York: Oxford University Press, 1960), pp. 56–59; David Quentin Voigt, *American Baseball*, vol. 1 (Norman: University of Oklahoma Press, 1966), pp. 23–24; Irving Leitner, *Baseball: Diamond in the Rough* (New York: Abelard-Schuman, 1972), pp. 83–97; Preston D. Orem, *Baseball (1845–1881)* (Altadena, Calif.: By the author, 1961), pp. 87–97, 100, 102–103. See also Harold Seymour, "Baseball's First Professional Manager," *Ohio Historical Quarterly* 64 (October 1955): 406–423; David Quentin Voigt, "America's First Red Scare: The Cincinnati Reds of 1869," *Ohio History* 78 (Winter 1969), 12–24, 68–69; Adelman, *A Sporting Time*, pp. 170–172. Nearly every popular history of the game includes several paragraphs on the team, and numerous articles talk about their contribution. Few of these accounts can be trusted.

6. Knickerbocker Base Ball Club of New York Club Book, 2 vols., 1854–1859, 1859–1868, cited in Seymour, "Baseball's First Professional Manager," pp. 406–407; John Kieran, "Henry Wright," *Dictionary of American Biography* (New York, 1936), 20:554.

7. For the nine of the Cincinnati Base Ball Club in the late 1860s, see Henry Chadwick, ed., *Beadle's Dime Base-Ball Player* (New York, 1870), pp. 61–62. For the Union Cricket Club players, see *Wilkes' Spirit of the Times*, August 4, 1866, p. 365. Actually, the Cincinnati Base Ball Club began to play on the grounds of the Live Oak Base Ball Club. It was not until the following year that the baseball club began to play on the cricket club's grounds. The arrangement was not simply fraternal: the ballplayers paid their cricket comrades $2,000 for the use of their field.

8. Joseph S. Stern, Jr., "The Team That Couldn't Be Beat," *Bulletin of the Cincinnati Historical Society* 27 (1969): 30; Seymour, "Baseball's First Professional Manager," p. 412; clipping from *New York Clipper*, August 1870, in John Hadley Doyle Scrapbooks, vol. 2, National Baseball Library, Cooperstown, N.Y.

9. *New York Clipper*, August 1870, in Doyle Scrapbooks, vol. 2.

10. *Ball Players' Chronicle*, August 18, 1867, p. 6; July 18, 1867, p. 2; July 25, 1867, p. 1.

11. Stern, "Team That Couldn't Be Beat," pp. 28, 30; *Ball Players' Chronicle*, October 31, 1867, p. 4; Henry Chadwick, ed., *Beadle's* (1870), p. 62 (emphasis in original). Recall also that, as indicated in the Judiciary Committee hearing cited in chap. 5, it was implied that every club had its wealthy backers—"a class of members in every club who do the paying part of the business, and but little else."

12. *Wilkes' Spirit of the Times*, April 4, 1868, p. 99; April 11, 1868, pp. 115–116.

13. Ibid., April 11, 1868, p. 116; May 30, 1868, p. 252.

14. Chadwick, ed., *Beadle's* (1869), p. 99. Uniforms of the 1860s and 1870s carried no numbers and no players' names. Both of these innovations—the former later in the nineteenth century, the latter not until the mid-twentieth—were accompanied by controversy. Some teams still do not put players' names on their uniforms.

15. *Wilkes' Spirit of the Times*, May 28, 1864, p. 196.

16. That gentlemen might not have been able to afford new uniforms raises an important issue. It is difficult to overstate the extent to which the misinterpretation of this term has skewed the popular and scholarly history of baseball. Most historians of the game have simply assumed that "gentleman" meant a member of the upper class, and have therefore argued that baseball was originally controlled by a genteel upper crust, and was gradually appropriated by the masses. Thus Harold Seymour describes the Knickerbockers as having "a distinctively exclusive flavor—somewhat similar to what country clubs represented in the 1920s and 1930s, before they became popular with the middle class in general." In this view, "the Knickerbockers wanted to restrict baseball to their own social class," but were eventually "thrust aside" by the Eckford Club, among others (Seymour, *Baseball*, 1:15, 23–24). Following Seymour's lead and making the argument much more strongly, David Quentin Voigt claims that the "aristocratic" Knickerbockers "took a condescending view of other clubs . . . and it soon became apparent that they were out to establish themselves as the social arbiters of baseball." This effort failed, according to Voigt, as the other clubs in the New York area, unconvinced of the Knickerbockers' "superior pedigrees," "bluntly rejected [them] as baseball's fashion dictators" (Voigt, *American Baseball*, 1:8). Melvin Adelman has demonstrated that these accounts are without historical foundation. After looking at the social composition of the early baseball clubs, including the Knickerbockers, Adelman concludes, first, that "gentlemen" referred primarily to the prosperous middle class rather than to an upper class, and second, that it had less of an economic meaning than a social one—that is, it was an indicator less of class than of culture (Adelman, *A Sporting Time*, pp. 122–125). Although this conclusion represents a real advance in baseball scholarship, it does not go quite far enough. There were well-off merchants and professional men in early baseball clubs who styled themselves "gentlemen," but there were also large numbers of clerks and skilled workers whose interest in being called gentlemen was attributable mainly to their desire for respectability. This longing for respectability, and not players' status as members of the prosperous middle class, presents the real key to the puzzle of "gentlemen." Gentility, understood as an upper-class Victorian delicacy and priggishness, played only a minor part in the culture of baseball during these years. The cult of respectability among artisans, clerks, and petty proprietors gave them just as much dread of "the poor" and the "roughs" as was expressed by those much farther up the class ladder.

17. In fact, given the common associations of the color, a surprisingly large proportion of the sporting and theatrical clothes offered by Peck & Snyder was partly or wholly made of bright-red material. It is tempting to speculate further about the psychological significance of this color in baseball, especially since to Chadwick it suggested children and the insufficiently repressed "yokels" and "roughs." Bright red had for many years been used to indicate sexual passion or sexual commerce. Red dresses (or petticoats) could identify prostitutes, who worked in red-light districts. Hester Prynne's badge of adultery partook of the same symbolism, as did the "lady of the scarlet petticoat" in Hawthorne's "My Kinsman, Major Molineux." Garish as well as naughty, red carried both meanings in the nineteenth century. Might the prominence of red in baseball uniforms and team names (the Red Stockings, the Red Sox, the Redlegs, the Cardinals, or Redbirds) have been a way of maintaining a relationship to a younger, naughtier culture, if only by a kind of visual suggestiveness? The political implications of the color, in any event, are a matter of

record. The Cincinnati Reds of 1944 changed their name to the Redlegs precisely to deflect public feelings about political "reds."

18. Or rather, the tour turned a profit of about $1,700. At the beginning of the 1869 season the club had incurred liabilities (including the current players' salaries) of over $15,000. By the end of the year all but about $1,000 of this debt had been paid off. See clipping from *New York Clipper*, August 1870, in Doyle Scrapbooks, vol. 2.

19. *Spirit of the Times*, June 5, 1869, p. 246.

20. Voigt, *American Baseball*, 1:27.

21. The only other team captain of long enough tenure to have "Captain" placed before his name in newspaper stories was Robert Ferguson of the Mutuals and Atlantics. Ferguson, however, was fully ten years younger than "Captain Harry," and though he commanded respect on the ballfield and off, he simply did not exercise the same authority as the Cincinnati (later Boston) captain.

22. Seymour, *Baseball*, 1:56–57; Voigt, "America's First Red Scare," p. 18.

23. Wage figures for these years vary a good deal, but some general ranges can be established. Though lower than they were in 1866–1867, wages were still relatively high in the late 1860s and early 1870s. We can calculate an upper limit on yearly income for five groups studied—blacksmiths, carpenters, engineers, machinists, and painters—by taking the highest daily wage earned in any of these occupations in the twenty-year period from 1860 to 1880 and multiplying it by the largest possible number of working days—312, at six days a week. The figure thus arrived at is just under $865. For a number of reasons this figure is much higher than what skilled craftsmen could expect to earn during these years. Few if any worked the maximum number of days, and most worked at well below this wage level. These calculations are based on Series D, 728–734, "Daily Wages of Five Skilled Occupations and of Laborers, in Manufacturing Establishments: 1860 to 1880," in *Historical Statistics of the United States, Colonial Times to 1870*, 2 vols. (Washington, D.C.: Bureau of the Census, 1975), 1:165; and two tables in Stephen Thernstrom, *Poverty and Progress: Social Mobility in a Nineteenth-Century City* (New York: Atheneum, 1970), pp. 93–94.

24. *Spirit of the Times*, June 12, 1869, p. 261; June 26, 1869, p. 291.

25. Joseph M. Overfield, "Baseball in Buffalo—1865 to 1870: Heyday of the Niagaras," *Niagara Frontier* 47 (1965): 10; *Spirit of the Times*, June 19, 1869, p. 281.

26. *Spirit of the Times*, June 26, 1869, p. 296.

27. Ibid., June 11, 1870, p. 263; June 18, 1870, p. 277.

28. *New York Clipper*, August 1870 and August 27, 1870, in Doyle Scrapbooks, vol. 2; Seymour, "Baseball's First Professional Manager," p. 415. Actually the club netted a total of $1.39 for the season.

29. The circular, dated November 21, 1870, was reprinted in the *New York Clipper*, December 3, 1870; the clipping is in Doyle Scrapbooks, vol. 2.

30. Voigt, *American Baseball*, 1:31–32.

31. There is some evidence that the club's stated inability to pay players' salaries was actually a negotiating ploy designed to force players to accept lower salaries: Seymour, *Baseball*, 1:59.

7. AMATEURS IN REBELLION

1. *Spirit of the Times*, November 26, 1870, p. 232.

2. Cited in ibid., November 26, 1870, p. 235.

3. Henry Chadwick Scrapbooks, 1:42, in Albert G. Spalding Collection, New York Public Library.

4. This account drew on the conflict between "English" and "American" cricket players, as well as on efforts to have professionals (who were otherwise accepted as normal parts of the game) barred from cricket matches. The latter question arose mainly because professionals were so much better than the other players that contests between clubs became, in effect, contests between a few professionals. These conflicts anticipated the debate over baseball's English or American origins, and provided it with some of its emotional fervor and vocabulary. The assertion that baseball was an American game (made frequently by Henry Chadwick) required the repression of the well-known English parent.

5. Chadwick Scrapbooks, 1:42.

6. I have used the term "amateurists" to indicate those who tried to create an ideology of amateurism. Their manifesto also helps to explain why so many people who write about baseball assume that such a period actually existed. Such allegations can clearly be traced to the "recollections" of men such as Jones of the Excelsiors, rather than to evidence drawn from the golden age itself.

7. *Spirit of the Times*, March 18, 1871, p. 70. The issue of admission fees had been of concern to the Stars for some time. At the 1869 New York State Association convention the Star delegates asked for a definition of professional and amateur clubs. After a "lengthy and very desultory debate," the convention managed to express its "diversity of opinion" in a resolution holding that "a club receiving gate money, so long as it was not devoted to remunerating players, was not a professional": *New York Clipper*, November 27, 1869, in John Hadley Doyle Scrapbooks, vol. 2, National Baseball Library, Cooperstown, N.Y. The same definition was adopted by the professionals themselves. See *New York Clipper*, January 14, 1871, also in vol. 2 of Doyle Scrapbooks.

8. *Spirit of the Times*, April 22, 1871, p. 148; April 29, 1871, p. 165; August 19, 1871, p. 16; June 22, 1872, p. 293.

9. Henry Chadwick, ed., *The Base-Ball Guide for 1869* (New York, 1869), p. 69.

10. Letter from a member of the Beacon Base Ball Club to the editor, *Spirit of the Times*, March 1, 1873, p. 35; ibid., September 20, 1873, p. 125; August 23, 1873, p. 42; October 3, 1874, p. 198. On September 27, 1873, the paper published a letter from the Beacon Club thanking it for covering amateur games, "for in the columns of the daily press but little space is given to our games" (p. 163).

11. Ibid., September 5, 1874, p. 81; September 12, 1874, p. 121; September 26, 1874, p. 156.

12. Ibid., July 25, 1874, p. 513. Note that this unfortunate infield was being analyzed as a piece of productive machinery—only machines need "overhauling."

13. Ibid., November 14, 1874, p. 335.

14. Chadwick Scrapbooks, 1:44.

8. Professional Leagues and the Baseball Workplace

1. Harold Seymour, *Baseball*, vol. 1 (New York: Oxford University Press, 1960), pp. 59–60; David Quentin Voigt, *American Baseball*, vol. 1 (Norman: University of Oklahoma Press, 1966), pp. 35–36, and *America through Baseball* (Chicago: Nelson Hall, 1976), pp. 42–46; Albert G. Spalding, *America's National Game* (New York, 1911), cited in Seymour, *Baseball*, 1:80.

2. *Spirit of the Times*, March 18, 1871, p. 70; Henry Chadwick, ed., *The Base-Ball Guide* (New York, 1872), p. 110; *Spirit of the Times*, March 8, 1873, p. 51; Chadwick, ed., *Base-Ball Guide* (1874), pp. 98–99, and (1875), p. 98; Chadwick, ed., *Beadle's Dime Base-Ball Player* (New York, 1872), p. 46 (emphasis added).

3. Ballfield performance also had an effect: all but one of the 1872 dropouts had a winning percentage under .300 at the time they quit.

4. Voigt maintains that the NAPBBP "failed" to control revolving by "trusting too much in the good faith of players and directors" (*American Baseball*, 1:37). The NAPBBP trusted no one. The simple structure legislated by the delegates proved inadequate principally because the problem of competition between clubs for players was so complicated that even after the institution of the reserve rule, it dogged professional league organizations all through the late nineteenth and early twentieth centuries.

5. *Spirit of the Times*, March 18, 1871, p. 70.

6. Ibid., June 3, 1871, p. 244. The exception, of course, had been the 1869 Cincinnati Red Stockings. Roy Rosenzweig writes about the class nature of enforced silence in cultural institutions, particularly the late-nineteenth-century working-class saloon and the early-twentieth-century movie theater; see his *Eight Hours for What We Will: Workers and Leisure in an Industrial City, 1870–1920* (New York: Cambridge University Press, 1983), pp. 185–186, 199–204, 215–217.

7. See, for example, Harry Wright to N. E. Young, April 26, and May 24, 1872; March 28 and June 21, 1873; Wright to Charles A. Hadel, Baltimore Base Ball Club, April 27, 1874; Wright to Fred W. Early, Chicago Base Ball Association, June 29, 1872; Wright to Benjamin Douglass, Mansfield Base Ball Club, Middletown, Conn., June 4, 1872; Wright to A. D. Warren, June 6, 1872; Wright to Horace B. Verny, June 26, 1872; Wright to C. A. Farnham, Resolute Base Ball Club, April 24, 1873; all in Harry Wright Papers, Albert G. Spalding Collection, New York Public Library.

8. Wright to N. E. Young, June 17, 1871, in Wright Papers.

9. Wright to Young, April 21, 1871, in Wright Papers.

10. *Spirit of the Times*, March 30, 1872, p. 100 (emphasis in original); Chadwick, ed., *Beadle's* (1873), pp. 44–46.

11. *Spirit of the Times*, March 18, 1871, p. 70. An excellent discussion of these relationships may be found in Paul E. Johnson, *A Shopkeeper's Millennium: Society and Revivals in Rochester, New York, 1815–1837* (New York: Hill & Wang, 1978), esp. pp. 37–61.

12. Chadwick, ed., *Beadle's* (1872), pp. 41–44. Ten to twelve years earlier, "men of forty years of age and upwards, could excel in it. . . . What a change has taken place in ten short years!": Chadwick, ed., *Base-Ball Guide* (1869), pp. 10–11.

13. Wright to N. E. Young, March 22, 1872, in Wright Papers.

14. Wright to Ross Barnes, December 22, 1872, in Wright Papers; emphasis in original.

15. Wright to Ross Barnes, December 22, 1872; Wright to James O'Rourke, December 8 and 27, 1872; all in Wright Papers. For the continuation of this quarrel and its result, see Wright to O'Rourke, December 31, 1874; January 29, 1875; February 8, 1875; and March 4, 1875, in ibid.

16. Wright to Benjamin Douglass, June 29, 1872, in Wright Papers; emphasis in original.

17. Wright to Chadwick, January 2, 1875, in Wright Papers.

18. Allen Guttmann, *From Ritual to Record: The Nature of Modern Sports* (New York: Columbia University Press, 1978), pp. 100, 113–114.

19. Chadwick, ed., *Beadle's* (1864), pp. 59–60.

20. Ibid. (1872), p. 33; unidentified clipping in Henry Chadwick Scrapbooks, 1:17, in Albert G. Spalding Collection, New York Public Library.

21. *Spirit of the Times*, October 5, 1872, p. 122.

22. Until 1870 a record of twenty-four runs scored in ten matches was cited as "two

and four over," rather than 2.4, and was thus not easily distinguished from a record of eighty-four runs in forty matches, also figured as "two and four over," not as 2.1: Chadwick, ed., *Beadle's* (1869), pp. 50, 74. The modern batting average, figured as the number of base hits per official time at bat and written as a three-figure decimal, first appeared in *New York Clipper*, July 20, 1872, p. 123. Thus a batter who had 100 base hits in 300 official chances batted an average of .333, an excellent mark for a professional player. Even though amateur baseball had many similarities to the professional game, the performance of amateur players received far less extensive statistical analysis. At this time, amateur productivity escaped some of the rationalizing thrust of the baseball marketplace. Modern amateurs, located mainly on college clubs, receive no such dispensation.

23. Wright to Charles H. Tubbs, December 2, 1874, in Wright Papers.

24. Voigt, *American Baseball*, 1:62. William A. Hulbert, secretary of the Chicago White Stockings, was furious at the association and at the Athletics because a disputed player, Davey Force, had been awarded to the Athletics. Harry Wright was outraged that the Athletics had been able to pack the Judiciary Committee, so that it ruled consistently in the Athletics' interest. See Seymour, *Baseball*, 1:79, and the following letters of Wright, all in Wright Papers: to Charles Gould, March 15, 1875; to W. A. Hulbert, March 15 and March 23, 1875; to Benjamin Douglass, March 22, 1875; to C. O. Bishop, March 23, 1875; to *New York Clipper*, March 26, 1875; to William Cammeyer, March 30, 1875; to Henry Chadwick, March 31, 1875.

25. Seymour, *Baseball*, 1:79–80; Voigt, *American Baseball*, 1:61–64.

26. *Constitution of the National League of Professional Base Ball Clubs* (Philadelphia, 1876), p. 11.

27. On the Boston Red Stockings, see Voigt, *American Baseball*, 1:57–58; Chadwick, ed., *Beadle's* (1876), p. 67. On the Athletics, see *New York Clipper*, November 30, 1872, p. 276. For salaries of the 1874 Chicago, Boston, Philadelphia, and Athletic Club players, see *Wilkes' Spirit of the Times*, February 21, 1874, p. 32.

28. Mills to O. P. Caylor, March 3, 1883; undated copy of a deposition of A. G. Mills, probably from the late 1880s or early 1890s; both in Abraham G. Mills Papers, National Baseball Library, Cooperstown, N.Y.

29. See John Montgomery Ward, "Is the Base Ball Player a Chattel?" *Lippincott's Magazine*, August 1887, pp. 310–319. For the formal introduction of the blacklist, see A. G. Mills circular to each League club president, December 22, 1883, in Mills Papers. For the National League owners' discussions and decisions regarding players fined, suspended, expelled, and blacklisted, see the copies of the National League meeting minutes in Mills Papers. See also the National League Minute Book in the National Baseball Library for a list of player fines, suspensions, and blacklistings during the 1880s.

30. Seymour, *Baseball*, 1:83, 90–93, 135–147; Voigt, *American Baseball*, 1:121–153. On Sunday baseball, see Steven A. Riess, *Touching Base: Professional Baseball and American Culture in the Progressive Era* (Westport, Conn.: Greenwood Press, 1980), pp. 121–149; John A. Lucas, "The Unholy Experiment—Professional Baseball's Struggle against Pennsylvania Sunday Blue Laws, 1926–1943," *Pennsylvania History* 38 (1971): 163–175. On the Players' League revolt, see Lee Lowenfish and Tony Lupien, *The Imperfect Diamond: The Story of Baseball's Reserve System and the Men Who Fought to Change It* (New York: Stein & Day, 1980); Seymour, *Baseball*, 1:221–250; Voigt, *American Baseball*, 1:154–169; and Peter Levine, *A. G. Spalding and the Rise of Baseball: The Promise of American Sport* (New York: Oxford University Press, 1985), pp. 56–66.

EPILOGUE

1. It was hardly coincidental that one of the best baseball writers in the country, with a sensitive appreciation for the two kinds of history I have described, wrote two of his finest articles that year about college and semiprofessional baseball. See Roger Angell, "The Web of the Game" and "In the Country," in *Late Innings: A Baseball Companion* (New York: Simon & Schuster, 1982), pp. 361–379, 391–429.

2. Bill James is the exception here, as in so many other ways. His article "Revolution" in *The Bill James Baseball Abstract: 1988* (New York: Ballantine, 1988), pp. 17–22, is a fascinating exploration of what might happen in professional baseball if the game's antitrust exemption were eliminated. For another, so far unsuccessful attempt to bring a different kind of power to bear on a professional baseball club, see Warren Goldstein, "Declaring Independence from King George (Steinbrenner)," *New York Times*, October 31, 1987.

Selected Bibliography

Adelman, Melvin. *A Sporting Time: New York City and the Rise of Modern Athletics.* Urbana: University of Illinois Press, 1986.

Alexander, Charles C. *Our Game: An American Baseball History.* New York: Henry Holt, 1991.

Angell, Roger. *The Summer Game.* Lincoln: University of Nebraska Press, 2004.

Berlage, Gai Ingham. *Women in Baseball: The Forgotten History.* Westport, Conn.: Praeger, 1994.

Block, David. *Baseball before We Knew It: A Search for the Roots of the Game.* Lincoln: University of Nebraska Press, 2005.

Bouton, Jim. *Ball Four.* New York: John Wiley, 1990.

Browne, Lois. *Girls of Summer: In Their Own League.* New York: HarperCollins, 1992.

Burgos, Adrian, Jr. *Playing America's Game: Baseball, Latinos, and the Color Line.* Berkeley: University of California Press, 2007.

Burns, Ken. *Baseball.* Florentine Films, 1994.

Echevarría, Roberto González. *The Pride of Havana: A History of Cuban Baseball.* New York: Oxford University Press, 1999.

Gorn, Elliott. *The Manly Art: Bare-Knuckle Prize Fighting in America.* Ithaca: Cornell University Press, 1986.

Gorn, Elliott, and Warren Goldstein. *A Brief History of American Sports.* New York: Hill & Wang, 1993.

Gregorich, Barbara. *Women at Play: The Story of Women in Baseball.* San Diego: Harcourt Brace, 1993.

Guttmann, Alan. *From Ritual to Record: The Nature of Modern Sports.* New York: Columbia University Press, 1978.

Hogan, Lawrence D., ed. *Shades of Glory: The Negro Leagues and the Story of African American Baseball.* Washington, D.C.: National Geographic Books, 2006.

James, Bill. *The New Bill James Historical Abstract.* New York: Free Press, 2001.

Kahn, Roger. *The Boys of Summer.* New York: HarperCollins, 2000.

Korr, Charles P. *The End of Baseball As We Knew It: The Players Union, 1960–1981.* Urbana: University of Illinois Press, 2002.

Kuklick, Bruce. *To Every Thing a Season: Shibe Park and Urban Philadelphia, 1909–1976.* Princeton: Princeton University Press, 1991.

Lanctot, Neal. *Negro League Baseball: The Rise and Ruin of a Black Institution.* Philadelphia: University of Pennsylvania Press, 2004.

Miller, James Edward. *The Baseball Business: Pursuing Pennants and Profits in Baltimore.* Chapel Hill: University of North Carolina Press, 1990.

National Baseball Hall of Fame and Museum. *Baseball as America: Seeing Ourselves Through Our National Game.* Washington, D.C.: National Geographic Books, 2002.

Rader, Benjamin. *American Sports: From the Age of Folk Games to the Age of Televised Sports.* Englewood Cliffs, N.J.: Prentice Hall, 1983.

——. *Baseball: A History of America's Game.* Urbana: University of Illinois Press, 1992.

Riess, Steven. *Touching Base: Professional Baseball and American Culture in the Progressive Era.* Westport, Conn.: Greenwood, 1980.

Ritter, Lawrence. *The Glory of Their Times: The Story of Baseball Told By the Men Who Played It.* New York: HarperCollins, 1992.

Rosenzweig, Roy. *Eight Hours for What We Will: Workers and Leisure in an Industrial City, 1870–1920.* New York: Cambridge University Press, 1983.

Ruck, Rob. *Sandlot Seasons: Sport in Black Pittsburgh.* Urbana: University of Illinois Press, 1987.

——. *The Tropic of Baseball: Baseball in the Dominican Republic.* Westport, Conn.: Meckler, 1991.

Tygiel, Jules. *Baseball's Great Experiment: Jackie Robinson and His Legacy.* New York: Oxford University Press, 1983.

——. *Past Time: Baseball as History.* New York: Oxford University Press, 2000.

Ward, Geoffrey C., and Ken Burns. *Baseball: An Illustrated History.* New York: Knopf, 1994.

Zimbalist, Andrew. *Baseball and Billions: A Probing Look inside the Big Business of Our National Pastime.* New York: Basic Books, 1992.

Index

Aces, 13
Active Club, 57, 80
Adelman, Melvin, 102
Alcohol, and baseball, 80–81
Amateur movement, 126–33
  and critique of professional baseball,
    120–26
American Bank-Note Co., 25
Angell, Roger, 3
Arlingtons, New York, 130
Athletics, Philadelphia, 21, 23, 41, 149
Atlantics, Brooklyn, 18, 21, 23, 24,
    33–34, 101
  dispute with Unions, 94–96
  vs. Excelsiors, 76
  vs. Mutuals, 67, 71

Ball Players' Chronicle, 67–68, 73
Balls, 13
Baltics, 24, 57
Barnes, Ross, 141, 143
Barzun, Jacques, 4
Baseball
  amateur movement in, 126–33
  as business, 134–42
  capital and labor in, 94–100
  cultural antecedents of, 27–31
  cultural conflict and division in, 75–83
  ethics of, 53–58
  and fly rule, 48–53
  growth of, 67–72; and fragmentation,
    72–75
  histories of, 1–6, 67–72
  as manly pastime, 43–48
  origins of, 10–14
  professional, critique of, 120–26

and rites of play, 17–20
Base Ball Club, Cincinnati, 104–5
Base Ball Club, New York, 57
Base-Ball Guide, 128
Baseball Hall of Fame, 70
Baseball statistics, origin of, 142–47
Baseball uniforms, 108–11
Batter, 13
Beacon Club, Boston, 129–31
Beadle's Dime Base-Ball Player, 34, 36,
    43, 54, 112, 123
Berra, Yogi, 2
Betting scandal, 90–92
Black list, 150
Blacks, excluded from NABBP, 88
Black Sox, 3
Boston Base Ball Association, 137
Boston Herald, 123
Bostons, 137–38
Boughton, Frederick, 38
Bound game vs. fly game, 49–50
Bowdoins, Boston, 20
Boyishness vs. manliness, 4, 43–48
Brainard, Asa, 142
Brine, Peto, 96–97
Brooklyn Eagle, 9
Brooklyn *Times*, 67
Brotherhood of Professional Base Ball
    Players, 150, 151
Buckeyes, Cincinnati, 105–7
Business, baseball as, 134–42

Called strike, 13
Capital and labor, 94–100
Captains, 18, 47–48, 152
Cartwright, Alexander, 12, 43

Chadwick, Sir Edwin, 9
Chadwick, Henry, 9, 11, 31, 34–37,
    43–44, 49–50, 52, 54–56, 67–68,
    71, 83, 87–89, 92, 105, 108–11,
    144–45
Champion, Aaron B., 106
Championship matches, 58–62
Chowder suppers, 29
Chronicle. See Ball Players' Chronicle
Clipper. See New York Clipper
Club rooms, 17
Clubs
    at home and away, 101–3
    vs. nines, 25
    and relationship with players, 94–100
    and rules of player conduct, 139–40
Columbias, Bordentown, 21
Competition, 70
    and behavior, 77
    problem of, 40–42
Control, agents of, 34–40
Cooperation among players, 22–23
Creighton, James, 70, 85
Cricket, 49, 52, 70, 103–4, 125, 128–29,
    144
Cultural antecedents, 27–31
Cultural conflict, and division, 75–83
Custom vs. reform, 53–58
Cuthbert, Ned, 136

Devyr, Thomas, 90–92
Division, and cultural conflict, 75–83
Doubleday, Abner, 11
Duffy, Edward, 90–92

Eastons, 132
Eagles, New York, 12
Eckfords, Brooklyn, 18, 20–24, 38, 58,
    75–76
    vs. Mutuals, 90–91
Eligibility, 89–90
Elysian Fields, Hoboken, 12, 23, 29, 104
Empires, New York, 12, 21, 38, 85
Engine Co. No. 34, 25
Entertainment, postgame, 18–19, 41,
    54–55
Ethics of baseball, 53–58
Eurekas, Newark, 41
Excelsiors, Baltimore, 18–19
Excelsiors, Brooklyn, 18–19, 21, 42, 46,
    55, 58, 132–33
    vs. Atlantics, 76
    vs. Knickerbockers, 50–52

Excitement, dangerous, 32–34
Exhibition games, 52–53

Fans, conduct of, 75–83
Fashion Course, 14, 70, 102
Ferguson, Robert, 135, 136, 142
Fines, 35
Fire companies, and baseball clubs, 25,
    28–30, 111
First nine, 17, 54
Flyaways, New York, 130
Fly rule, 48–53
Forest City Club, Cleveland, 139
Fragmentation, baseball growth and, 72–75
Friendly games, 17
Fultons, Hoboken, 23, 90

Gambling, 33, 71, 90–92
Gate-money system, 84
Gifford, Mr., 94–96
Gorman, Arthur Pue, 73
Gorn, Elliott, 31, 40
Gothams, New York, 21
Gould, Charley, 105, 140
Graftons, Worcester, 130
Growth of baseball, 67–72
    and fragmentation, 72–75
Guttmann, Allen, 143–44

Hatfield, John, 107
Hawks, Dr., 19
Histories, 1–6, 67–72
Hobsbawm, Eric, 78
Home-and-home series, 18
Hose Co. No. 55, 25
Hospitality, 18–19
Hulbert, William, 147

Illinois Association of Base-Ball Players,
    74
Irvingtons, 80–81

Jefferson Club, 24
Jewett, Nat, 85
Jones, Dr., 19, 86–87, 123–25
Junior Association, 44–47
Junior clubs, 44–47
Juveniles, 46–47

Kelly, M. J., 88
Knickerbockers, New York, 11–12,
    55–57, 76, 104, 128
    vs. Excelsiors, 50–52

Labor and capital, 94–100
Lafayette Engine Co. No. 19, 25
Leggett, Joseph P., 76
Leonard, Andrew, 141
Localism, 101–3

McKeever, William, 33–34
McVey, Cal, 143
Management
    of Cincinnati Red Stockings, 1869–1870,
        112–119
    and players, 5
Manliness
    and boyishness, 4
    and fly rule, 48–53
Manly pastime, baseball as, 43–48
    restoring, 126–33
Martin, Alphonse C. (Phonny), 85
Massachusetts game, 13, 87
Match games, 18
Men and boys, in baseball, 43–48
Mercury, 33
Military companies, volunteer, 30
Miller, Marvin, 154
Mills, Abraham G., 10–11, 149–50
Mills, Charles, 136
Money, and baseball, 69–71
Muffin match, 80
Muffin nine, 17
Mutual Hook and Ladder Co. No. 1, 28, 30
Mutuals, New York, 28, 30, 33–34, 85,
        127, 136
    vs. Atlantics, 67, 71
    and betting scandal, 90–91
    vs. Eckfords, 90–91
    vs. Irvingtons, 80–81

Nameless Club, Brooklyn, 131
National Association game, 13
National Association of Amateur Base Ball
        Players, 126
National Association of Base Ball Players
        (NABBP), 12, 25, 44–45, 48–49,
        54–55, 62, 82, 125, 134–36, 147
    decline of, 84–94
National Association of Professional Base
        Ball Players, 5, 97, 134, 146
National Bank-Note Co., 25
National League of Professional Base Ball
        Clubs, 5, 97, 134–35, 147–50
National Police Gazette, 7
Nationals, Washington, 104, 105, 138
    vs. Cincinnatis, 104

National Typographical Union, 26
New York Clipper, 32, 36–38, 46–47,
        50–53, 57, 59–62, 75–77, 105
New York Club, 12
New York Daily Times, 25
New York Sunday Mercury, 9
Nines vs. clubs, 25

O'Brien, Peter, 47
Oceana Hose No. 36, 25
Ohio State Base-Ball Association, 106
Olympics, Philadelphia, 12, 60, 80, 105,
        137
Olympics, Washington, 109, 138
O'Rourke, James, 143

Page, Mr., 94–96
Pearce, Dickey, 47, 70, 145
Peck & Snyder, 30
Pidgeon, Frank, 20, 76
Players
    and alcohol, 81
    and clubs, 94–100
    and management, 5
    and rules of conduct, 139–40
    separation of, from clubs, 97–100
    and women, 20
    and workers, 24–27
Players' League, 150, 154
Porter's Spirit of the Times, 7–8, 52
Practice, 20–24
Practice days, 17–18
Practice games, 56–57
Printing trades, and baseball clubs, 25–26
Prizefighting, and baseball, 28, 30
Prizes, 18
Professionalism, 88–89
    and revolving, 97
Providence Journal, 21
Putnams, 23

Queen, Frank, 8, 60

Reach, Al, 70, 85, 151
Red Stockings, Boston, 135, 140, 148–49
Red Stockings, Cincinnati, 5, 70
    birth of, 103–8
    vs. Buckeyes, 105–7
    management of, 1869–1870, 112–19
Red Stockings, St. Louis, 130
Reform
    vs. custom, 53–58
    fruits of, 58–63

Reserve clause, 6, 149–50
Resolutes, Fall River, 131
Revolving, 84–85, 89, 96–97, 116,
    135–36
Rites of play, 17–20
Rivalry, 101–3
Rounders, 10, 43, 44
Rules, 55–56
    as agents of control, 34–36
Runs, 13

St. George Cricket Club, 103–4
Salaries, 84, 89, 99, 114, 117–18, 149
Sands, George F., 74
Second nine, 17
Shelley, Mr., 94–96
Smith, Charley, 47
Sociability, 29
Social games, 17
Socializing, 29, 55, 57
Spalding, Albert G., 11, 134–35, 150, 151
Spectators, conduct of, 75–83
Spirit of the Times, 7–8. *See also Porter's
    Spirit of the Times; Wilkes' Spirit of
    the Times*
Stars, 21, 46, 126, 128, 137
Start, Joe, 47, 70, 136
State associations, 86–87
Staten Island Club, 129, 130, 131
Statistics, 68–69
    origin of, 142–47
Sterry, Tull V., 94–95
Striker, 13
Subterranean, 7

Tammany Hall, 30
Third nine, 17

Thompson, E. P., 10
Town ball, 87
Tweed, William Marcy, 30

Umpires, 47–48
    as agents of control, 35–38
Uniforms, 108–11
Union Cricket Club, 104–5
Unions, Morrisania, 105
    dispute with Atlantics, 94–96

Victory, hard work and, 20–24

Walsh, Mike, 7
Wansley, William, 90–92
Washington Club, 12
Waterman, Fred, 85
Westerns, Keokuk, 130
White Stockings, Chicago, 11, 109, 136
Wildey, John, 92, 93, 98
Wilkes, George, 7–8, 111, 122
Wilkes' Spirit of the Times, 7–8, 21, 41,
    50, 56–57, 69, 71, 80, 93, 107, 109,
    120–21, 123, 126, 127, 130, 132, 139,
    140
Women
    as agents of control, 38–40
    and players, 20
Workers, and players, 24–27
Wright, George, 104, 140
Wright, Harry
    as manager, 112–14, 135, 137–42, 151
    as player, 103–4, 107
Wright, Sam, 103

Young, Nick, 138